BEFORE JACKIE

ADVANCE PRAISE FOR *BEFORE JACKIE*

Your excellent book, which I like very much, is solid, thoughtful, and creative—full of useful suggestions for classroom teachers in high schools and even elementary schools. It provides an ingenious teaching guide that shows ways to spark students' interest in history and enhance their understanding of it by using examples from baseball—specifically, examples indicating how baseball can be a major source of insights into the history of race, segregation, and integration. You also include fine information on gender issues.

Among the book's strengths are its outstanding photos and images, its useful suggestions regarding secondary and primary sources (including, for example, *The Green Book*, films, and novels), and its discussion of specific pedagogical strategies. It is, in sum, a wonderful teaching tool, full of ideas about how to engage students and increase their awareness of history's relevance.

Mainly I want to congratulate you for your accomplishment. My guess is that teachers on a number of levels will eagerly turn to *Before Jackie* as a terrific guide to how they can introduce students to central historical themes and experiences, especially those involving race, gender, civil rights, inequities, injustices, and dramatic struggles to realize the American dream.

LeRoy Ashby, Ph.D.
Claudius O. and Mary Johnson Distinguished Professor of History
Washington State University Regents Professor, Emeritus

Dr. Mary Corey and Mark Harnischfeger's book *Before Jackie: The Negro Leagues, Civil Rights and the American Dream* could not be more timely for students in the United States. Weaving together critical legacies of sports culture and racial injustice, the book frames segregated baseball in an approachable, documented format that never shies from the stark realities of Jim Crow, yet celebrates black ownership and achievement as transcendent power. I'll be delighted to adopt this book for my sports history courses at both Georgetown and George Washington Universities.

Bonnie J. Morris, Ph.D.
Professor of Women's Studies and Sports History

A must read for every educator, parent, student, and school board member. As the authors' state, the struggle was "... a journey to develop a civil rights consciousness . . ." *Before Jackie: The Negro Leagues, Civil Rights, and the American Dream* is designed to help teachers take students on that journey. Rich with meaningful content and value-based activities, it provides an enduring understanding of the multi-generational process of African-American activism that took a national approach through the sport of baseball.

Dr. Aggie Seneway
Vice President, Hilton Central School District Board of Education, Hilton, NY
Past President, Monroe County School Boards Association, Rochester, NY

A must teaching resource for teachers at all levels! With engaging lessons that build critical thinking skills, *Before Jackie* addresses the under-representation of African Americans in traditional social studies textbooks and spans the post-Civil War period to the pre-Civil Rights era. Teachers will benefit from the strong foundation in the teaching of the material that the authors provide; students will benefit from exposure to social history which draws upon a sports narrative that highlights the importance of individuals working toward incremental societal changes. Dr. Corey and Mr. Harnischfeger have created an important work that aids our understanding of America as a multi-cultural society.

Tricia J. Stewart, Ph.D.
Associate Professor, Educational Policy, Educational Leadership, Policy, and Law
Alabama State University

BEFORE JACKIE

The Negro Leagues, Civil Rights and the American Dream

A Social, Political and Economic History
of the Negro Leagues Era for Teachers of
Social Studies and American History

Mary E. Corey
and
Mark Harnischfeger

Paramount Market Publishing, Inc.

950 Danby Road, Suite 136

Ithaca, NY 14850

www.paramountbooks.com

Voice: 607-275-8100; 888-787-8100   Fax: 607-275-8101

Publisher: James Madden

Editorial Director: Doris Walsh

Copyright © 2014 Mary E. Corey and Mark Harnischfeger

Printed in USA

ISBN-10: 0-9851795-4-6 | ISBN-13: 978-0-9851795-4-0

All rights reserved. No part of this book may be reproduced, stored in a retrieval system, or transmitted in any form or by any means, electronic, mechanical, photocopying, recording, or otherwise, without the prior written permission of the publisher. Further information may be obtained from Paramount Market Publishing, Inc., 950 Danby Road, Suite 136, Ithaca, NY 14850.

All trademarks are the property of their respective companies.

Every reasonable effort has been made to trace the ownership or the source of photos and illustrations used for this volume. If you are the copyright holder of an unattributed image or excerpt, please contact the publisher so that appropriate credit(s) can be arranged.

On the cover: The Negro Leagues All-Star East-West Game, August 23, 1936,
Comiskey Park, Chicago

On the title page: Satchel Paige, Kansas City Monarchs, 1942

Publisher's Cataloging-In-Publication Data
(Prepared by The Donohue Group, Inc.)

Corey, Mary E.
    Before Jackie : the Negro leagues, civil rights and the American dream / Mary E. Corey and Mark Harnischfeger.

        p. : ill. ; cm.

    "Includes lesson plans that allow students to engage with a wide variety of resources and gives teachers valuable assistance in making social studies come alive for teaching at all grade levels."-- Publisher.
    Includes bibliographical references and index.
    ISBN-13: 978-0-9851795-4-0
    ISBN-10: 0-9851795-4-6

    1. Negro leagues--Social aspects. 2. Negro leagues--Political aspects. 3. Civil rights--United States--History. 4. Baseball--United States--History. 5. Negro leagues--Study and teaching. I. Harnischfeger, Mark. II. Title.

GV863.A1 C67 2013
796.357/64/0973

To all the players and managers, owners and fans —
all who played in or supported the Negro Leagues —
for your grace, your talent, your pride, and your dignity,
thank you.

Contents

Foreword

"Four score and eight years" is a mere measurement of time, more than half a century, but it represents my life, the 88 years of my journey thus far. Born into a family of seven who lived in a small community on the west side of Atlanta, I soon learned the importance of family unity.

My parents helped me form character during what would later be known as one of the most challenging times in all of American history—the Jim Crow era of 20th-century racial segregation. They often reminded my brothers, my sisters, and me that we were each someone special, that we were neither defined by nor limited to the conditions of our living environment.

The street that we lived on was referred to as "The Alley." It was an offshoot from the main road, the road that led the way to a series of white- and colored-only signs that defined our place in the community. These signs separated people merely on the basis of the color of their skin and they were everywhere—on the main streets' buildings, over bathrooms, on buses, street cars and at water fountains, and because of these blatant symbols of discrimination, many blacks were treated as less than human. My parents taught me that in spite of our living

Authors' Note: We would like to thank Ora Morgan Jerald, Director of the William H. Greason Foundation Project, for her kind introduction to Rev. William H. Greason and for her efforts as our liaison throughout the process culminating in this Foreword he has written on behalf of our work. Rev. Greason was one of the pioneering members of the Negro Leagues. He was a pitcher for the Birmingham Black Barons, the St. Louis Cardinals, and one of the Montford Point Marines. On May 30, 2011, he was honored for his service to his country during World War II with the Congressional Gold Medal. We are humbled that he has honored us with his willingness to tell you a bit about his life's journey and share his thoughts about our work.

environment and the times in which we lived, I could and would be the "somebody special" that I was created to be.

The love of God was at the center of my family and I was taught that this love must also come first in my own life. Next must come humility—something I must strive to achieve and to then practice in all my affairs. If I were to add strong personal determination to these first two actions, I could move up in life, out of "The Alley" and away from the negative attitudes and behaviors present there that would otherwise limit both my vision and my potential. I could rise up in character and in dignity and in doing so, I could leave "The Alley" behind.

God was good to my family. We worked hard and with His grace we were able to move to a better neighborhood on the "avenue." As chance would have it, the young Rev. Dr. Martin Luther King and his family lived across the street from us. His words in later years would help to define my own journey—that with determination and the love of God, I might be judged "not by the color of my skin but by the content of my character."

I was thrust into manhood during the 1940s when I experienced the harsh reality of World War II as a Montford Point Marine. As a Marine I fought in the Battle of Iwo Jima where two of my best friends were killed. Because we were the first Negro Marines, we were told from day one that we had to "prove ourselves." And we did! I realized if I were to make it off that island alive, I would have to persevere, to maintain team discipline, and first and foremost pray to God with a commitment to serve Him and Him alone. Seven thousand of my fellow Marines were killed on that island and an additional 20,000 were injured. My life was spared and God's tender mercies were to follow me through my subsequent service in the Korean War in the early 1950s. It appeared that God had other plans for me.

I had always loved the game of baseball and God blessed me with the talent to become a pitcher. I started to play more seriously in 1947 while still in the military and baseball would go on to form the next chapter of my life. As a pitcher on the Marines' team, I was the only black player on the squad. I recall our wins vividly. We won nine games and lost only three. In my sixteen innings of pitching, I struck out twenty men! I was truly blessed! I would survive my wartime experiences and with an honorable discharge behind me and my baseball skills on the rise, I moved forward in my baseball career with intensity and determination. I would go on to enjoy a professional career in the Negro Leagues, where I would have the opportunity to play with some of the best ballplayers of all time.

I was fortunate to play professional baseball for a number of years in the Negro Leagues with teams such as the Nashville Black Vols and the Asheville Blues. I won the 1948 Black World Series against the Kansas City Monarchs while playing with the renowned Birmingham Black Barons under the leadership of Piper Davis. In addition to my time in the Negro Leagues, I also played two years in the Mexican Leagues, eight in the Minors, and five in the Winter Leagues from 1953 to 1958 while in Cuba and Puerto Rico. I broke the color barrier as the first black to have played for AA teams in Oklahoma City—the Oklahoma City Indians—and with the Houston Buffs. Later, I played with the Columbus Red Birds before I moved on to the Major Leagues with a brief stay with the St. Louis Cardinals. I also played with the Rochester Red Wings in the beautiful city of Rochester, New York, before ending my career there under the management of Ellis Cot Deal. I am privileged to have played alongside many greats such as my dear friend, the late Roy Campanella, Willie Mays, Satchel Paige and a host of other All-Star, Hall of Fame players.

Throughout my baseball career, I never lost sight of the personal responsibility I felt to rise above the social-economic restraints of my childhood and I knew that education would be the key to my achieving this goal. I pursued higher education and earned a Bachelor's Degree in Theology, a Bachelor of Arts Degree, and an Honorary Doctorate of Divinity from the Birmingham Easonian Baptist Bible College. In addition, I also earned a second Bachelor's in Theology and an advanced Diploma of Christian Training from Sanford University, then known as Howard College, and have since taken additional coursework there. I hold education in the highest regard.

I view my accomplishments through the years as merely incidental events in the saga of my life. I've always believed that God has called me to a higher purpose. While I aspired to be greater than my opponents on the baseball field, I desired to be an even better leader in the community and church. After I retired from baseball, I joined the historic Sixteenth Street Baptist Church in Birmingham, Alabama. It was after this that God called me into the ministry in 1967. Today, I am serving as the pastor of Bethel Baptist Church and have been blessed with this privilege for the past 41 years. I am also currently teaching at the Birmingham Easonian Baptist Bible College and find time to work with the youth of my community through my foundation. I am often asked how I manage to accomplish and maintain this wide range of activity. My response is simple: "When you serve the King, you live like a King."

Like so many others, I have strived to exhibit my character and the substance of my being in ways beyond any accolades or awards that might come my way. However,

I am particularly proud to have recently received the Congressional Gold Medal. In receiving this award, I'm not sure what is most gratifying: the fact that I received this honor alongside other decorated soldiers, the fact that I received the medal from an African-American, four-star General, or the fact that I received it from the highest office of our country from a President who just happens to look like me—African and American. Times have certainly changed since my childhood days in the "Alley" and I am grateful to have been blessed with the opportunity to experience and to participate in this change. I hope that this phase of my journey echoes words of hope regarding the endless possibilities that one might attain through dedication and self-sacrifice, a lesson my mother taught me well.

The main reason I am especially pleased that I can share some of my life story through this textbook for educators is because certain things which I believe should not be forgotten might be remembered and preserved through its use. Many things that have not been included in mainstream history textbooks may become new again to a new generation of Americans. It bridges a gap in American history, telling a previously untold story of those who accomplished remarkable feats during days of incredible social and economic duress, days when I happened to be a baseball player in the Negro Leagues.

This book provides insight into those "foot soldiers" who sacrificed their personal interests and in many cases, their lives, for the cause of social and civil justice. Their historic contributions are uncelebrated as they were cast into the shadows of Jim Crow segregation and discrimination. But the dignity, integrity, and the character of Negro League Baseball, its players, and its supporters, provided both a voice and a direction toward a better America. These were the voices heard in the shouts of a home run and a stolen base, on the street corner and in the market place. These were the businessmen, the patriarchs, the moms and dads, the "common" people—pioneers all—the true soldiers upon which the civil rights movement was built.

The common thread that leads us all to have hope in our future is the desire to build a movement out of the ashes of ignorance with a spirit to educate, enlighten, and guide our young people into truth. As a sourcebook for educators, this text serves as a beacon for the next generation of readers, professors, teachers, students, and even baseball enthusiasts alike.

As I consider my life's journey, nothing is more inspiring than to reflect upon the monumental moments of personal sacrifice and dedication of those whose lives were forgotten and who have been tragically omitted from our history texts. This work seeks to correct that injustice. The omission of those men and women who were not only athletes, but also social and civil heroes of this Renaissance era, has been

Tribute to Rev. William H. Greason, May 20, 2011 www.youtube.com/ watch?v=78z32Zim 2uM a travesty. This is why I am very pleased and honored to support and commend the authors, Mary Corey and Mark Harnischfeger, for this truly exceptional chronicle of the character and contribution of both African Americans and other minorities who helped shape our nation's foundation. Like my life, it describes interests and activities that go far beyond simple baseball statistics. It will ignite the imagination, inspire the soul, and etch its way into the memories of its readers for generations to come.

Rev. Dr. William H. Greason
Birmingham Black Baron
St. Louis Cardinal
Montford Point Marine

Preface

The one constant through all the years has been baseball. America has rolled by like an army of steamrollers. It's been erased like a blackboard, rebuilt, and erased again. But baseball has marked the time. This field, this game, is a part of our past. It reminds us of all that once was good, and what could be again.

—James Earl Jones as Terrance Mann in *Field of Dreams*

Social studies is one of, if not *the most* important subject kids need to learn and learn well. Everything else they need to learn can be categorized as simply subsets of the great human pageant and can be taught through the lens of history. The ancients knew that. The great storytellers of the past knew that the oral histories of their people were more than mere entertainment, they were absolutely critical to their survival. The same is true today. One need only glance through the daily news to see how misunderstandings, incorrect information, and unchallenged distortions of the past lead to poor decision making and policy choices in the present. (We also believe that the groundwork for successful social studies teaching begins in the elementary and middle school grades and depends on well-prepared teachers.) This book is therefore designed to help pre-service teacher candidates as well as practicing teachers.

The two problems working against teachers we have identified and addressed are:

- inadequate social studies textbook narratives of the African-American experience; and

- inadequate social studies methods texts used for teacher preparation, especially those directed toward preparing elementary social studies teachers.

We see these as critical issues because they lead to:

- disaffection for social studies by most students;

- a disproportionately higher disaffection for social studies among African-American students and other students of color;

- a wider achievement gap in social studies assessments between African-American students and other students.

Methodology

To address these problems and suggest new directions for teaching social studies at all levels, we draw on both experience and research. We propose that the answer lies with on-going professional development but in an area that professional development too often overlooks—content area professional development. Because social studies is so critically important to the development of personal narratives that will form the foundation of a student's view of both their country's narrative and their place in that national story, it cannot be overemphasized as the singular most important place for this type of professional development to focus.

The resources in this book provide the type of professional development we suggest. They focus on African-American history in an effort to reach students demonstrating the highest levels of disaffection for social studies. And, they offer elementary and middle school pre-service and practicing social studies teachers background readings and teaching materials that span a significant time period in American and African-American history—the post-Civil War period to the pre-Civil Rights era. So, this book is designed to do two things:

- cover a significant period of time where textbooks have the widest gaps in their narratives about African-American history, and

- help teachers striving to teach a multicultural curriculum.

Misunderstandings and Misconceptions

Anecdotal evidence, and research, indicates that students leave elementary social studies with many misunderstandings and misconceptions about much of American history: names and dates. More damaging, these misunderstandings and misconceptions coupled with the very limited time devoted to social studies in the elementary classroom, leave students with the impression that social studies is of little importance and less than interesting.[1] "These same types of evidence indicate that professional development also neglects content."[2]

In working with elementary-level social studies teachers, many admitted they did not feel social studies was their strong suit. And when asked to identify the three most important reasons why they found teaching social studies to be difficult for them, their own experiences led them to the same answers a number of researchers have identified:

1. Some school districts have stopped teaching social studies and have replaced it with what is being called non-fiction studies. As troubling is a new category of children's and YA literature shelved as "non-fiction social studies." Does that imply there is such a thing as "fictional social studies?" www.goodreads.com/shelf/show/non-fiction-social-studies

2. A survey of teacher education programs for elementary level teacher candidates reveals that formal preparation to teach social studies often requires no more than one, possibly two classes in American or world history, and frequently requires no coursework in history at all.

3. James Leming, Lucien Ellington, and Mark Schug, "The State of Social Studies: A National Random Survey of Elementary and Middle School Teachers," *Social Education*, Sept., 2006, 70 (5), 322-327. June R. Chapin, "The Achievement Gap in Social Studies and Science Starts Early, Evidence from the Early Childhood Longitudinal Study," *The Social Studies*, Nov./Dec., 2006, 97 (6), 231-238. Jeff Passe, "New Challenges in Social Studies," Sept./Oct., 2006, 189-192.

4. Chapin, p. 236.

5. Margit E. McGuire, "What Happened to Social Studies? The Disappearing Curriculum," *Phi Delta Kappan*, April 2007, 620-624.

6. Anne-Lise Havorsen, "Back to the Future: The Expanding Communities Curriculum in Geography Education," *The Social Studies*, May/June, 2009, 115. Havorsen defines "expanding communities" as ". . . the theory that young children learn best when they study what is most familiar and immediate to them and then gradually expand outward from that personal context. In practice, the curriculum uses the structure of child-centered, concentric 'social domains' or 'communities'—from family to nation—with each domain or community enlarging the previous one. For example, in kindergarten, children

- lack of time,
- feelings of discomfort about the content itself, and
- unhappy memories of their own experiences as students in social studies classes.[3]

Their responses paralleled the research exactly.

A brief review of some of the more salient findings of recent research supports their experience. June Chapin's work shows that on average, 42.2 percent of elementary teachers reported that they spend between 1–30 minutes a day, and 32 percent reported spending between 31–60 minutes a day, teaching social studies. Chapin qualifies her findings by adding,

> Given the wide range of thirty or fewer minutes, it is difficult to ascertain if most first-grade teachers taught social studies on average for 5 minutes or twenty minutes per day. A further difficulty in interpretation is that social studies could have been integrated with reading or other subject areas. . . . Thus, it is not possible to say how much social studies is being taught in kindergarten and first grade.[4]

This is supported by Margrit McGuire's study in which she notes:

> A closer examination of the curriculum that is supposed to teach social studies reveals that teachers are indeed teaching social studies topics solely as a literacy endeavor.
>
> And, she argues that "social studies is more than reading for comprehension."[5]

James Duplass raises similar concerns by challenging the "expanding communities"[6] approach in place for over half a century.[7] His critique challenges the "trivial and redundant" textbook content supporting "expanding communities," in particular their reliance on a 1950's model of "what and when students encounter information that is no longer valid." Children of the 1950s had many fewer opportunities to encounter information whereas today's children have "greater exposure to the world through the Internet and television" with hundreds of channels as compared to the two or three of the 1950s. In addition he critiques the disjointed "vignettes" of information offering tidbits of information with little sequence or substance.[8]

Each of these and other studies speaks directly to the concerns of student teachers. Pressured to focus on literacy, the time they spend exclusively on social studies is negligible, much of their own understanding of social studies content is based on the textbooks they use, and, raised themselves on the "expanding communities" model, they viewed social studies as, if not trivial, not a priority.[9]

Teacher Preparation

Students, when questioned why they were uncomfortable with the content of social studies and why they often relied on the textbooks for their students along with the ancillary materials provided by textbook publishers for their content, opened up questions about how teachers are prepared to teach social studies.[10] The answers are complicated. Elementary teachers are expected to teach well across disciplines. So in programs that require a major in a particular discipline, they may have depth in one area but lack it in all the others. For example math majors may be very well equipped to teach elementary math but be deficient in social studies, English, and science. Or they may have a major in an area that has little or no direct connection to the elementary curriculum they will be teaching.[11] Other elementary education teacher preparation programs offer a major in education and require 9–12 hours in each of the four main disciplines. In this scenario, depth is replaced by superficial breadth.

In the case of middle school teachers, many teacher education programs accept students with any social science major and some arbitrary number of history courses. Changing either type of program is next to impossible. It would simply be impractical to require elementary level teacher candidates to have at least a minor in the four main discipline areas on top of all of the other requirements for both college graduation and credentialing that would include their general education requirements and as many as 15 credit hours of special education classes.

Methods classes address some of the weaknesses in the content areas, but without strong background knowledge of the discipline, all the methods classes in the world won't make you a confident teacher in any field you know only a little about. Except in the case of a student who had chosen to pursue an undergraduate history major, none of my students had more than six credit hours in history, the number that their preparation programs had required.

Now for Something Completely Different

While nothing could be done about students' memories of the ghost of social studies past, the future was theirs to create. Together we decided to focus the class on content and they trusted us to bring them worthwhile materials. This included introducing an eclectic variety of readings designed to cover a significant amount of content and do it with readable, provocative, and engaging materials. The response was overwhelmingly positive. They loved feeling they left the class with a much firmer grip on what they needed to teach, and with some important new ways of approaching their curriculum. After exploring Native American history, one teacher said to the class, "After reading

study themselves, their families, and their homes; in first grade, the school; in second grade, the local community . . ."

7. James E. Duplass, "Elementary Social Studies: Trite, Disjointed, and in Need of Reform?" *The Social Studies*, July/August, 2007, 137-144.

8. *Ibid.*, 138.

9. One of the reasons consistently cited by respondents and my students for the small amount of time devoted exclusively to teaching social studies and their use of the strategy of folding it into literacy exercises was the pressure from administrators to meet NCLB requirements measured on standardized tests that do not directly test social studies content. Again, if it isn't tested, you'd be hard pressed to convince an administrator that there is justification for teaching it.

10. M. Ogawa, 2001. *Building multiple historical perspectives: An investigation of how middle school students are influenced by different perspectives.* ERIC Document Reproduction Service No. ED453108; T. Goodland, *A Place Called School: Prospects for the Future.* (New York: McGraw-Hill, 1995); and others cited in Duplass, 138.

11. The following are all New York State approved majors for elementary education teacher candidates: Arts for Children,

Biological Science, Chemistry, Earth Science, English, French, Geology, Health Science, History, Mathematics, Meteorology, Physics, Political Science, and Spanish.

12. Walter C. Parker, *Social Studies in Elementary Education;* Arthur K. Ellis, *Teaching & Learning Elementary Social Studies;* Thomas N. Turner, *Essentials of Elementary Social Studies;* George W. Maxim, *Dynamic Social Studies for Constructivist Classrooms;* David Warren Saxe, *Social Studies for the Elementary Teacher;* James J. Zarrillo, *Teaching Elementary Social Studies, Principles and Applications;* June R. Chapin, *Elementary Social Studies, A Practical Guide;* Cynthia Szymanski Sunal, and Mary Elizabeth Haas, *Social Studies for the Elementary and Middle Grades, A Constructivist Approach.*

13. Walter C. Parker, *Social Studies in Elementary Education,* (NJ: Merrill Prentice Hall, 2001) p. 111.

14. Penelope J. Fritzer and Ernest Andrew Brewer, *Social Studies Content for Elementary and Middle School Teachers,* 2nd Ed. (New York: Allyn & Bacon, 2009). This is a step in the right direction, but only a surface coverage is achieved in its modest 144 pages. June R. Chapin, "Achievement gap starts early in social studies and science."

this I'm actually embarrassed about the way our school teaches about Thanksgiving. I'll never do the paper hats and feathers thing again."

If we take seriously the truism that you can't teach what you don't know, we must grapple with this. We must question past practice in the design of programs preparing elementary teachers. Further, if it is understood that you can't teach what you don't know, it also needs to be understood that you can teach quite well that which you have misunderstood, partially understood, and that which is incorrect. It is critical that we take seriously that *what* you teach is just as important as *how* you teach. What good is facility with methodology if you are ill-equipped to challenge the textbook or enrich it for your students?

Further exacerbating the problems discussed above, are the texts used in elementary social studies education methods classes. A survey of a representative sampling of textbooks focusing on social studies teaching methods reveals that they all make the same assumption: that the students in these methods classes already have the necessary content. That's a huge assumption and a faulty one.[12] For example, in a section on how to teach history, one author offers guidelines for selecting literature. Among other criteria listed, he asks the teacher to ask him/herself, "Is the interpretation sound?"[13] This is terrific advice. In fact for someone with a rich and deep understanding of history and historiography, it's an excellent question to ask oneself before choosing a piece of literature for classroom use. However, for someone with perhaps only three to six credit hours of college level history, how would that person begin to determine whether or not the interpretation is sound?[14]

You Can't Bore Them into Submission

Clearly a new approach is necessary. The evidence is overwhelming; by the time students reach middle and high school they don't like social studies classes. They routinely characterize them as boring. But, however wide the general distaste for it is, among African-American students it's palpable, and, as a result, the achievement gap is strikingly wider in social studies than that found with any other subject.[15] This special disinterest and distaste for American history has been identified by a number of scholars and led to a state-wide initiative to address it in New York. The necessity for this initiative is explained by the New York State Education Department:

"In recent years, data gathered from international, national, and state assessments and studies have indicated a need for strengthening student performance in social studies, particularly for students in high-need districts. However, even low-need districts often see significant achievement gaps in social studies."[16]

High needs districts are frequently those found in urban areas where the percentage of students of color is high. The report went on to say:

On the 1998 NAEP Civics Assessment, 70 percent of students in grades 4, 8, and 12 were at the "basic" level in civics performance; female students had lower scale scores than male students in grades 8 and 12; and higher percentages of white and Asian/Pacific Islanders were at or above the "proficient" level than black, Hispanic, or Native American Indian students.[17]

In her groundbreaking book, *Why Are All the Black Kids Sitting Together in the Cafeteria?* Beverly Daniel Tatum writes, "Too often I hear from young African-American students the embarrassment they have felt in school when the topic of slavery is discussed . . . [they are] uncomfortable with the portrayal of their group as helpless victims—the rebellions and resistance offered by the enslaved Africans are rarely discussed—they squirm uncomfortably as they feel the eyes of White children looking to see their reaction to the subject."[18] It seems reasonable that the same could be said for the portrayal of African Americans during the years following Reconstruction.

James W. Loewen asserts in his introduction to *Lies My Teacher Told Me*, "African American, Native American, and Latino students view history with a special dislike." Going further he recounts asking students, "What images come to your mind about [Reconstruction]? The class consensus: Reconstruction was the time when African Americans took over the governing of the Southern states . . . but they were too soon out of slavery so they messed up and reigned corruptly, and whites had to take back control of the state governments." After offering a necessary corrective to this misinformation he says, "For young African Americans to believe such a hurtful myth about their past seemed tragic. It invited them to doubt their own capability, since their race had 'messed up' in its one appearance on American history's center stage. It also invited them to conclude that it is only right that whites be always in control."[19]

Unfortunately, even the current best practice remedies that promise to better engage our disaffected students will do little to address the special enmity of African-American students. Merely enlivening the teaching strategies will do little if the content sends the same debilitating messages. And, as important as rethinking how we teach the past may be, if we are to ever truly reach our African-American students, the fact is that the message as it stands now is just as damaging to our white students. History that portrays African Americans only as victims denies them their full humanity again, rendering them as one-dimensional scenery for a story in which only whites have historical agency. This is bad history for everyone. It wipes from the historical

www.eric.ed.gov/ERICWebPortal/custom/portlets/recordDetails/detailmini.jsp?_nfpb=true&_&ERICExtSearch_SearchValue_0=EJ773749&ERICExtSearch_SearchType_0=no&accno=EJ773749

15. www.emsc.nysed.gov/ciai/socst/ssinitiative.html

16. *Ibid.*

17. *Ibid.*

18. Gloria Daniel Tatum, *Why Are All the Black Kids Sitting Together in the Cafeteria,* (New York: Basic Books, 1997, 2003,) p. 41.

Understanding White Privilege by Frances E. Kendall includes a poignant, but by no means exceptional, story of her own "crucible" upon discovering she had been taught a sanitized version of American history designed to uphold white supremacy. She says she felt as though, "my legs had been knocked out from under me." Textbooks that reinforce this sanitized perspective undermine the integrity of their narratives.

19. James Loewen, *Lies My Teacher Told Me,* (New York: Touchstone, Simon&Schuster, 1995, 2007), pp. 1, 157.

record the wit and courage that resistance required from African Americans to make change happen; actions to be admired by all students and to which all can turn and draw inspiration. It prevents us from appreciating the contributions of an important segment of the American family and privileges a few, to everyone's detriment in a multicultural world.

Furthermore, even the language used in our standard narratives describing the situation faced by African Americans is passive. "Segregation" is used to identify a state of being rather than an action. This can lead students to think of segregation as merely the separation seen in the ubiquitous illustrations of whites-only water fountains and streetcar seating. Bad enough, to be sure, but failing to convey the full scope of the dynamic power wielded over African Americans making, by omission, the many acts of courage it took to stand up against it seem less courageous than they were. Loewen agrees and argues, for example, that texts almost unanimously focus on the fact that under the doctrine of "separate but equal," facilities were never equal; thus missing the point that "there could never be such a thing as 'separate but equal' facilities. When any race was kept apart from another, it was deprived of its equality . . ." He suggests instead this sociological definition, ". . . segregation: a system of racial etiquette that keeps the oppressed group separate from the oppressor when both are doing equal tasks, like learning the multiplication tables, but allows intimate closeness when the tasks are hierarchical, like cooking or cleaning for white employers. The rationale of segregation thus implies that the oppressed are a pariah people. 'Unclean!' was the caste message of every 'colored' water fountain, waiting room, and courtroom Bible. 'Inferior' was the implication of every school that excluded blacks (and often Mexican, Native Americans and 'Orientals')."[20]

In order to begin re-envisioning the narrative, segregation needs to be appreciated in all of the ways that it intimidated African Americans. But, *resistance* also needs to be an integral part of the story: how African Americans, often at great risk to themselves, resisted the system while at the same time creatively taking advantage of any and all room within the system to ultimately prevail over it. The textbooks will always have pictures of "whites only" water fountains but they will not have this joyous testimony:

Poet Amiri Baraka recalls what going to see the Newark Eagles meant to him:

> . . . the most special feeling of [my] childhood was when my father took me down to Ruppert Stadium some Sundays to see the Newark Eagles. Very little in my life was as heightened (in anticipation and reward) for me as that.[21]

Baraka described the Eagles as "legitimate black heroes," and the team as "pure love."

20. *Ibid.,* p. 163.
21. Anthony Venutolo, "The African-American Newark baseball team was a source of pride and identity in segregated times,"*The Star-Ledger,* February 12, 2009. http://blog.nj.com/ledgerarchives/2009/02/the_africanamerican_newark_bas.html

In the laughter and noise and colors and easy hot dogs, there was something of us celebrating ourselves," he wrote. "In the flying around the bases and sliding and home runs and arguments and triumphs there was more of ourselves in celebration than we were normally ever permitted. It was ours.[22]

You can count on the textbooks to include pictures of "whites only" water fountains or waiting rooms but this, too, is the African-American experience:

"... black kids, especially those who played baseball, 'idolized' the Eagles players," according to Ronald Murphy of Newark, who was the Eagles' bat boy in 1946 and 1947. Sunday games were quite the event. The games started at 2 p.m. to allow churchgoers time to reach the ballpark. Fans came dressed in their Sunday best—women with fashionable flowery hats, men in jackets and ties.

"One hardly saw any casual attire at the ball games," recalled Edwin Burks of East Orange, whose father would take him to Eagles games when Burks was a 10-year-old. "People came dressed to the nines for this social event.

"You always knew when the Eagles were in town—the No. 31 bus, which ran down South Orange Avenue, was jammed with riders on their way to Ruppert Stadium."

"There were big write-ups in the paper about the Eagles," Murphy said. "Why go to Yankee Stadium when you could see the Eagles? They were right here, in Newark."[23]

Cathartic anger that militates against the standard narrative of African-American passivity comes from Troy, the main character in August Wilson's powerful play, *Fences*. For African-American students, indeed for all students, understanding Troy's rage is a necessary antidote to a narrative that rarely if ever includes the righteous anger of the oppressed. Anger is uncomfortable, but change requires discomfort and Troy embodies it.

Troy is a former Negro Leagues player, still angry at having been barred from the majors. Now his son wants to play football; Troy sees that as pursuing a dream that will lead nowhere, just as his did. When Rose, his wife, and his friend Bono tell him that the times are different now (the 1950s), Troy explodes:

Troy: How in hell they done changed?

Rose: They got lots of colored boys playing ball now. Baseball and football.

Bono: You right about that, Rose. Times have changed, Troy. You just come along too early.

Troy: There ought not never had been no time called *too early!*

22. *Ibid.*
23. www.amnh.org/ exhibitions/baseball/ index.html

Changing the Point of View

Joy, delight, and rage are active responses to the circumstances of your life. None of that filters through the standard social studies narratives that African-American, indeed, all kids suffer through. Bad for all, worse for black kids. How to change it? Reposition the camera, choose a new angle, turn up the volume, turn on music!

That changed focus and angle is for us, the story of the Negro Leagues. No other part of the African-American community, save school and the church, were as long lived, accessible, and important. But baseball had a singular dimension that school and church lacked; it was national. Long before black players were organized into the Negro Leagues, black players were playing baseball. And, long before black players were segregated, they were playing baseball on integrated teams. Because of the inclusive and less organized early history of baseball before it too followed the national pattern toward a systematically segregated nation, the history of baseball is also a case study of the history of the creation of Jim Crow, and ultimately its end. It's a complex history and often not a very pretty tale. But it's one that needs to be told.

We are recommending, then, a historically layered approach that takes students on a journey to develop a civil rights consciousness, to make the African-American experience the central narrative through the lens of the Negro Leagues. We know teachers need to and want to reach diverse student populations and be knowledge-able about what they are teaching. The reality is that they do not have the time to do this type of research themselves. We have the same goals and have invested the time to do this important work for them. We hope this type of resource will do good things for all our students and, in particular, help close the achievement gap for our African-American students.

Chapter Overview

Baseball was re-integrated a decade before the impact of *Brown* v *Board* would be felt. It was integrated before the armed forces were integrated. It led the way. We see that fact as one of great consequence. By exploring why that was the case we can use it as a lens through which we can see the evolution of a larger definition of what we meant when we agreed that "all men are created equal." History is often told as the story of great leaders and great movements. History is all that, but much more. It is the cumulative result of decisions made by ordinary people in all walks of life. The integration of baseball in the modern era stands as a monument to some of the most important individual decisions in American history.

Preface

A brief comment on textbooks and teaching inclusively.

Introduction

This section invites readers into an alternate vision of the Jim Crow era, one in which African Americans are the change agents and the baseball diamonds of the Negro Leagues are home to some of the most dynamic movers and shakers driving that change.

Chapter 1. A Game of Base Ball: Early Innings

This section describes the early years of baseball in America and reflects the ways that the game mirrored the America in which it was played. It also introduces some of the early stars of the game and the powerful player/manager, Cap Anson, who led the movement to exclude black players from the newly forming baseball leagues. His leadership effectively excluded black players from access to the mainstream of what was to become one of the most American of sports, its self-proclaimed national pastime: baseball.

This decision did not happen in a vacuum. New laws specifically designed to segregate African Americans were being enacted all over the southern United States. Their constitutionality was ultimately decided and confirmed in the Supreme Court case of *Plessy v. Ferguson* in 1898. A workshop refresher on the case for teachers on the wide-ranging national implications of this decision will help lay a firm foundation for teaching the rest of the lessons.

Chapter 2. Andrew "Rube" Foster, Red Summer, and the Birth of the Negro Leagues

The focus of this section is on the vision and work of Andrew Foster. This section also gives an overview of the parallel baseball world of the Negro Leagues and their role in accelerating the momentum toward expanded civil rights for African Americans while at the same time accommodating the restrictions of Jim Crow America.

In an age of inequality and in spite of it, one of the most vibrant economic institutions of African-American life grew during this time period, largely due to the single-minded efforts of Foster. He saw the way organized leagues could work like other multiplier enterprises. By organizing leagues using the model provided by white leagues he insisted that the nature of the sport and the needs of the teams would lead to growth in other black-owned businesses: restaurants, hotels, stores, and entertainment. His goal was to keep African-American money within the African-American community. Although some saw him exercising dictatorial control, no one can deny the effectiveness of his vision or the effectiveness of its fruition. Overlapping the years of the Harlem Renaissance, the rich traditions of the Negro Leagues enhanced and were enhanced by an age of African-American achievement.

Chapter 3. Barnstorming into History

From the earliest years of black baseball when barnstorming carried the day to the creation of the leagues and the tradition of the East-West Championships, African-American baseball centered community attention on an institution that more than any other displayed achievements at the highest levels. This chapter debunks the mythology of "barnstorming" in favor of a clearer telling of the lives of these journeying baseball players. It also focuses on an important artifact of the era, *The Negro Motorist Green Book*. Like the Fodor's *Guides* of today, *The Green Book* listed places to stay for African-American travelers. But unlike a Fodor's, it also listed places where you could get a haircut, buy gasoline, use the restrooms, buy a shirt, or buy an ice cream for your child. In a Jim Crow society, the freedom to choose from among the array of accommodations available to other travelers was severely restricted. *The Green Book* was a necessary traveling companion and offers some devastating, disturbing, and amazing insights into the American scene circa 1949, the year the edition we use here was published.

Chapter 4. South of the Border: Winterball in Latin America

Sometimes the best way to understand your own world is to spend time in another. The opportunity to do exactly that was offered to the players of the Negro Leagues. Although they faced all of the well-known limitations of life for African Americans in the United States, limitations that prevented them from playing in the major leagues, no such limitations existed in the countries of Latin America. There they were superstars. The names of players like Satchel Paige and Josh Gibson were known throughout Latin America and their experiences there changed forever how they would view their lives back in the United States.

Chapter 5. The Women of the Negro Leagues

Effa Manley is the only woman ever to be inducted into the National Baseball Hall of Fame. Her skills as both an owner and manager of the Newark Eagles were legendary. Her willingness to buck powerful men like Branch Rickey and others in major league baseball when they began raiding the Negro League teams after Jackie Robinson re-integrated major league baseball, showed her to be as fierce an advocate for the players then as she had been when she organized against the stores in Harlem who refused to hire African Americans. She earned her title as the "Queen of the Negro Leagues" and hers is a story worth telling.

Second basemen Toni Stone and Connie Morgan, and pitcher "Peanut" Johnson were the only women who ever played on Negro League teams. From 1953 to 1955 they played for the Indianapolis Clowns and the Kansas City Monarchs, two iconic teams of the era. Like Effy Manly, they struggled to use their talents when the odds were against them. While they were at first considered novelties, signed to attract fans in the waning days of the Leagues, they proved to be skilled and talented athletes, comparable to their teammates, and better than some.

Chapter 6. Jack Roosevelt Robinson

Signing Jackie Robinson was Branch Rickey's gift to all Americans. Jackie's gift was his greatness of heart and determination of spirit. In this chapter teachers will gain a greater appreciation for a man whose place in baseball history is already well-known. What is not as well-known is his role after his baseball years were over as a leader and activist on behalf of civil rights. For many, the story of Jackie Robinson ends once the integration of baseball is accomplished and other black players are signed around the major leagues. But, that is just the beginning of the accomplishments and legacy of the man.

Part 1. The Player
Part 2. "Dear Mr. President . . .": The Civil Rights Years

Chapter 7. The Post-Game Show

The consequences of integration brought both positive and negative changes in African-American life and American life. This chapter will be an overview of these changes and culminate with the 2006 induction of Negro League players into the National Baseball Hall of Fame, and the Life Achievement Award for John "Buck" O'Neil, Negro League Ambassador of Good Will.

Chapter 8. Sacrifice Bunts

This section stitches together a dozen short snapshots of telling moments as recalled by players and others that offer insights into African-American life. This is the only section of the book that actually explains anything about playing baseball or a specific baseball game! We also include here a suggestion for helping students think about their own "sacrifice bunts" or those of people they know.

Appendixes
Learning Standards
Readings and Resources

Introduction

VISUALIZE AN ARCHIPELAGO—a vast expanse of sea dotted with islands. That was the situation for African Americans in the United States between the Reconstruction Era, following the Civil War, and the beginnings of the Civil Rights Movement. Enclaves of African-American life and culture dotted the landscape of the United States, separated from each other and segregated from the rest of American life by law and tradition. It was during this time that one of the most important social, cultural, and economic institutions of black life knit these islands together. Between the end of the 19th century and the middle of the 20th century, the teams of the Negro Leagues crisscrossed the country, navigating the many and varied limitations on black life. By doing so, they brought a shared national experience to the entire African-American community and were integral to sowing the seeds of change. We propose that an important current of American history lay in exploring what these teams meant to the African-American community and how they helped nurture a sense of pride and determination in it. It is, in fact, not too much to say that this history involves every important dimension of a century of African-American history and ultimately renders a richer telling of American history.

Our decision to write this history using the lens of the Negro Leagues as its central organizing theme stemmed from a growing enthusiasm about the rich civil rights history embedded in it. This perspective offered seemingly endless opportunities for teachers to use it to reach all of our increasingly diverse student populations. We then decided to include teaching materials that would encourage using this alternative narrative. Teachers know, and studies continue to confirm, that the achievement gap among African-American students and other students of color has been resistant to every pedagogical remedy attempted. We think it's time to address not just how we are teaching, but what we are teaching.

Before we started working on this book, even we didn't realize how integral to the story of America between the Civil War and the Civil Rights era the story of African Americans in American life was. The reality is that African-American history *is* American history and cannot be separated from it without destroying the integrity of the whole.

Moreover, based on recent studies demonstrating how positively the Mexican-American Studies program in Tucson affected Mexican-American students, significantly raising both test scores and graduation rates, it stands to reason that weaving African-American history into social studies classes on a regular basis, would *do the same.*

> "[A] Tucson Unified School District audit found its Mexican American Studies program gives students a measurable advantage over their peers. The audit was conducted by David Scott, the district's director of accountability and research. In it, he wrote, 'Juniors taking a Mexican American Studies course are more likely than their peers to pass the [state's standardized] reading and writing . . . test if they had previously failed those tests in their sophomore year," and that "Seniors taking a Mexican American Studies course are more likely to persist to graduation than their peers.'"[1]

1. Cited in: http://americanindians inchildrensliterature. blogspot. com/2012/01/ teaching-critical- thinking-in-arizona. html

Probably the most important thing teachers want from a book like this is usability —good solid information *and* strategies to easily incorporate it into over-crowded curriculums. Because we appreciate that teaching is a full-time enterprise we have attempted to tackle three goals. First: to provide an engaging narrative augmented by as many teaching strategies and resources as possible; second: to bring a fresh perspective to an area that is a standard part of the social studies curriculum, Recon-struction to Civil Rights; and third: to address in a concrete way one of the knottier problems of teaching social studies—cultural relevancy. The history we've written was done with the express intent of reaching African-American students with a narrative of important contributions and accomplishments too often overlooked, to the detri-ment of all students.

Each chapter is followed by as many as four different teaching strategies, each with its own introduction and the materials necessary to bring it into the classroom. In this way we hoped to further assist teachers in their efforts on behalf of inclusive classroom practices. And, although, our work is fairly comprehensive, the world of Negro League baseball history is vast, so for those who want to know more about a particular topic, we've included suggestions for further reading.

Conceptual Constructs

Three conceptual constructs for our approach are used. The first is a narrative of deeply layered historical change. Teaching history from this perspective helps students see the past as incremental rather than a series of unconnected convulsive events. It is a perspective that shows all historical events are the story of incremental change and allows a number of important elements to be added to the story. For example, the integration of major league baseball in 1947 with the signing of Jackie Robinson to play for the Brooklyn Dodgers was received then, and is sometimes still portrayed, as a bolt from the blue. It was no such thing. In order for Jackie Robinson to be chosen, there had to be capable players to choose from. In order for other teams to follow the Dodgers, there needed to be dozens of capable players from which to choose. A deeply layered approach includes the back story, so that important change can be seen as something that is constructed. In the instance of expanding civil rights, the incremental changes required efforts large and small. In this way the story can illuminate the power of individual action. We want young people to see that they *can* make a difference, because every step forward no matter how large or small, is a necessary part of the journey.

The second conceptual construct we use comes from James M. Washington's, *Martin Luther King, Jr.: I Have a Dream, Writings & Speeches That Changed The World*. At a time when Martin Luther King, Jr. has been too often reduced to "I have a dream," Washington takes the reader on King's journey instead—his pilgrimage to his philosophy of non-violence—and reminds us that before the events there was the "rising tide of racial consciousness." Again, the emphasis is on a narrative of incremental, participatory change.

The third, and perhaps the most important, construct that we use has been identified as "culturally relevant teaching." This model is based on the work of Gloria Ladson-Billings. In her study, *The Dreamkeepers: Successful Teachers of African American Children* she explains, ". . . culturally relevant teaching is a pedagogy that empowers students intellectually, socially, emotionally, and politically by using cultural referents to impart knowledge, skills and attitudes. These cultural referents are not merely vehicles for bridging or explaining the dominant culture; they are aspects of the curriculum in their own right." Drawing from her own experience she recalls her fifth grade teacher,

Mrs. Benn. ". . . Mrs. Benn opened up the world of U.S. history. . . She was a great storyteller and, unlike any teacher I had ever known before, *she made a point of telling us about what 'the colored folks' contributed to this story.*"[2]

2. Gloria Ladson-Billings, *The Dreamkeepers: Successful Teachers of African American Children*, p. 19.

This is where our work enters the picture. We hope it will provide teachers and teacher candidates with the means to teach their students a good deal "about what *'the colored folks'* contributed to the story."

By weaving the three central constructs of our argument together, what we have written is a history and resource that we hope will enrich the understandings of teachers about a significant portion of American history, 1865–1965; provide readers with stories, primary documents, music, and film; focus specifically on the incremental changes over time that ultimately led to the Civil Rights movement; and do it from the perspective of African Americans acting on their own behalf.

Goals

Our goals for the book, then, are twofold. The first goal is to challenge the current textbook narrative about Jim Crow America and to explore that world through the lens of Negro League baseball as both a reflector and generator of American culture, values, and change over time. We provide both the history and teaching materials needed to paint a more complete picture of this era. Because the era spans a lengthy period of time, we have used a framework that would allow chapters to be taught sequentially and embedded in each successive era of the standard periodization used in textbooks.

Our second goal is to enrich teachers' understandings about a significant portion of the American past, one that directly relates to a more robust rendering of the American experience because it includes the African-American experience. We propose to do this by tapping the rich history of Negro Leagues baseball, paying particular attention to its place in the American experience. Integration as a self-evident goal in all walks of life was the singular struggle of African Americans and their allies during this time period. But, as critical to progress as large events like *Brown v. Board of Education* were, other equally important forces were also at work. One of those forces was the desire for full access to the American pastime. In order to understand why it was so important to African Americans, it's important to see the ways in which it was important to all Americans.

Teaching Strategies

Research-based teaching strategies that have proven track records for improving student learning are used throughout. Although we have emphasized to this point the necessity for teaching content that will offer a perspective that minority students will find more engaging, it is clear that how any materials are presented to students is also critically important, if students are to construct their own understandings. In an important addition to the kit-bag of all teachers, Robert J. Marzano, Debra J. Pickering, and Jane E. Pollock have distilled decades of education research into "nine broad teaching strategies that *have positive effects on student learning:*"

- Identifying similarities and differences
- Summarizing and note taking
- Reinforcing effort and providing recognition
- Homework and practice
- Non-linguistic representations
- Cooperative learning
- Setting objectives and providing feedback
- Generating and testing hypotheses
- Questions, cues, and advance organizers.[3]

These strategies are used throughout the book so that teachers can be assured that the projects and activities were designed to maximize student learning in ways that we know work.

Primary and Other Sources Included

Using the black press, biographies, plays, poems, music, memoirs, children's and YA literature that reflect the teams and the players as important measures of pride, passion, and engagement, we provide teachers with the background, teaching strategies, and resources necessary to enrich the narrative of the Jim Crow era. The Negro Leagues were a symbol of the community's active challenge to Jim Crow throughout their existence. Somewhere between the rosy past of Buck O'Neil's "best hotels and best restaurants" and the hardscrabble and dangerous world that other players remember is the fascinating story of how the leagues, the travel, and the players heightened the aspirations of, and impelled to action, African Americans in all walks of life.

We hope teachers will use these tools to help all their students see their lives and their potential as very much like a baseball game. It's a team sport but it's also a compilation of individual efforts. No one wins the game alone and each play has consequences for both the individual and the team. It's a game where home runs *and* sacrifices make a difference. And, while it's true that not every year ends in winning the World Series, each year brings new opportunities to swing for the fences.

3. Robert J. Marzano, Debra J. Pickering, and Jane Pollock, *Classroom Instruction that Works: Research-based Strategies for Increasing Student Achievement*, ASCD, 2001, Back Cover.

• • •

A number of further considerations recommend a historically layered approach that describes the journey to a civil rights consciousness through the lens of the Negro Leagues and goes beyond Mrs. Benn to tell more than what "the colored folks' contributed," to make the African-American experience the central narrative.

- More than any other sport, baseball has evolved as we as a nation have evolved. Its position as the most financially important institution within the black community and its wide-ranging impact makes it an ideal vehicle for the deeply layered historical approach we are positing. Over the past several years the National Baseball Hall of Fame has sponsored a traveling exhibit called, *Baseball as America*. The literature describing the exhibit says, "Baseball came of age amid the inventive exuberance of 19th-century America, and continued to mature during the rapid change of the 20th. Our growth as a nation and a people is mirrored in the dugout, on the diamond, and throughout the bleachers. In baseball, one can glimpse our entrepreneurial spirit, our values and self-image, the tensions and triumphs of embracing diverse traditions while forging a sense of community."[4] We agree.

- Baseball is a sport, but more than a sport. Walt Whitman loved baseball. Baseball has been the subject of poetry, literature, film, and drama. It was recently the subject of a documentary by Ken Burns. Major League Baseball has just launched a network solely devoted to the game. The 2009 Coretta Scott King Award for young adult literature was awarded to *We Are the Ship: The Story of Negro League Baseball*. And, it is a sport that, perhaps more than any other, remembers its past.[5]

- The history of Negro Leagues baseball is local history wherever social studies is taught. As early as the mid-1800s baseball was played in towns large and small across the country. The participation of African Americans is integral to that history. The story is accessible.

- Race has been, and continues to be, one of the great unresolved issues of life in America. Baseball, and the story of the Negro Leagues, offers opportunities for teachers to enrich their teaching with voices from the African-American community. It's not always a comfortable story; often it's a painful story. But, it is also a story that is populated by people who struggled daily and in so doing laid the groundwork for change; people who undermined the racist ideology of black inferiority through the witness of their lives.

4. *www.amnh.org/ exhibitions/baseball/ index.html*

5. See *www.baseballmovie. com/baseball-movies. php* for a list of popular movies about baseball.

- The scope of the work spans a significant portion of American history, the mid-19th century to the mid-20th century, thus lending itself to on-going inclusion of African-American history throughout a good portion of the school year.

In addition to the materials for working with students, we've included a teacher workshop with Chapter One. It was designed as a "refresher course" on *Plessy v. Ferguson,* the case that installed "separate but equal" as the law of the land for over sixty years. It can be used individually or with colleagues who may want or need an opportunity to review or better understand the impact of *Plessy v. Ferguson.* We know teachers need to and want to reach diverse student populations and be knowledgeable about what they are teaching. The reality is that they often do not have the time to do this type of research themselves. We have the same goals and invested the time to do this important work for them. We hope this combination of history and resources will do good things for all our students and, in particular, help close the achievement gap for our African-American students.

A Game of Base Ball: Early Innings

In our sundown perambulations of late through the outer parts of Brooklyn, we have observed several parties of youngsters playing 'base,' a certain game of ball. Let us go forth awhile, and get better air in our lungs. Let us leave our close rooms. The game of ball is glorious.

—Walt Whitman, 1846

THE AMERICAN NATIONAL GAME OF BASE BALL.

Spring holds special promise. It's a time of rebirth, a time when the first crocuses peek from beneath the snow to reassure us that warm days will follow. It's a time when sunny afternoons and frosty nights assure us that maple syrup will be ours again. As February snows bluster, then yield to the final parries of March, we know the punch of winter has become like that of a flabby old boxer ready to hang up his gloves. It's all that, but more; it's the beginning of baseball season. To an aficionado of the game the off-season void yields to the magic of some of the most wonderful words in the language: Pitchers and catchers report on the 1st!

No one knows for certain when baseball truly began. We know it did not begin in Cooperstown and that Abner Doubleday did not invent the game.[1] We do know that variations of the game were played during the Civil War and some claim Washington's troops played a game of "base" even earlier. In those days it wasn't organized as we know it today and in some ways it was probably more fun. It was certainly more democratic. Everybody played baseball.

1. Dean A. Sullivan, editor of *Early Innings: A Documentary History of Baseball, 1825-1908*, places the earliest documented reference to baseball at 1825. This reference culminates with the creation of the Doubleday Myth. Ironically enough, one of the great Negro League players, John W. "Bud" Fowler actually grew up in Cooperstown.

35

2. Lawrence Hogan, ed., "Early Days," James Overmyer, *Shades of Glory: The Negro Leagues and the Story of African-American Baseball* (Washington, DC: National Geographic Society, 2006), p. 5.

James Overmyer reports that—

Some of the earliest black baseball was played by slaves. Between 1936 and 1938 the federal Writers' Project set down the reminiscences of several former slaves who recalled baseball, or something like it, having been played in their youth. Sam Scott of Russellville, Arkansas, remembered, 'I never did dance, but I sure could play baseball and make home runs!' John Cole of Athens, Georgia, recalled life on a plantation . . . "always on Saturday afternoon you would have 'til 'first dark' for baseball . . ."[2]

Circa 1870s

It was a game for boys and "white and Negro[3] boys played ball together," not unusual at the time. The rules, however, would change as boys became men and as the game itself became an organized business.

3. The use of the term "Negro" is used in keeping with the usage of the time period being discussed and the standard usage of historians writing about the Negro Leagues.

The State of Play, c. 1865 – 1890

Our story begins in the years immediately following the Civil War before the game was completely segregated and before the Negro Leagues were formed. Over the course of the late decades of the 19th century as the country itself moved toward the separation of citizens that came to be known as Jim Crow America, and as baseball became less of a recreational activity and more of a business, the newly organized teams and leagues reflected the racism of the time and attempted to prevent African Americans from playing on these new "professional" teams. But there were always exceptions to integration. In part this stemmed from the short-lived duration of many of the early teams and leagues. For example, in 1867, the National Association of Base Ball Players, the first organized league, decided without a trace of self-consciousness to exclude the Pythian Club, an all-black team from Philadelphia. Its explanation reads in part ". . . to bar the admission of any club which may be composed of one or more colored persons . . . if colored clubs were admitted there would in all probability be some division of feeling, whereas by excluding them no injury could result to anyone."[4] Such was the casual racism of the time that even the possibility of injury to the Pythians themselves never occurred to the NABBP. Drawing the color line in the short-lived NABBP had little immediate effect but set a precedent for excluding black players in the future. When the next association, The National Association of Professional Base Ball Players, organized itself two years later in 1871, the written decision of the earlier association didn't require codification. By then a "gentlemen's agreement" made admitting Negro clubs or clubs with Negro players unthinkable. But, as can be seen in the picture below, it did not prevent talented black players from playing on professional clubs.

4. Peterson, Robert, *Only the Ball Was White*, (New York: Oxford University Press, 1970).
5. *Ibid.*, p. 20.

The first known professional African-American player, John W. "Bud" Fowler, is pictured below with the 1885 Keokuk's from Keokuk, Iowa. Part of the Western League, the team was 29-8, due in large part to the talents of Fowler, its star player, when the league broke up on June 29th. Fowler went on to play for a number of teams including the Orion (Colored) Club of Philadelphia, a team in St. Joseph, Missouri and the Pueblos in Colorado as well as the Smoky City Giants, the All-American Black Tourists, and the Kansas City Stars. But as the color line gelled, finding a spot on the predominately white teams became increasingly difficult. Fowler was widely acknowledged as one of the best second basemen around, but was frequently out of work. *Sporting Life*, (the *Sports Illustrated* of its day) put it this way:

John W. "Bud" Fowler, 1885 Keokuks

> Fowler, the crack colored second baseman, is still in Denver, Colorado, disengaged. The poor fellow's skin is against him. With his splendid abilities he would long ago have been on some good club had his color been white instead of black. Those who know say there is no better second baseman in the country; he is besides a good batter and fine base-runner.[5]

During the early years of professional baseball, leagues as well as teams organized and broke up with stunning regularity. It made the life of every baseball player uncertain, at best. For African-American players it made a bad situation just that much worse. Besides being a "crack" second baseman, and the acknowledged inventor of shin guards, Fowler played more seasons and more games during his career than any other African-American player until Jackie Robinson played his final season in 1956. After a career spent bouncing from team to team, in 1894 he organized and became a player-manager for the Page Fence Giants, one of the notable teams of its era. But even then the uncertainties of the financial footing that defined baseball during these early years forced the team, after three successful seasons, to fold.[6] Anecdotal evidence suggests there were other black players on white teams during the 1870s and 1880s, but the next that can be placed with certainty is Moses Fleetwood Walker.

Moses Fleetwood Walker was an unlikely candidate for immortality as one of baseball's greats when he entered Oberlin College in 1877. There he was a good, but

not outstanding, student who studied Greek, philosophy, mathematics, and French, and pondered his future. As luck would have it, in his third year at Oberlin, the school organized a baseball team. College baseball was becoming all the rage and Moses joined the team. There, his natural athletic ability helped him become a first-rate catcher and find his calling. His younger brother Weldy Wilberforce Walker patrolled right field. They would become the first and second African-American major league players. Fleetwood is seated on the left in the second row and his brother Weldy is standing in the back row in the picture at left of the Oberlin Varsity ball club.

Oberlin Varsity Team, 1881

After college, Fleet joined the Toledo team of the Northwestern League. The following year, 1884, when the Blue Stockings joined the three-year-old American Association, Fleet became the first African-American major leaguer. His appearance brought mixed reviews. *Sporting Life* reported, "In Baltimore three thousand people turned out to view the curious spectacle of a Negro playing with whites. Every good play by him was loudly applauded."[7] But the real test came in Richmond, Virginia. The manager of the Toledo team, Charlie Morton, received a letter in September in anticipation of a scheduled October series:

> We the undersigned warn you not to put up Walker, the negro catcher . . . as we could mention the names of 75 determined men who have sworn to mob Walker if he comes on the ground in a suit . . . We only write this to prevent bloodshed, as you alone can prevent it.

But the signers of the letter had no connection to anyone on the Richmond team. As it turned out, Walker wasn't able to play because of a broken rib from a foul tip. So we'll never know how determined the mob may have been.

Fleet's brother Weldy entered major league baseball a year later, in 1884. Again, one

6. In spite of Fowler's short time with the Keokuk's, he is prominently featured on *The History of Keokuk, Iowa* website along with a homage to Roger Maris www.keokuk.net/baseball/index.html#1885

7. Peterson, Robert, *Only the Ball Was White*, (New York: Oxford University Press, 1970), p 23.

of the Walker brothers was in the right place at the right time. The Blue Stockings were short handed due to a rash of injuries thus opening the opportunity for Weldy to play. He played in six games and "play[ed] well" according to *Sporting Life.*[8]

Peterson reports, "Fleet Walker and Bud Fowler were the only Negroes in organized white leagues, although Weldy Walker was apparently playing somewhere because in a later report to the Oberlin College alumni office, he said he was in baseball that year."[9] Over the next few years the records show that only a handful of African-American players were still on the rosters of white teams, "important minor league teams." The designation of minor league needs to be explained. As teams organized and folded along with leagues, there was little difference between what was considered minor versus major. That said, the four players that can be identified included Bud Fowler, batting .309 for Topeka in the Western League, joined by George Stovey, "the first great Negro pitcher," in the same league. "*Reach's Official Base Ball Guide* for 1887, reporting on the 1886 season reports Stovey faced 1,059 batters and gave up 177 hits for an ERA of .167."[10]

Fleet Walker caught 32 games and hit .209 in Waterbury for the Eastern League. The fourth, Frank Grant, was so good he became known as "the Black Dunlap," after the spectacular St. Louis Cardinal second baseman, Fred Dunlap. Grant played with the Meriden, Connecticut team until it folded in July, and was picked up by the Buffalo Bisons where the Buffalo *Express* introduced him as a "Spaniard" because of his light complexion. The following season found all four playing in the International League, Fowler in Binghamton, Walker and Stovey with Newark, and Grant in Buffalo. Sol White, who later became the first chronicler of the early years of black players and teams, also entered professional baseball that year, playing for Wheeling. The year 1887 also saw the organization of the first legitimate minor league for black clubs.

Peterson speculates, perhaps too optimistically, that had the League of Colored Base Ball Clubs succeeded, it may have eventually become a feeder for the major leagues. "It is impossible to believe that as a legitimate minor league it could have been ignored completely as were the Negro circuits of a later era."[11] Looking back on the short tenure of the new league Sol White later commented that although short-lived it, "served to bring out the fact that colored baseball players of ability were numerous."[12] The records of the players support his statement and may have been the single most important reason why serious rumblings among white players led to the overt discontent that would bar African-American players from white baseball by the end of the century. Typical of the rebellions among white players was this incident: Dug Crothers, a player for the Syracuse Stars was suspended for refusing to sit for the team photograph because one pitcher was "colored." Leading the headlines in the June 11, 1887, issue of the *Sporting News*, the Syracuse correspondent reported:

8. *Ibid.,* p. 24.
9. *Ibid.,* p. 24.
10. *Ibid.,* p. 25.
11. *Ibid.,* p. 27.
12. *Ibid.,* p. 27.

The Stars have broken out in a new spot. Manager Simmons last Saturday told the members of the club to put in an appearance Sunday morning at Ryder's photograph gallery to have a group picture taken. All the members reported except Pitcher Crothers and left fielder Simon. The manager surmised at once that there was a 'nigger on the fence' and that those players had not reported because the colored pitcher Higgins, was to be included in the club portrait.[13]

13. *Ibid.,* p. 28.
14. *Ibid.,* p. 28.

Drawing the Color Line: Whites Only Baseball

By July the International League's directors met and agreed that the discontent among white players had reached a point that many were ready to leave because of the presence of the "colored element" and "directed Secretary White to approve no more contracts with colored men."[14]

Because these types of incidents and decisions led to the rapid installation of the color line in baseball, in spite of the obvious abilities of the black players, or perhaps because of them, it's easy to see that the prevailing Jim Crow culture of the time made the decision predictable and inevitable.

Sol White's History of Colored Base Ball reserves the leading role in the final ringing down of the color line to National Baseball Hall of Famer, Adrian Constantine "Cap" Anson, one of the greatest players in baseball history, its first superstar, and one of the most outspoken and virulently racist players of his time. He gets little argument from contemporary historians. But, ironically enough, when Anson is remembered today, it is not as much for his status as a superstar but in conjunction with Fleet Walker and with Anson's single-minded mission to keep blacks out of "white" base-ball. His sense of entitlement knew no bounds. The game was his property, and he was unwilling to share.

Historians have speculated that his background may account for his extreme racism, remarkable even at a time when racism was prevalent. He was born in Marshalltown, Iowa in 1852 only five years before the infamous Dred Scott Decision declared [blacks] were "so far inferior [to whites] that they had no rights which a white man was bound to respect." Certainly the prevailing racism of the time had its effect on the young Anson. Sol White was puzzled by Anson's bias:

Adrian "Cap" Anson

Just why [Anson] was so strongly opposed to colored players . . . cannot be explained. His repugnant feeling, shown at every opportunity . . . was a source of comment throughout every league.

White concludes that, "with his great popularity and power in baseball circles, [Anson] hastened the exclusion of the black man from the white leagues."

The irony is that there's no evidence that the Scott Decision and the prevailing racism of the time played a significant part in Anson's early years. He spent his childhood playing with Pottawatomie Indian children who lived in the area of Marshall-ville, Iowa, with few occasions for contact with African Americans. So it's unclear, and probably always will be unclear, why his racism was extreme enough to generate comment at a time when racism was a given in American society.

Peterson agrees that Anson's attitude *"was* strange" but disagrees that Anson had, or needed, the power to force blacks out of the white leagues. By 1887 most white players, North and South, opposed the continued or expanded integration of the game.[15] Ten years after the end of official Reconstruction, Jim Crow America was nearly completely crafted as the American way.

Showdown in Newark

Anson's attempts to oust black players dates from as early as 1883 when he tried to prevent Fleet Walker from playing in an exhibition game between the Toledo Blue Stockings and the Chicago White Stockings, precursor of the Chicago Cubs. The Toledo manager responded saying that Walker would play or there'd be no game. That time Anson relented rather than lose his share of the gate. Later it was revealed that the Toledo team hadn't planned to have Walker catch the game because of a sore hand. It was Anson's threat that determined that Walker would catch, or else. The Toledo folks had no intention of letting Anson think he was calling the shots. By 1887, however, he and his team successfully prevented George Stovey from pitching with the same threat that the White Stockings would refuse to play if Stovey pitched the game. Such were the changes in baseball's climate in the few short years since he tried it against Walker, that the Newark Little Giants yielded, releasing a report that Stovey had "complained of sickness." Another version of the incident reports that when Stovey heard about Anson's threat, he announced he wouldn't play against any team Anson was a part of. What we do know with certainty is that Stovey didn't pitch and another strike was called against integrated baseball.

Even those who celebrate Anson, like Brad Wackerlin, creator of the website *The Life and Times of Adrian "Cap" Anson,* acknowledge the troubling legacy of Anson. In his Chapter Four, "Cap's Great Shame," he presents a balanced appraisal of Cap's culpability, as well as the culpability of baseball owners, fans, and the temper of the times:

> It would be an injustice to the memories of the many thousands of talented black ballplayers that never played a game in the major leagues to exclude a conversation about Cap Anson's role in helping draw the baseball color line that existed from 1887 until 1947. Anson was clearly a racist and one of the most vocal proponents of the exclusion of blacks from organized baseball. By

15. *Ibid.,* p. 31. Two months after Anson's successful barring of Stovey from the game in Newark, a scheduled game between the St. Louis Browns and the all-Negro Cuban Giants was canceled at the last minute because the Brown's manager received a note from his "players which read: 'We the undersigned members of the St. Louis Base Ball Club, do not agree to play against negroes tomorrow. We will cheerfully play against white people at any time, and think, by refusing to play, we are only doing what is right, taking into consideration and the shape the team is in at present.' Of the eight players that signed the note, four were native to the North; a fifth was born in Canada."

Cap Anson and Negro League Founder Andrew "Rube" Foster seemed unlikely friends

both word and deed, Anson revealed himself as a bigot on and off the field. Yet it is unfair to make Anson the exclusive scapegoat for the color line when a number of contributors are to blame.

Wackerlin also notes:

. . . that Anson's racism may have mellowed with age. As coach of the semipro Anson's Colts, he took to the field against many black players. He was often seen talking baseball strategy with the great black manager Andrew "Rube" Foster, the "Father of the Negro Leagues" and later coach of the Chicago American Giants, an all-black team.

And, he disagrees with fans who

. . . believe Anson should be banned from the Hall of Fame because of his racist legacy. This seems an extreme measure, but it does beg a larger question —is it okay to be a fan of Cap Anson in this more enlightened age? Each fan will have to make up his or her own mind. The facts show that Anson was not alone in segregating baseball; that with or without his influence baseball was destined to be segregated due to the prevailing attitudes of the time. Anson was no saint, but neither were the majority of his peers.

He concludes by saying, "In the end, Anson should be remembered as a talented yet flawed individual, a relic of his times. His story has lessons for us all, and he is worthy of both our admiration and contempt to equal degrees."[16]

By the end of the century a called third strike against black players completely segregated professional baseball. But that is both the bad news and the good news. It's the bad news, of course, because it underscores the terrible injustices of Jim Crow America. But, it also ushered in the era of the great Negro Leagues. Later we will see just how important these leagues were to African Americans, indeed to all Americans, when this era plays its final innings.

16. www.capanson.com/chapter4.html

Constructing Jim Crow America: The "Nadir" of Race Relations[1]
A Workshop for Teachers

In order to put Negro League baseball during the Jim Crow era in context, students will need to understand the full sweep of restrictions on African Americans through means both legal and extra-legal, those enforced by law and those enforced by tradition and custom. Although it is an unpleasant truth, until the successes of the Civil Rights era, the United States was an unselfconsciously racist society in ways that were qualitatively and quantitatively more repressive than many of today's students can imagine. Therefore, in order to approach helping them achieve a clear understanding of the national dimensions of this era a firm contextual foundation must be built. Although most textbooks do a very good job of delineating the most obvious abuses of this era, they falter in at least three important ways.

First, when it comes to describing the physical boundaries of Jim Crow, the framework is too narrow. For most, with the possibility of rare exceptions that we have yet to find, the physical boundary of Jim Crow America is limited to the South. Nothing could be further from the truth. By the end of the 19th century Jim Crow was the American way.

Second, because of the periodization followed by textbooks, another problem with understanding the Jim Crow era is that clear references to it are in large

The regrettable Hotel Clark, Memphis

1. James Loewen, *Teaching What Really Happened,* (New York: Teachers College) 2010. Loewen's Chapter 10 offers an excellent analysis of "the Nadir of race relations" during this period and its on-going relevance to teaching about these years, approximately 1890 to 1940.

part confined to the post-Reconstruction era, 1877 to about 1900 when, in fact the America African Americans experienced as Jim Crow America reached well beyond those years; extending into the 1960s and shaping public and private policy in every facet of American life. This was true for both African Americans and white Americans. It confirmed, accelerated, and reinforced an undeserved position of inferiority for African Americans and confirmed, accelerated, and reinforced an undeserved position of privileged superiority for white Americans.

And third, throughout the story African Americans are portrayed as having no historical agency. With the exceptions of Booker T. Washington and W.E.B. DuBois (portrayed as antagonists) and perhaps Ida B. Wells Barnett, African Americans are not seen as acting on their own behalf. The entire entry regarding the 1896 case of *Plessy v. Ferguson* in one standard textbook is two sentences long and is used as a backdrop to a short discussion of the work of Washington and DuBois during the Progressive Era.

Curiosity alone might lead an astute student to inquire, "Who was Plessy?" An even more astute student might go farther to wonder, "What did he do? What was the case about? It takes money to take a case to the Supreme Court, was he wealthy? Did he have supporters? What arguments were put forth on both sides? What did the Court base its decision on?" Answering just these questions would go a long way toward helping students begin to understand the sweep of civil disabilities inflicted on African Americans by the Court and implemented as the law of the land; a ruling that stood for nearly sixty years. In addition, a close reading of the Dissent by John Marshall Harlan would help students see the connections between his dissent and the arguments that built upon it in later cases up to and including

the decision in *Brown v. Board*. In addition, it will demonstrate to students that African Americans took an active role in struggling for their rights long before the Civil Rights era of the 1960s.

Before students can fully appreciate the hardships and limitations that Jim Crow America imposed on the Negro Leagues, they need to be immersed in that America. The following readings and internet-based activities are designed to enhance familiarity with how segregation was constructed in the United States and the totality of the alternate America through which the teams traveled and played. To do this we use a variety of the important building blocks of segregation including the Louisiana Separate Car Law; the 14th Amendment; the ruling in *Plessy v. Ferguson* and the Dissent to *Plessy* by John Marshall Harlan; and the images, artifacts, and film collection of Ferris State University's online Jim Crow Museum of Racist Memorabilia and from the oral history project at American Public Media, "Remembering Jim Crow."

Workshop Objectives:

- Participants will read and interpret Part I of the 14th Amendment, and place it in its historical context, i.e., the specific historical circumstances of its inclusion in the Constitution.

- Participants will be able to identify and explain the three promises contained in the 14th Amendment with regard to citizenship, both state and national.

- Participants will be able, based on their understanding of the 14th Amendment, to explain how the 14th Amendment protects citizens from possible abuses by state governments in the same way that the Bill of Rights protects citizens from possible abuses by the federal government.

- Participants will be able to analyze the Louisiana Separate Car Act of 1890 in order to draw conclusions about the implicit intent of the law.
- Participants will be able to read and interpret the decision in *Plessy v. Ferguson* written by Justice Henry B. Brown.
- Participants will be able to read and interpret the Dissent to *Plessy* written by Justice John Marshall Harlan.
- Participants will then be able to compare their understanding of the 14th Amendment and the Louisiana Separate Car Act of 1890 to the Supreme Court's interpretation of both in the majority decision in *Plessy v. Ferguson* handed down by Justice Henry B. Brown and the dissenting opinion submitted by Justice John Marshall Harlan.

Part 1
Working with Primary Documents:
The Fourteenth Amendment and *Plessy v. Ferguson*

DOCUMENT A
SOURCE: UNITED STATES CONSTITUTION

AMENDMENT XIV, SECTION 1. 1868

All persons born or naturalized in the United States, and subject to the jurisdiction thereof, are citizens of the United States and of the state wherein they reside. No state shall make or enforce any law which shall abridge the privileges or immunities of citizens of the United States; nor shall any state deprive any person of life, liberty, or property, without due process of law; nor deny to any person within its jurisdiction the equal protection of the laws.

---

1. Section 1 of the 14th Amendment states that all persons born or naturalized in the United States have two citizenships. They are **citizens** of

_____

and

_____,

2. Under this amendment no **state** can

_____

or

_____

any law that will abridge (lessen) the privileges or

_____

of citizens of the United States.

3. What **group** was especially in danger of losing their rights as citizens through state laws when this amendment was passed?

4. Under this amendment, no state shall deprive any person of life, liberty, or property **without**

_____ ;

nor deny to any person within its jurisdiction the

_____

protection of the laws.

5. What do these promises **guarantee** to all United States citizens?

6. **Making comparisons:** This section of the 14th Amendment defines who is considered to be a citizen of the United States and makes three important promises to those citizens. How is this section of the 14th Amendment **similar** to the Bill of Rights in its protections for citizens?

DOCUMENT B
SOURCE: LOUISIANA SEPARATE CAR ACT 64, 1890

To promote the comfort of passengers on street railways, requiring all street railways in this state to provide equal but separate accommodations for the white and colored races, by providing separate cars or compartments so as to secure separate accommodations . . .

Section 1 . . . That all street railway companies carrying passengers . . . shall provide equal but separate accommodations for the white and colored races by providing two or more cars or by dividing their cars by wooden or wire screen partitions . . . no person or persons shall be permitted to occupy seats in cars or compartments other than the ones assigned to them on account of the race they belong to.

Section 3 . . . all officers and directors of street railway companies that shall refuse or neglect to comply with [this] act shall upon conviction . . . be fined not less than $100, or be imprisoned in the parish (county) jail not less than 60 days and not more than 6 months . . .

. . . nothing in this act shall be construed as applying to nurses attending children of the other race.

1. What must all street railways **provide** for passengers in Louisiana?

2. What **penalties** may be enforced if the street railways do not comply with this law?

3. What **exception** to the requirements of this law is made in Section 3?

Critical Thinking

1. This law asserts that it was passed in order to promote the **comfort** of passengers. Based on your knowledge of the legislature of Louisiana in 1890, what is your best hypothesis regarding which Louisiana citizens' comfort was the primary concern of this legislation?

2. One **exception** to this law is contained in Section 3. Based on your understanding of Louisiana society in 1890, does this exception allow "colored" nurses to sit in "white" cars if they are caring for white children OR white nurses to sit in "colored" cars if they are caring for colored children? Why might the legislature of Louisiana in 1890 make this exception?

3. How does this exception to the law reveal **whose comfort** the law was meant to protect?

DOCUMENT C
SOURCE: JUSTICE HENRY B. BROWN'S DECISION ON BEHALF OF THE SUPREME COURT IN
PLESSY V. FERGUSON, 1896

So far, then, as a conflict with the Fourteenth Amendment is concerned, the case **reduces itself to the question whether the statute of Louisiana is a reasonable regulation,** and, with respect to this, there must necessarily be a large discretion on the part of the legislature. **In determining the question of reasonableness, it is at liberty to act with reference to the established usages, customs, and traditions of the people, and with a view to the promotion of their comfort and the preservation of the public peace and good order.** Gauged by this standard, we cannot say that a law which authorizes or even requires the separation of the two races in public conveyances [p551] is unreasonable . . .

We consider the underlying fallacy of the plaintiff's argument to consist in the assumption that the enforced separation of the two races stamps the colored race with a badge of inferiority. If this be so, it is **not by reason of anything found in the act, but solely because the colored race chooses to put that construction upon it.**

Legislation is powerless to eradicate racial instincts or to abolish distinctions based upon physical differences, and the attempt to do so can only result in accentuating the difficulties of the present situation. . . . If one race be inferior to the other socially, the Constitution of the United States cannot put them upon the same plane.

Justice Brown writes in the first paragraph that the case reduces itself to a question of whether the Louisiana law is reasonable. In order to answer that question the court says that if the law is in agreement with "established usages, customs, and traditions of the people" then the Court "cannot say that it . . . is unreasonable."

1. Based on your knowledge of Louisiana society in 1890, why might local "usages, customs, and traditions" be a **poor** standard by which to measure the reasonableness of the law?

2. In the second paragraph Justice Brown writes that, "the assumption [is] that the enforced separation of the two races stamps the colored race with a badge of inferiority. If this be so, it is not by reason of anything found in the act, but solely because the colored race chooses to put that construction upon it."

   Justice Brown is saying that if the "colored race" thinks being separated stamps them as inferior, it's because they choose to think that way. Based on your knowledge of Louisiana society in 1890, what might convince African Americans that separation was, in fact, designed to **enforce** an inferior status for them in that society?

3. In the last paragraph of this excerpt from the full decision, the Supreme Court held that if one race were socially inferior to the other, the Constitution was powerless to do anything about it. With this decision the court affirmed the validity of the Louisiana Separate Car Law of 1890 and established "separate but equal" as the law of the entire United States.

   Why is it important for you to understand that when the Supreme Court, the highest federal court in the United States, hands down a ruling that ruling becomes the law for the **entire** country?

4. *Trick question:* Which Supreme Court judge do you think would be most likely to disagree with the court's decision—Henry B. Brown of Massachusetts, who had gone to Harvard, or John Marshall Harlan from Kentucky, whose family had owned slaves and was educated at the tiny law school at Transylvania University in Kentucky? Answer below.

Answer to the "trick" question: the dissenting justice was the one who was raised in a slave-holding family, Justice John Marshall Harlan.

DOCUMENT D
SOURCE: J. M. HARLAN, DISSENTING OPINION, 1896

In respect of civil rights common to all citizens, the Constitution of the United States does not, I think, permit any public authority to know the race of those entitled to be protected in the enjoyment of such rights. . . . I deny that any legislative body or judicial tribunal may have regard to the race of citizens when the civil rights of those citizens are involved. Indeed, such legislation as that here in question is inconsistent not only with that equality of rights which pertains to citizenship, National and State, but with the personal liberty enjoyed by everyone within the United States.

The white race deems itself to be the dominant race in this country. . . . But in view of the Constitution, in the eye of the law, there is in this country no superior, dominant, ruling class of citizens. There is no caste here. Our Constitution is color-blind, and neither knows nor tolerates classes among citizens. In respect of civil rights, all citizens are equal before the law. . . . It is therefore to be regretted that this high tribunal, the final expositor of the fundamental law of the land, has reached the conclusion that it is competent for a State to regulate the enjoyment by citizens of their civil rights solely upon the basis of race.

The arbitrary separation of citizens on the basis of race while they are on a public highway is a badge of servitude wholly inconsistent with the civil freedom and the equality before the law established by the Constitution. It cannot be justified upon any legal grounds.

If evils will result from the commingling of the two races upon public highways established for the benefit of all, they will be infinitely less than those that will surely come from state legislation regulating the enjoyment of civil rights upon the basis of race. We boast of the freedom enjoyed by our people above all other peoples. But it is difficult to reconcile that boast with a state of the law which, practically, puts the brand of servitude and degradation upon a large class of our fellow citizens, our equals before the law. The thin disguise of "equal" accommodations for passengers in railroad coaches will not mislead anyone, nor atone for the wrong this day done.

1. In his dissent, Justice Harlan writes, "the Constitution . . . does not . . . permit any public authority to **know** the race of those entitled to be protected in the enjoyment of their civil rights." What does this statement mean?

2. According to the last sentence of the first paragraph, legislation that separates people on the basis of race goes against what **two** basic principles?

3. Justice Harlan disagrees with the majority of the court regarding whether or not separating the races implies inferiority for the non-dominant race. On the basis of the third paragraph, what is his opinion?

4. According to the last paragraph, what consequences does Justice Harlan conclude will be the lasting effect of the majority decision on American freedom?

5. Based on the last sentence, what is Justice Harlan's opinion of **qualifying** "separate" with "equal"?

Part 2
Using Biographical Sketches

The following biographical sketches will help participants get to know a bit about each of the three most important actors involved in the case of *Plessy v. Ferguson*: Homer Plessy, Justice Henry B. Brown, and Justice John Marshall Harlan.

Directions

After participants read each of the biographical sketches, have them work together with either a partner or in groups to generate a list of things that they would like to know more about each of them. Provide internet access, a text set, or other research materials so they can begin answering their own questions. Have each pair or group share what they discover with the rest of the class.

Jason Feldt,, "Homer Plessy: Pioneer in Civil Rights," *Iowa Council for the Social Studies Journal,* Fall, 2006.

Homer Plessy: Pioneer in Civil Rights

In 1890, a law for racially segregated facilities was written into Louisiana state law. Laws such as this became known as Jim Crow laws. This law included the Separate Car law that called for the segregation of passenger trains traveling within the state of Louisiana. This law sparked the concerns of a group of citizens fighting for the rights of all people. This group called themselves the Citizens' Committee. The group planned strategies to challenge segregation laws in the courts. They hired Albion Tourgee, a white New York attorney who had previously fought for African Americans, to come to Louisiana and lead the challenge. In 1896, the group asked Homer Plessy to act against the state law by sitting in a railcar designated for white people only. He was then arrested and jailed but released the next day on a $500 bond.

Homer Plessy went to court on the basis that the law had violated his 13th and

14th amendment rights. Judge John Howard Ferguson oversaw the court case that was titled, *Plessy v. Ferguson*. After listening to the case made by Homer Plessy's lawyer, Judge Ferguson found Homer Plessy guilty. The case eventually was decided by the Supreme Court.

Henry B. Brown, 1891–1906

Henry B. Brown was born in South Lee, Massachusetts, on March 2, 1836. After graduation from Yale College in 1856, he studied abroad for one year. Upon his return to New England, Brown began reading law in Ellington, Connecticut, and then pursued further studies at the law schools of Yale and Harvard. In 1859, at age 23, Brown moved to Detroit, Michigan, and was admitted to the bar. He then established a law practice and developed a specialty in maritime law. In the first year of his practice, Brown was appointed a Deputy United States Marshal for Detroit. Three years later, he was appointed an Assistant United States Attorney for the Eastern District of Michigan. Brown also held an interim appointment as Circuit Judge for Wayne County in 1868. In 1875, President Ulysses S. Grant appointed Brown to the United States District Court for Eastern Michigan, where he served for fourteen years. President Benjamin Harrison nominated Brown to the Supreme Court of the United States on December 29, 1890, and the Senate confirmed the appointment seven days later.

www.supremecourthistory.org/ history-of-the-court/associate-justices/henry-brown-1891-1906/

John Marshall Harlan, 1877–1911

Justice Oliver Wendell Holmes called his colleague John Marshall Harlan the last "tobacco chomping justice." Born in 1833 in Boyle County, Kentucky into a family that had owned slaves, Harlan not only chewed tobacco, but drank bourbon, played golf, loved baseball, and wore colorful clothing not often associated with Supreme Court justices. Although sometimes a terror to attorneys while on the bench, Harlan was approachable in person. A man of middle-class values, Harlan alone among the justices of his era was comfortable socializing with Hispanics, Negroes, and Chinese.

Harlan is best known for his eloquent dissent in the 1896 case, *Plessy v. Ferguson*, which upheld a Louisiana law requiring blacks and whites to ride in separate railroad cars. Harlan criticized the Court's adoption of the "separate but equal" doctrine in these memorable words: "Our Constitution is color blind and neither knows nor tolerates classes among citizens."

http://law2.umkc.edu/faculty/ projects/ftrials/shipp/harlan. html

Part 3
Incorporating Technology: Internet Sources and Film

Participants should tour the following website and select a representative number of links to explore in detail.

A. Ferris State University Jim Crow Museum of Racist Memorabilia

www.ferris.edu/jimcrow/what.htm

For each linked site chosen they should address the following prompts in their notebooks:

> Title
>
> Author or designer (if available)
>
> Author or designer's ethnic background (if available)
>
> Date of the artifact, film, etc.
>
> Overview of contents
>
> Time period it represents
>
> Is it still relevant today? (For example, if it's a film, is it still available, being shown?)
>
> What overarching message does the material at the link you've chosen send?

Closure

Each home page lists a number of objectives that the site's authors hope to accomplish through their research and presentation of these materials. Based on their study of the site's materials, participants can evaluate in what ways the site's materials successfully meet these objectives, and present their conclusions in a class discussion.

B. American Public Media *"Remembering Jim Crow"*

http://americanradioworks.publicradio.org/ features/remembering/index.html

With partners, or in groups, participants can explore this website and select a representative number of links to the slideshows, documents, and interviews. After they've had a chance to familiarize themselves with what it has to offer, they can prepare a short presentation in which they recommend something on the site that they think the others in the class would be interested in. They should be encouraged to incorporate sound clips from the tapes or other materials available on the site to enrich their presentations.

C. Thinking About Segregation

For this activity, participants will organize their understanding of the ruling in *Plessy v. Ferguson.* In order to visualize the way this decision affected American life, especially for African Americans, participants will consider the guide questions and reflect on their answers after viewing the film, *A Class Divided*, to reach a variety of affective objectives such as empathy and concern for others.

GUIDE QUESTIONS

- Based on the "equal protection" clause of the 14th Amendment, was it Constitutional to separate street car passengers based on their race?

- How do you think it would it feel to be separated from the mainstream of American life?

Film: *A Classroom Divided*

One day in 1968, Jane Elliott, a teacher in a small, all-white Iowa town, divided her third-grade class into blue-eyed and brown-eyed groups and gave them a daring lesson in discrimination. This is the story of that lesson, its lasting impact on the children, and its enduring power decades later.

http://video.google.com/videoplay?docid=618999171263 6113875#

Before showing the film ask participants to consider the following questions:

- What does "equal protection" of the laws mean to you?

- Since the color of your eyes or your skin aren't things you can control, would a school rule that separated participants by the color of their eyes be okay? Explain your response.

- Let's add another layer. Would this kind of separation be okay if one group was given more privileges because they had brown eyes instead of blue? For example, if just the brown-eyed participants were allowed to go to lunch early, or got the new books would that be okay? Explain your answer.

- What kinds of groupings do seem fair to you? Explain.

Watch the film and as you watch, be attentive to the behavior of **both** the brown-eyed and blue-eyed third graders.

- The participants who were part of this experiment got together years later and reflected on the impact of the lesson on the rest of their lives. What are some of their comments that really seemed surprising or important to you?

- How has the experiment been used in the years since 1968? Did any surprise you? Explain.

- What did the film add to your understanding of segregation?

WRAPPING IT UP, BRINGING CLOSURE TO THE WORKSHOP:

Summarizing

In order to help participants pull all of the workshop components together, ask them to synthesize their learning by addressing the following prompt:

In the court case *Plessy v. Ferguson,* the court ruled that it was okay to separate street car passengers based only on the color of their skin. Now that you've had a chance to think about your answers to the questions above and watched the film, what is your response as to the validity of the court's ruling?

Predicting

Now that participants have completed these assignments they will be able to begin predicting some of the challenges the teams of the Negro Leagues would have encountered as they traveled across the country. Help participants generate a list of those challenges. After they have completed the list, help them anticipate how the teams will meet these challenges by posing the question:

What strategies do you think the teams might be able to utilize in order to meet these challenges?

This should make them start thinking about the ways that these African-American historical actors traveled through Jim Crow America as decision makers, initiators, and challengers of that world.

Andrew "Rube" Foster, Red Summer and the Birth of Negro League Baseball

NEGRO LEAGUES BASEBALL   NEGRO LEAGUES BASEBALL

When Rube Foster strode into a room, it belonged to him. And so it was on February 13, 1920, when he stood to face the gathered owners of the teams that would soon become the first organized Negro League, his vision made manifest. Physically imposing at 6'4", tall, muscular, and weighing in at over 200 pounds, Andrew Foster was a presence. This was a man who had weathered a sickly childhood to become the pre-eminent pitcher of his era. He had endured the hardships—physical, mental, and emotional—of a barnstorming career that spanned over fifteen years. He had cultivated and maintained an aura of intimidation on the baseball field, rattling the opposition hitters from the mound by boasting of his team's abilities and the inevitability of their winning the game. He brooked no compromises; his intensity to dominate, to win, knew no bounds. Legend has it that once he actually pitched with a loaded revolver strapped to his hip just to intimidate the opposition. Over the course of his playing career, he met the physical, mental, and emotional challenges of his life and prevailed by conquering them all and gaining a respect and notoriety that crossed racial lines. Although his pitching career was over, his real legacy and the purpose for the meeting, was waiting in the wings.

By 1919, Andrew Foster was not only a celebrity in Chicago; he had achieved a healthy measure of recognition nationally within the African-American community. Reporters from African-American newspapers felt privileged to be in his company, let alone be granted an occasional interview. Every quotation was a trophy and stories about him and his various baseball activities frequently found their way to the front page, trumping both local and national news stories. He was visible and active in his community, playing a strong role in his church and Chicago civic organizations. The society column of *The Chicago Defender*, the leading national African-American newspaper of its day, regularly reported on the social activities of both Foster and his wife. "Sightings" of the couple in the Chicago area signaled an "event."

It is not too much to say that Andrew "Rube" Foster was one of the most influential African-American leaders of the early 20th century. Though less recognized today than W.E.B. DuBois or Booker T. Washington, in his day he was the very embodiment of African-American ingenuity and activism against the segregationist practices that stand today as a humiliating blot on the national character. As his biographer, Robert Charles Cottrell, stated, ". . . without Foster's vision and organizational acumen, [Satchel] Paige, [Josh] Gibson, Buck Leonard, and even Jackie Robinson would likely have remained mere footnotes in American sports history."[1] His point is that without the Negro leagues Foster organized, black baseball would have never achieved the level of success and financial stability necessary to highlight the talents of these players. They, like the many talented players before them, would have faded into the same obscurity.

Moreover, Andrew "Rube" Foster is in a class all to himself as an architect of race relations and social progress in American baseball. His most enduring legacy was the founding of the Negro National League in 1920, which provided opportunities for an entire generation of African-American athletes.[2] Sports historian Jules Tygiel agrees, "Rube Foster ranks with Charles Comiskey, Connie Mack, and John McGraw as one of the founding giants of modern baseball. As player, manager, owner, and executive he set the standard for baseball in black America during the early twentieth century."[3]

"Foster's importance ultimately reached well beyond his own lifetime, as his league [and the leagues that it inspired], other than a yearlong hiatus at the height of the Great Depression, remained in existence until the color barrier was broken in organized baseball. From the time of its founding, the Negro National League [and later, the Negro American National League] served as vehicles through which the finest black baseball players showcased their considerable talents."[4] It was from these leagues that Branch Rickey could choose Jackie Robinson. A look back to the years before baseball was re-integrated will show just how he did it.

When Foster called, people listened. So when he called for a meeting of all the team owners in the Spring of 1920, the response was immediate. Excitement was palpable. Foster trumpeted the event with several articles he wrote for *The Chicago Defender* and the newspaper was heralding the meeting with a number of columns and articles of its own in the weeks leading up to it. The invited team owners Foster had selected for his league needed no coaxing to attend. Foster was considered the foremost authority on all facets of the game of baseball, and on African-American baseball in

1. Robert Charles Cottrell, *The Best Pitcher in Baseball: The Life of Rube Foster, Negro League Giant,* (New York: NYU Press, 2001) p. 5.

2. Phil S. Dixon, *Andrew "Rube" Foster: A Harvest on Freedom's Fields,* (New York: Xlibris, 2010).

3. Review of *The Best Pitcher in Baseball,* amazon.com.

4. Cottrell, p. 4.

particular. His status and reputation in the sport was such that any endorsement by him signaled a stamp of approval. Foster and the other owners were met in Kansas City with some considerable fanfare and celebration by the African-American community. Their initial evening in town was highlighted by a formal dinner at the elegant home of a prominent African-American socialite and her businessman husband, where all were treated to what was considered a very special dinner—opossum, with all the trimmings. It was an event worthy of an extensive report in the society column of Kansas City's black newspaper, *The Kansas City Call.*

The Impact of World War I and the Great Migration

The timing of this event was anything but random. The impact of World War I on the African-American community receives far less attention than that of World War II, the latter characterized by the "Double-V" campaign, the GI Bill, the desegregation of the American Armed Forces, and the subsequent arrival of Jackie Robinson to previously all-white Major League baseball. However, the legacy of WWI was no less significant in informing the civil rights issue. Organizing African-American baseball was neither a new idea nor sudden revelation for Foster. As early as 1913 he had expressed the sentiment: "Organization is the only thing that will save black baseball."[5] Although it would be another seven years before the idea came to fruition, he chose an ideal time to act. It was against the backdrop of WWI's legacy and the Great Migration that Andrew Foster launched the Negro National League in 1920.

World War I was a watershed experience for the African-American community. The following, from the National Archives, outlines the impact of the war:

> During World War I, 380,000 African Americans served in the wartime Army. Approximately 200,000 of these were sent to Europe. More than half of those sent abroad were assigned to labor and stevedore battalions, but they performed essential duties nonetheless, building roads, bridges, and trenches in support of the front-line battles. Roughly 42,000 saw combat.
>
> American troops arrived in Europe at a crucial moment in the war. Russia had just signed an armistice with Germany in December 1917 freeing Germany to concentrate her troops on the Western Front. If Germany could stage a huge offensive before Americans came to the aid of her war-weary allies, Germany could win the war.
>
> The 369th Infantry helped to repel the German offensive and to launch a counteroffensive. General John J. Pershing assigned the [all-black] 369th to the 16th Division of the French Army. With the French, [this unit nicknamed] the Harlem Hellfighters fought at Chateau-Thierry and Belleau Wood. All told

5. *Indianapolis Freeman,* Dec. 20, 1913.

they spent 191 days in combat, longer than any other American unit in the war. "My men never retire, they go forward or they die," said Colonel Hayward. Indeed, the 369th was the first Allied unit to reach the Rhine.

The extraordinary valor of the 369th earned them fame in Europe and America. Newspapers headlined the feats of Corporal Henry Johnson and Private Needham Roberts. In May 1918 they were defending an isolated lookout post on the Western Front, when they were attacked by a German unit. Though wounded, they refused to surrender, fighting on with whatever weapons were at hand. They were the first Americans awarded the *Croix de Guerre*, and they were not the only Harlem Hellfighters to win awards; 171 of its officers and men received individual medals and the unit received a *Croix de Guerre* for taking Sechault.

In December 1917, when Colonel Hayward's men had departed from New York City, they had not been permitted to participate in the farewell parade of New York's National Guard, the so-called Rainbow division. The reason Hayward was given was that "black is not a color in the rainbow." Now Colonel Hayward pulled every political string he could to assure his men would be rewarded with a victory parade when they came home in February 1919. Crowds thronged New York City's Fifth Avenue as the 369th marched to the music of their now-famous regimental jazz band leader, James Reese Europe. After the parade, city officials honored the troops at a special dinner. But what kind of America had they come home to?[6]

6. www.archives. gov/education/ lessons/369th-infantry/

The close of hostilities in 1918 contributed to significant racial tension across America. Hundreds of thousands of soldiers, both white and black, were rapidly demobilized without any specific plan or legislation to cope with their assimilation back into American society or its economy. The Great Migration of African Americans from the South to the industrial cities of the North had begun in earnest around 1910 and would continue through the next decade. Fueled by expanding opportunity for jobs, as well as a desire to escape oppression in their daily lives, the migration swelled the population of African Americans in many northern cities. Chicago alone saw its population of African Americans increase from 40,000 to 110,000 during the decade.

The "Red Summer" of 1919

Such a burgeoning presence helped to create significant social and economic tension. City services, particularly housing, were over taxed as the competition for jobs intensified. Tensions escalated quickly, particularly in the increasingly over-crowded cities, where racial and ethnic groups were suddenly pushed together in fierce competition for jobs and for social advancement. Entering this arena was the African-American WWI veteran, exhibiting a higher level of militancy and pride, with expectations for full citizenship after having served his country in war. He was victorious and he had contributed and he was not content to return as a second-class citizen. Lemuel Moody, a soldier who served overseas, reflected that his experience was, "altogether improving and broadening . . . [it]changed my outlook on life. I see things now with different eyes."[7] Various white ethnic groups strongly resented this new attitude, as well as the increasing African-American presence in general and began to focus on the black community as the object of their increasing frustration.

The year 1919 *appeared* destined to become one of triumphant peace and universal fellowship. The Great War, World War I, "the war to end all wars," had ended with a ringing defeat of German autocracy and the world was once again "made safe for democracy." A triumphant Woodrow Wilson confidently predicted that the international unity that had led to military victory would expand and prosper, the product of a new "moral force that is irresistible."[8]

But the America encountered by returning African-American war veterans in 1919 was one that neither embodied nor embraced the unity that was championed in Wilson's words. Instead the summer of 1919 witnessed one of the worst seasons of racial conflict in American history. Indeed, John Hope Franklin called it the worst.[9] From April 13 through October 1, "race riots" occurred in 34 cities and towns across America. Author and social activist James Weldon Johnson, the secretary of the newly minted NAACP in 1919, coined the phrase "Red Summer" to describe the period, the word "red" referring to the degree of violence and bloodshed that characterized the conflicts. The violence enveloped towns, counties, and large cities from Texas to Nebraska, Connecticut to California—no section of the country was spared from the violence and destruction. Hundreds died, thousands were injured and made homeless, and countless businesses and farms were burned or destroyed. Yet today, the season is only a footnote in America's historical narrative and a glaring omission from our classrooms and from our national conscience.

Several factors arranged themselves into a perfect storm to create the tinderbox of racial unrest that characterized the America of 1919. Jim Crow had been strengthened and emboldened throughout the country subsequent to the *Plessy v. Ferguson* Supreme Court decision of 1898. The Great Migration north of hundreds of thousands of blacks had created a new urbanization that taxed receiving areas' abilities to provide adequate housing, sanitation, and other vital services. Finally, there was both a local and national economic downturn as the nation struggled to cope with the many thousands of returning job-seeking World War I veterans. African Americans were

7. http://exhibitions.nypl.org/africanaage/essay-world-war-i.html

8. Cameron McWhirter, *Red Summer: The Summer of 1919 and the Awakening of Black America* (New York: Henry Holt & Co., 2011), p. 12.

9. John Hope Franklin, in Phil S. Dixon, *Andrew "Rube" Foster: A Harvest on Freedom's Fields,* (New York: Xlibris, 2010), p. 114.

targeted by many as being primary contributors, if not the actual causative agents, of the stress and frustration felt by the larger white population. The racial violence that ensued was not a virulent contagion that spread from one area to the next but rather a symptom of a tension that gripped the entire nation. An alleged crime, a neighborhood argument, a routine building inspection or traffic stop—any of these could, and in fact did, provide flashpoints for interracial conflict.

While many historians use the term "race riot" to describe the events that summer, the term is in reality a misnomer as so applied. Most of the "riots" were, in fact, confrontations initiated by whites and characterized by roving gangs of white males systematically seeking out African Americans and physically attacking any they found. Author Gunner Myrdal was particularly opposed to the term "riot" when applied to America's Red Summer, describing the interracial conflicts as "a terrorization or massacre" and considered it "a magnified, or mass lynching."[10] When occurring in the larger cities, particularly in Chicago, the gangs were frequently organized around ethnic identity. Areas of black settlement were literally invaded and hundreds of black homes and businesses were burned to the ground or otherwise destroyed. To many it seemed as if the white mobs were literally attempting to drive the black community from their presence.

Of all the violence that occurred that summer, the violence in Chicago is generally considered to have been the worst and was certainly the most prolonged. Its flashpoint was the drowning death of black teenager Eugene Williams who disappeared under the waves when he was pelted by rocks being hurled at him from the beach by a white adult male. The sweltering heat had drawn hundreds of Chicago residents to the beach that afternoon and there had already been some minor interracial conflict earlier in the day between the swimmers at the adjoining segregated beaches of South Chicago. The story is that Eugene and his friends apparently strayed too close to the "Whites Only" signs for the comfort of the rock-thrower. Segregated crowds of angry blacks and whites gathered as his body was pulled from Lake Michigan and the name-calling and verbal abuse directed at each other's group turned into explosive violence by nightfall. Eight days of rage resulted in several dozen fatalities and hundreds of injuries, the overwhelming majority of whom were African American. When calm was finally restored and the burning fires extinguished, the Black Belt of Chicago, where in 1919, 90 percent of the black population of Chicago resided, ironically resembled one of the war-ravaged cities of Europe after World War I.

In Chicago, and in a number of other cities and towns across America, something profound and fundamentally different occurred in 1919. In these new urban settings a new generation of African Americans resisted white violence with organized violence of their own, and did so in large numbers. This marked a turning point for

10. Gunnar Myrdal, *An American Dilemma: The Negro Problem and Modern Democracy*, (New York: Harper, 1944), p. 566, cited in Robert A. Gibson, *The Negro Holocaust: Lynching and Race Riots in the United States, 1880-1950*, Themes in Twentieth Century American Culture, 1979, Vol. 2 (New Haven: Yale Teachers Institute, 1979), and www.yale.edu/ynhti/curriculum/units/1979/2/79.02.04.x.html

black communities as they actively defended themselves during the Jim Crow era. As previous generations had resisted the Klan during Reconstruction, this generation demonstrated its willingness to fight back—to band together for physically safety and to fight for their civil rights. With this kind of organized resistance, the seeds of a renewed sense of pride, shared identity, and determination were planted in the black community, and a newly energized activism was about to emerge.

The black community in America received support and encouragement for its retaliatory action from several of its prominent leaders. W.E.B. Dubois was one of those who advocated self-defense against mob attack as early as October, 1916. From the pages of his newsletter, *The Crisis*, he wrote:

> In God's name, let us not perish like bales of hay. . . . Lynching [will only stop] when the cowardly mob is faced with effective guns in the hands of the people determined to sell their souls dearly.[11]

A. Phillip Randolph, speaking as editor of *The Messenger*, wrote:

> The black man has no rights which will be respected unless the black man enforces that respect. . . . We are consequently urging Negroes and other oppressed groups concerned with lynching and mob violence to act upon the recognized and accepted law of self-defense.[12]

Even the fledgling NAACP, considered by many in the black community to be a moderate voice, defended the legality of black retaliatory self-defense from mob attack.[13]

Despite the political and cultural significance of the Red Summer of 1919, the events have not found a significant place in history textbooks or the social studies classroom, and many teachers may be unaware of this historical episode. This is neither a shock nor surprise, since history is, after all, often said to be the written domain of its victors. African Americans have rarely, if ever, been in a position of either power or influence to advocate for their inclusion in the historical narrative. Many of the involved localities have chosen to erase that summer's events from their collective memory. Many of their residents, some of whom are descendents of victims or perse-cutors, are unaware of their families' histories, having learned long ago that the subject was "not something we talk about." Everyday lives were restored, burned businesses rebuilt, and a five-month span of American history was sealed and paved over.

Consequently, a full accounting of African-American causalities from the Red Summer remains elusive. The NAACP records 77 lynchings in 1919, up from 64 in 1918. Especially shameful and poignant were the murders of the ten veterans still wearing their World War I Army uniforms.[14] Anecdotal evidence from each individual

11. W.E.B. DuBois, *The Crisis*, October, 1916, in Gibson.

12. *Ibid.*

13. *Ibid.*

14. http://exhibitions.nypl. org/africanaage/essay-world-war-i.html

event renders a conservative toll of at least 100 dead and thousands injured and left homeless. Similar evidence reveals only a handful of white causalities and significant exclusion from the devastating property damage visited upon the black community.

Cameron McWhirter summarized the significance of the summer's events:

> Yet something amazing happened as the mobs rose up. They encountered black men and women transformed by their experiences during the war, whether in European trenches, on the factory floors of northern cities, or in the cotton fields of the South. The economic, social, and political dynamics of black-white relations were changing. African Americans fought back in large numbers. They retaliated immediately, picking up guns and firing on approaching mobs. They organized and transformed political organizations, primarily the NAACP, to challenge the violence in the political arena and the courts. The white attacks, and importantly the black reaction to them, emboldened blacks across the country and made 1919 a turning point in American race relations.[15]

Jamaican-born poet, Claude McKay, captured this new militant spirit of the black community in his 1921 poem:

> *If We Must Die*
> If we must die, let it not be like hogs
> Hunted and penned in an inglorious spot,
> While round us bark the mad and hungry dogs,
> Making their mock at our accursed lot.
> If we must die, O let us nobly die,
> So that our precious blood may not be shed
> In vain; then even the monsters we defy
> Shall be constrained to honor us though dead!
> O kinsmen we must meet the common foe!
> Though far outnumbered let us show us brave,
> And for their thousand blows deal one deathblow!
> What though before us lies the open grave?
> Like men we'll face the murderous, cowardly pack,
> Pressed to the wall, dying, but fighting back![16]

The new narrative needs to demonstrate that African-American activism for social justice and civil rights did not burst spontaneously onto the American stage with Jackie Robinson's integration of the major leagues in 1947 or because of the *Brown v. Board of Education of Topeka, Kansas* decision of 1955. It was a process that spanned the generations, and the story of the Civil Rights movement is incomplete without

15. McWhirter, p. 14.

16. *Harlem Shadows: The Poems of Claude McKay* (New York: Harcourt, Brace and Co., 1922) in Gibson. Originally published in *The Liberator Magazine*, a monthly socialist publication.

the inclusion of the Red Summer of 1919. The summer's events signified a national call to the black community, a call taken to heart by Andrew Foster and his vision for a Negro League.

This, then, was the backdrop for the events to follow. When, in July, Foster's Chicago American Giants returned from a road trip to the West Coast, they returned to a Chicago in chaos and "their park . . . occupied by the tents of National Guardsmen."[17] Foster was instrumental in accelerating this new attitude in the African-American community of Chicago. Already a semi-regular subject of and contributor to Chicago's *Defender*, his columns increased that fall and into the following spring, when he actively reinvigorated his campaign for organized black baseball. Strong themes of activism, identity, and pride had for years characterized his writing and now it seemed that his words had helped create a sense of strength among his readers. Whether by coincidence or by opportunity, it is clear that his words, his passion, and his ideas were reaching a different audience than that of the previous year. Brutal as it was, the summer's agony had opened an opportunity for further change. Speaking to this new activism, Foster had their rapt attention. Working in concert with community support, steps were being taken that would both influence and create the civil rights contests to come. Whether either Foster or the community was aware of it at the time, they had their champion—he would not let them down.

Andrew Foster made his home in Chicago and lived through that "Red Summer of 1919." One can only ponder his response and reaction to the events, but as a keen businessman and student of his community, it is a fair assumption to make that the lessons and legacy of that summer were not lost to him. While he applied his "need to organize" message to baseball, it is not difficult to recognize that he was also talking to a larger audience. When he wrote and spoke to the black community he focused on issues of pride and identity. His National League, he argued, would be something that "we can look to and be proud of." His expressed goals for his league further reinforced this ideal: "to create a profession that would equal the earning capacity of any other profession . . . to keep colored baseball from the control of whites and do something concrete for the loyalty of the Race."[18]

Negro League Baseball Is Born

The morning of February 13, 1920, dawned dark and cold in Kansas City, Missouri. Light flurries fell on the awakening city and there was a hint of heavier snow to come in the air. In a small room at the Paseo branch of the south side YMCA, Andrew Foster gathered a group of team owners to talk about the future of baseball, specifically African-American baseball. It was only six months since the race riots that shook

17. Hugh Davis Graham and Ted Robert Gurr, *Violence in America,* (New York: Praeger, 1969) in Gibson

18. Sports.JRank.org

Chicago the previous summer in July of 1919, hence a neutral location; Chicago was still too hot even in February.[19] Moreover, the Paseo YMCA was one of the very few "Negro" YMCAs. "Ten years earlier [1910] Julius Rosewald, a Jewish philanthropist challenged the city to raise $75,000 to build a Negro YMCA, to which he would add $25,000. The funds were raised in less than ten days by the black community."[20] Laying out a new way for African Americans to assert themselves was still risky, but Foster was determined and very persuasive. His campaign to organize black baseball was aided by one of the most influential black newspapers of the time, *The Chicago Defender.* From October, 4, 1919, through February, Foster had filled his column in the sports pages of the paper with persuasion and exhortations on the necessity for organization. Other sports writers agreed. On October 4, 1919, Cary B. Lewis of the *Defender* wrote that the season had been "so prosperous" and attendance "so great" that a "colored league" seemed inevitable and that Foster was "the man responsible for the proposed circuit."[21] Lewis continued, "No man in baseball has more influence than Rube Foster."[22]

With this gathering of owners, Foster finally had the opportunity to talk with them as a group, openly and candidly, and they had made enough of a commitment to hear him out. He was about to share a vision. His words described a vision that would forever change the game of black baseball. What had been a fairly disorganized and perennially shoe-string operation was about to become Negro League baseball. It would be a vision, in fact, that would forever impact the black community and in that sense, the landscape of civil rights in America. Andrew Foster, the father of Negro League baseball, was about to speak.

Andrew Foster's presence in that small room at the Y that February morning was both physically and personally commanding. With his ever-present pipe clutched in one hand, his presence alone was inspiring. Exhibiting a warm and gregarious personality that included calling everyone "darlin'," he presented the essence of self confidence and self assurance wherever he went. He knew the game of baseball and he knew it well. But most important to the confidence and assurance of the men he had assembled, was that Andrew Foster knew himself and he knew what he wanted. In order to assuage any misgivings about the plan, he came to the meeting well prepared for them. According to the *Freeman,* Foster "possibly had 'more at stake than any fifty men in baseball that could be named' and delivered this bombshell: "Gentlemen, the assets of the baseball club which I represent is more than all the Negro baseball clubs in existence . . ." With that, they understood he was ready to put it all on the line for the sake of all of them. He then "revealed that he had obtained a corporate charter 'for a National Negro Baseball League. The participants were purportedly astounded when he produced the actual document, which proved

19. For more information on this early race riot see: William M. Tuttle, *Race Riot: Chicago in the Red Summer of 1919,* (New York: Atheneum, 1970), Illini Books edition, 1996 and Cameron McWhirter, *Red Summer: The Summer of 1919 and the Awakening of Black America,* (New York: Henry Holt & Co., 2011).

20. Larry Lester, *Rube Foster in His Time: On the Field and in the Papers with Black Baseball's Greatest Visionary,* (Jefferson, NC: McFarland, 2012), p. 125.

21. Cottrell, p. 142.

22. *Ibid.,* p. 142.

23. *Ibid.,* p. 150.

24. Elisha Scott of Topeka, Kansas, was the attorney who wrote the constitution and by-laws for the new association and his son, Charles S. Scott, later served with Thurgood Marshall in the landmark 1954 case of *Brown v. Board of Education of Topeka, Kansas,* in Lester, p. 177.

25. Source lost.

to be a masterstroke. The league, it turned out, was *already incorporated in Illinois,* Michigan, Ohio, Pennsylvania, New York, and Maryland."[23] Details were arranged over the next months and included a constitution with a "baseball bill of rights."[24] His motto, "We are the ship, all else the sea," exactly represented how he saw the centrality of the African-American community that this new league would strive to embody. Success would lead to more leagues organized in the East and the South modeled after Foster's vision that would add their weight to the inevitability of the reintegration of major league baseball.

Establishing the Rules

In Foster's mind teams needed to adhere to a non-negotiable set of rules. He insisted on a strict style of behavior that every team in his league would practice; respectability in the eyes of the public was critical. In addition he insisted that baseball be played *his* way, "the right way." It was a style of baseball that emphasized speed and that relied heavily on the bunt, stolen base, sacrifice, and the hit-and-run. While the white major leagues focused on power, the black teams would be honing skills that would make them the dominant players in the major leagues in the decade following the modern era's desegregation of the game. Foster focused on manufacturing runs and in the process he was manufacturing a new style of play, a style that would revolutionize all of baseball after the re-integration of the sport. It's no accident that most of the important baseball awards went to African-American players in the first decade after Jackie!

His rules extended to off-the-field behavior as well. He made sure his players were well dressed, and alcohol was banned from the dugout. To the greatest extent possible, he also made sure that the players arrived for each game in suitable and appropriate transportation. This latter effort was a major departure from the jalopies and beat up busses that had characterized earlier years. Rube Foster's vision for the first organized Negro League was clearly set up as a training camp to prepare black America to enter white society. Many years earlier Frederick Douglass had commented that, ". . . the image of the black ballplayer was one of inferiority to much of white America."[25] Douglass also recognized the political and social impact of image. Years later, Andrew Foster took heed and was determined to shape the image of black ballplayers to exceed those of white players. He was a keen student of the segregated society in which he lived and he so fervently believed in the eventual re-integration of the white major leagues, he would do everything in his power to prepare them for that time.

Douglass, however, had also cautioned that African Americans displaying too "white" an image could prove unsettling and confrontational, acting uppity, to white

Americans. In this sense, Foster's insistence on a strict dress code and code of conduct for all players, as well as the act of organizing itself, was, in effect, *a form of activism* for the black community. Foster had put black and white America on notice—black baseball was no longer to be a disorganized novelty act operating on the fringe of black society.

Baseball players in general did not enjoy a positive image in 1919 America. The Chicago Black Sox betting scandal that was to emerge later that year only confirmed the nation's opinions. The image of the Negro ballplayer suffered an even more negative fate. With but a brief nod to the actual reality of the situation and owing much to prevailing racial stereotypes, the black ballplayer was largely characterized as hard-drinking, amoral, reckless, and unsocialized, causing him to be seen as inherently unpredictable and undependable, if not outright dangerous. Thus the argument for complete and continued segregation was bolstered. Foster recognized that if his league and his players were to approach any semblance of acceptance by white baseball and white America, he would have to address the image issue and do so directly and without compromise.

And, Foster did his part to make sure they looked sharp on the field, too. His teams were outfitted with new uniforms and he insisted that they were to be kept clean and in good repair. He also provided several buses, not only to ease some of the discomforts of travel but to also bolster the image of organization and professionalism of the league. It was quite probably a source of pride for the black community, and perhaps some surprise for the white, to witness a bus pull up to a stadium and discharge a group of neat, well-dressed gentleman ballplayers ready to play a Negro League game.

Dress the Part

Andrew Foster's attention to image had a significant impact in several areas. The first was simply one of presentation. Whether on the road to the next game or their arrival at the stadium, the image of neatly dressed players, many wearing sport coats and all wearing ties, was not only an impressive sight but one that directly confronted racial stereotypes. News photography, whether candid or staged, brought this image to the black press and opened the potential opportunity for an occasional "white" newspaper to publish as well.

A second positive effect of the dress and behavior codes was on both team and league unity and identity. The codes spoke loudly and in no uncertain terms—this is serious business, we are professional ballplayers, we take our jobs seriously, we respect ourselves, the game, and our league. The league had an identity, an image it could portray to both white and black audiences, and within each team, a strengthened sense of unity and cohesiveness.

Black America in the 1920's rose in celebration, pride, and support for their new Negro National League. The community's pride was reflected in their own appearance at the games. Recalls Stanley "Doc" Glenn: "Women came to the ballpark in their Sunday best, high-heel shoes, silk stockings, and they had hats on their heads, and long-sleeved gloves. . . . They would be dressed to kill. You would think you were at a cotillion." Men would attend in suits and ties and fashionable hats. The crowd was then entertained by professional ballplayers, in neat, clean uniforms, playing a style of baseball unique to them. The impact on community cannot be overstated. Slowly but surely, a rising tide of African-American pride and unity was building and Andrew Foster's Negro National League was playing an important role.

Who was Andrew "Rube" Foster?

Foster was a prime example of the opportunities his league would soon provide for others. Born the son of a preacher in rural Texas in 1875, one would expect that his lifetime experiences and opportunities were bound to be limited and local in nature. But he could play baseball and by the age of seventeen he was pitching for an all black team in Ft. Worth, Texas. City life would be a new and challenging experience for him but the bright lights he saw there were about to become brighter. By the age of twenty, Foster was pitching in Chicago and the following year found him in Philadelphia where he would remain for the next seven years. A rural African American from the Deep South had hit the big city and he rapidly became the dominant icon of turn-of-the-20th century African-American baseball.

His pitching prowess soon became legendary and gave him the credibility he needed to convince others that his vision of a Negro League was not only possible but critically necessary. By the time his playing career was over in 1917 his reputation was widely admired by baseball fans of all colors and was firmly cemented in the eyes of the power brokers of both black and white baseball. The statistical record strongly supports the then-prevailing opinion that he was the best pitcher of his era, black or white. However, he was not content to let his reputation rest just on the ball field. Before ending his playing career Foster began to manage the teams he played for and from there it was only a small step to becoming a team owner. He quickly established as strong a reputation in the roles of manager and owner that had characterized his playing career. One suspects that his vision for Negro League baseball had been evolving for some time but he now had the power and the influence and the identity to make it happen.

At a time when calling a black ballplayer the "black Babe Ruth" or the "black Lou

Gehrig" was considered to be quite an honor, it's unclear just how Andrew Foster earned the nickname Rube. Some say he earned it after besting the then predominant pitcher in the white major leagues, Rube Waddell, of the New York Yankees in an exhibition match. Others say he had the nickname "Rube" before the exhibition game was ever played. Whether or not the name originated in legend or was a reference to his early childhood, one thing is for certain, Andrew Foster embraced his nickname so much so that he adopted it as his official middle name later in life. Was he celebrating his heritage or his accomplishments? One can certainly argue for either. But on whichever side the evidence falls, both indicate a fierce sense of pride, self assurance, and identity. All were to serve him well in his future role as the "Father of Negro League Baseball."

Foster never lost sight of what he considered to be his responsibility to the African-American community. Living in Chicago in 1919, he was an active member of the church and a variety of all the important civic clubs. "The highlight over many seasons was raising funds for Provident Hospital which provided services at a time when most hospitals in Chicago would not treat African Americans."[26] With his reputation solidly founded on his place in the community, he set about to change the practice of black baseball depending on white booking agents and stadium owners. He foresaw the income generated from black baseball and a need to return this money to the black community. His plan for organization in 1920 was predicated on black team owners, black booking agents (himself as the primary agent), and black stadium ownership. His big city experience had prepared him well for the task.

26. Lester, p. 40.

Integrating the Major Leagues

After organizing the Negro National League, Foster began his more important crusade, integrating the major leagues, using the forum of the largest black newspaper in the country, *The Chicago Defender,* to advocate for his cause. He was convinced that there would come a time in the not too distant future when African Americans would be admitted to major league baseball. His ultimate goal was that the major leagues would consist of three leagues, the American, the National, and the Negro League. As such he patterned his proposed organization after the structure of white baseball. It would be organized, it would have a published schedule, it would be profitable, and most importantly, it would be respectable.

Considered by some to be a tyrant and by others the savior of black baseball, Foster passed away on December 9, 1930 in a Chicago sanitarium. He had been confined there for over four years since a gas leak in an Indianapolis hotel room rendered him unconscious and permanently altered his mental status and behavior. There had already been some obvious and unanswered questions about his mental status for many years owing to his intensity and single-minded, dictatorial personality. But despite his illness and despite being out of the public eye and away from the game he loved and helped transform for almost five years, the people remembered. People stood in line for hours in an icy Chicago rain for one last glimpse of the man they loved. Over 3,000 people filed past as his body lay in state for three days.

For too long Foster was the forgotten giant of Negro League baseball. But, beginning with Robert Peterson's, *Only the Ball was White,* Foster has begun to receive the attention he deserves. In Peterson's chapter, "Rube from Texas" he opened with this: "If the talents of Christy Mathewson, John McGraw, Ban Johnson, and Judge Kenesaw Mountain Landis were combined in a single body, and that body were enveloped in a black skin, the result would have to be named Andrew (Rube) Foster."[27]

Rube's Legacy

Despite a burgeoning library about the sport in recent years, much of the work has devoted considerable effort to recovering and documenting the statistical history of players and teams, with less emphasis on the biographies of individual players. A notable exception is the work of the Society for American Baseball Research through its Baseball Biography Project available at http://sabr.org/bioproject now boasting over 1700 biographical sketches. Happily, a recent biography of Foster, *Rube Foster In His Time, On the Field and in the Papers with Black Baseball's Greatest Visionary,* by Larry Lester has added much to the available scholarship about him. A measure of how little was appreciated about the man who singlehandedly created the Negro Leagues, was his delayed induction into the National Baseball Hall of Fame. In an interview his brother, Willie Foster, told historian Charles Whitehead, "Rube should have been the first Negro into the Hall of Fame. He organized the Negro Leagues and some say he revolutionized the game. He should be credited with the catcher running down to back up the first baseman on a hit ball. Pitchers throwing sliders, drop balls, or drag bunting? [The implication is that these were all innovations created by Foster] Rube had a great personality and would treat you fair. He wouldn't cuss anybody and paid your salary on time. You had to respect the man, and love the man."[28] Foster wasn't alone in receiving long-delayed recognition by the Hall. Even when it began redressing its sins of omission in the early 1970s, it moved at a painfully slow pace. A sportswriter at the time criticized the pace as, ". . . perpetuate[ing] and glorify[ing] in bits and dribbles, one of the great American tragedies—the time spanning the first 47 years of this century when blacks weren't allowed in the major leagues—is as disgraceful as the original injustice." And, one of the major issues was the fact that Foster was not the first to be inducted.[29] But it should also be noted that when he was selected,

27. Robert Peterson, *Only the Ball Was White: A History of Legendary Black Players and All-Black Professional Teams,* (New York: Oxford University Press, 1970), p. 103.

28. Charles E. Whitehead, *A Man and His Diamonds: The Story of Rube Foster* (New York: Vantage Press, 1980), p. 139.

29. John Hall, *Los Angeles Times,* quoted in Cottrell, p. 186.

due in large part to the efforts of "Tweed Mack, noted St. Louis historian and Rube Foster advocate, he was selected by the Veterans Committee, and not by the special Negro Baseball Leagues Committee, created in 1971."[30]

When A.S. "Doc" Young wrote *Great Negro Baseball Stars i*n 1953, he called Rube Foster "the first great pitcher, next a superb manager, and finally an outstanding administrator . . . he lost the most by the Jim Crow bar, for it was he who had the most to offer." Acknowledging that comparisons between past and present players is always subjective, he modified it in the case of Rube, "Rube still towers over the field of past and present Negro baseball personalities as a giant Sequoia dwarfs a pine."[31] He was, as Young concludes, "born too soon." But, as Troy roars in August Wilson's *Fences* when he was told he came along too early, "There ought not never had been no time called too early!"[32]

Rube Foster's legacy is that of an accomplished visionary. He saw far into the future to a time when baseball would be truly what it claimed to be, the national pastime. Until black players were playing in the major leagues there was a lack of integrity present in the sport that everyone acknowledged but few felt compelled to address, at least not publicly. When that time came, Rube wanted his players to be ready for it.

Since the recent airing of Ken Burns' documentary, *Baseball,* Negro League baseball and its beloved spokesman, John "Buck" O'Neil, have become more familiar to us. In an interview done with PBS as part of the materials produced to go with the documentary, O'Neil was asked, "What motivated Rube to keep black baseball going in the face of all the difficulties he encountered?" Buck's answer confirms the astonishing breadth of Foster's dreams and is a poignant assessment of his character.

> Rube was a great organizer and Rube wanted to put not just a team in organized baseball. No. Rube wanted to put a league into organized baseball. Period. Rube didn't want Rube to play with the New York Giants. Rube wanted all of the guys that could play to have a chance to play in organized baseball.[33]

He lived Booker T. Washington's adage, "Lift as you climb."

Finally, in 1981, Andrew Rube Foster was inducted into the National Baseball Hall of Fame and more recently, December 30, 2009, he and Negro League baseball were honored with a postage stamp. At a time when America looks to its past for guidance, the true heroes elevating American social consciousness need to be recognized. Rube Foster is one of those heroes.

30. Lester, p. 181.
31. Cottrell, p. 183.
32. Cottrell, p. 183 and August Wilson, *Fences*, Act One.
33. www.pbs.org/kenburns/baseball/shadowball/oneil.html

Lesson 1: Rube Foster's Rage and August Wilson's *Fences*

Cathartic anger that militates against the standard narrative of African-American passivity comes from Troy, the main character in August Wilson's powerful play, *Fences*. For African-American students, indeed for all students, understanding Troy's rage is a necessary antidote to a narrative that rarely if ever includes the righteous anger of the oppressed. Anger is uncomfortable, but change requires discomfort and Troy embodies it.

In this lesson students will have the opportunity to reflect on the disappointments in Rube Foster's life and career and compare the tone and emotion of August Wilson's character, Troy, in order to draw conclusions about the time in which Rube lived and the time Troy is living in this play. Students should be able to discuss and explain, on an emotional level and with empathetic understanding, how Jim Crow affected African Americans beyond the inconveniences of everyday life.

Troy is a former Negro Leagues player, still angry at never having had a chance to play in the majors because of his race. Now his son wants to play football and he sees it as pursuing a dream that will lead nowhere, just as his did. When Rose, his wife, and his friend Bono tell him that the times are different now (the 1950s), his playing days came before the war, Troy explodes:

Troy: How in hell they done changed?

Rose: They got lots of colored boys playing ball now. Baseball and football.

Bono: You right about that, Rose. Times have changed, Troy. You just come along too early.

Troy: There ought not never had been no time called too early! Now you take that fellow . . . what's that fellow they had playing right field for the Yankees back then? You know who I'm talking about, Bono. Used to play right field for the Yankees.

Rose: Selkirk?

Troy: Selkirk! That's it! Man batting .269, understand? .269. What kind of sense that make? I was hitting .432 with 37 home runs! Man batting .269 and playing right field for the Yankees! I saw Josh Gibson's daughter yesterday. She walking around with raggedy shoes on her feet. Now I bet you Selkirk's daughter ain't walking around with raggedy shoes on her feet! I bet you that!

Rose: They got a lot of colored baseball players now. Jackie Robinson was the first. Folks had to wait for Jackie Robinson.

Troy: I done seen a hundred niggers play baseball better than Jackie Robinson. Hell, I know some teams Jackie Robinson couldn't make! Jackie Robinson wasn't nobody. I'm talking about if you could play ball then they ought to have let you play. Don't care what color you were. Come telling me I come along too early. If you could play . . . then they ought to have let you play.

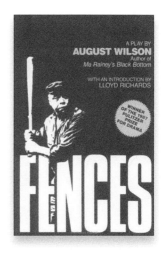

FENCES by August Wilson, copyright © 1986 by August Wilson. Used by permission of Dutton Signet, a division of Penguin Group (USA) LLC.

Questions for discussion

1. After reading about Rube Foster's life and career and reading this short excerpt from August Wilson's play, *Fences*, what parallels do you see between the two men?

2. What is the source of Troy's deeply felt anger?

3. Why does Selkirk's batting average enrage Troy?

4. What is his point about Josh Gibson's daughter, and by extension the children of all the former Negro Leagues players?

5. What, if anything, would you say to Troy if you were Rose or Bono? Explain.

6. What does this excerpt help you understand about Jim Crow America that goes beyond the everyday humiliations and inconveniences already discussed in earlier lessons?

7. Troy uses the word "nigger." Does it make a difference that August Wilson, the author, was an African American? Why might he have decided to have Troy use this freighted word? Does the context of the period in which the play is set, and Troy's emotional state, make it appropriate?

Lesson 2: The Multiplier Affect— Growing the Black Community

Think about the last time you attended or watched on TV any kind of sporting event. Now think about all the people involved in bringing that event to the public. A short list might look like this:

Parking lot attendants

Concession stand operators

Food service workers/ushers

Merchandise salespeople

Program printers and distributors

Custodians

Landscaping, field maintenance

Locker room help

Laundry

Advertisers

Play-by-play radio announcers on local radio and TV

Scorekeepers

Umpires, referees, judges

Administrative staff, secretaries, writers

Managers, coaches, physical therapists, doctors, EMT stand-bys

That's just a partial list of all the people involved in bringing a sporting event together. Now, let's move outside the stadium, ballpark, or court and think about the place where the team plays, its home field. A short list of the people involved in getting folks to the games and making them comfortable while they are there would include:

Hotel and motel workers—the people at the front desk, custodians, maids, pool keepers, and more

Restaurant personnel, chefs, waitstaff, reservations people, custodians, and more

Entertainment: movies, theaters, nightclubs, tourist attractions

Taxi drivers and maintenance staff

City bus drivers and maintenance staff

Hospitals

Emergency vehicles

Police

Firefighters

When a team makes its home in a city or town, the services the people living there and associated with the team would also have to include:

newspapers	barbers
hairdressers	clothing stores
doctors	lawyers
schools	child care
grocery stores	hospitals

For example, let's look at a recent article in *The Boston Globe:* "NBA lockout squeezes service workers near TD Garden" illustrates the value a team brings to a community.[1] When the basketball lock-out was in progress, parking lot attendants, bartenders, ticket managers, and local restaurants were all feeling the loss. "It's horrible," said Michael Ferragamo, market manager at Tickets of Boston in Allston. Early sales are down about 15 percent from last year, and the ticket agency had to lay off two part-time salespeople." The parking lot "will be empty," said Kevin Innes. "This is our season to make money . . . [we] count on the $100 a night we get when the Celtics are in town." The bartender at The Four's on Canal Street said "he was already on a 'bare bones' budget; now he won't even take any extra days off."[2] "For a server at The Four's, a Celtics game can mean $200 a night in tips . . ."[3]

In short, communities need to provide all the facilities that people have come to expect would be available in any town or city—but more of them are necessary to accommodate the team's personnel and their fans. As you can see, whenever a team sport is part of a town or city landscape, it generates jobs in all kinds of services. That's why they are called multipliers. Rube Foster was determined to keep as much of the revenues generated by all of these peripherals within the black community. His vision was much farther reaching than simply what was good for his baseball team. He wanted to positively impact his entire community.

Activities

Using a map of Chicago and a diagram of Comiskey Park, students can generate a visual representation of this army of people servicing the park, the team, and the fans coming to see the games. Since we know that the gate topped 50,000 each year for the Negro League's all-star game, the East-West Classic, we have some idea of what Chicago needed to offer to accommodate all these fans. Students can use magazines and pictures from the internet to find pictures of service workers to place on the map and diagram. When they are done, (and they can put a reasonable representation on their maps and diagrams so they don't become too crowded) they should be able to evaluate the value of a team to its host city.

Culminating evaluation and assessment

In a well-written essay, explain how Rube Foster's team, The Chicago American Giants, was a multiplier for the African-American community of South Chicago.

---

1. Johnny Diaz, "NBA lockout squeezes service workers near TD Garden," *Boston Globe*, October 28, 2011, Sports, 1.

2. *Ibid.*, p. 2.

3. *Ibid.*, p. 3.

Lesson 3: Using Historical Newspapers— The Black Press

The Black Press: Soldiers Without Swords

Produced and directed by Stanley Nelson
Written by Jill Nelson, Stanley Nelson, Lou Potter, and Marcia Smith

California Newsreel
Run time: 86 minutes, 1998
http://newsreel.org/video/THE-BLACK-PRESS-SOLDIERS-WITHOUT-SWORDS

Clip (2.2 minutes) available at:
www.youtube.com/watch?v=ruQarGb3368&feature=mfu_in_order&list=UL

The typewriter, too, is mightier than the sword. In a groundbreaking documentary, *The Black Press: Soldiers Without Swords,* the narrator's first remarks offer a succinct and pointed reason why the black press was so important to the black community during the early years of the 20th century. "We didn't exist in the other papers. We weren't born, we didn't get married, we didn't fight in any wars . . . we were truly invisible, unless we committed a crime."

The trailer for that documentary (*see link at left*) sets the stage for entering a world many students will be unfamiliar with. What an adventure!

As you will see in chapter three, the black press was a powerful advocate for the Negro Leagues and played an important role in chronicling the day to day history of the teams, players, and important events. Pioneering newspapers like *Freedom's Journal, The North Star, The Chicago Defender, The California Eagle, The Pittsburgh Courier, The Atlanta Daily World, The New York Afro-American,* and others brought news of consequence to a community that rarely, if ever, saw itself reflected in a positive way in any media devoted to the public arena—newspapers, movies, or general circulation magazines.

Because of this, for this lesson, we're going to take a short step away from the friendly confines of the ballpark to explore the wider world African Americans navigated during this time, to see how vital the black press was. The internet fairly bristles with materials, to be sure, but locating solid, reliable, teacher and student friendly sites can be a daunting task for busy teachers. One site that meets all these criteria is the site constructed as a "go with" for the documentary *Soldiers Without Swords* that can be found at:

www.pbs.org/blackpress/index.html

The clip offers just a tantalizing glimpse of the fine film that this is, so we would recommend it without reservation as a very good addition to a classroom library of resources. If, however, purchasing the film is not possible, the website alone offers a treasure trove of excellent materials.

Excerpts from the website

The following excerpts are good examples of the essays by historians and journalists that this site contains. They offer a solid overview of the history of the black press in the United State, and include short biographies of journalists, past and present, and other tools teachers will find useful in building their own familiarity with the long tradition of the black press as well as offering students opportunities to listen to interviews with modern journalists in the site's video archive.

The black press came to life in 1827, when a group of African American New Yorkers, no longer able to tolerate constant denigration of the black population in the pages of the mainstream press, pooled their resources to found *Freedom's Journal*. John Russwurm and Samuel Cornish, the editors of *Freedom's Journal*, proclaimed in their first issue that black Americans would now have a means by which to "plead our own cause"; they would no longer have to depend on white abolitionists to speak for them in the white press. *Freedom's Journal* ceased publication after only two years, but broke new ground both as an experiment in black entrepreneurship and as the inaugural instrument for public expression by African Americans where none had existed before.

Between 1827 and 1861, when the Civil War began, some two dozen black-owned and -operated newspapers were founded in Northern cities. *The North Star*, edited by Frederick Douglass, was the most influential. Its readership included not only African Americans but also Presidents and members of Congress, who used the paper to keep abreast of the activities of the antislavery movement. Under Douglass's visionary leadership, *The North Star* firmly established the black press as an indispensable tool of abolitionism. It would also provide a model for generations of black political and social activism to come.

Phyl Garland
www.pbs.org/blackpress/reslinks/index.html

After the Civil War, black newspapers flourished:

By 1910, over 275 black newspapers were being published in cities throughout the United States, reaching a cumulative circulation of half a million readers.

One of the most influential of these papers was the *California Eagle,* founded in 1879 by John James Neimore. The *Eagle* served as a catalyst in the growth of African American communities in Los Angeles. It reached out to African Americans in the rest of the nation, calling for them to seize opportunities available in the growing cities of the West, especially Los Angeles. When Neimore died in 1912, he turned control of the paper over to Charlotta Spears Bass. Mrs. Bass, as she was known, had joined the *Eagle* a few years earlier, selling subscriptions and working her way up its ranks. She was a deeply committed publisher and editor, as well as a dynamic community activist and leader. Through the newspaper and other public forums, Mrs. Bass spoke out on issues facing Los Angeles' black communities, from police brutality to discrimination in housing. She even took on the nascent film industry, leading a boycott that spread nationwide against D.W. Griffith's *Birth of a Nation,* an epic that celebrated the founding of the Ku Klux Klan.

Meanwhile, in the Midwest, Robert S. Abbott founded *The Chicago Defender.* Abbott had made Chicago his home after hearing Frederick Douglass's inspirational speech at the 1893 Columbian Exposition. Abbott composed and published the first issue of the paper in his landlady's kitchen in 1905, and sold issues on the street. It later made him a millionaire.

Timuel Black
www.pbs.org/blackpress/reslinks/index.html

Estimating the impact of a newspaper like *The Chicago Defender* is tricky; the number of people who read the paper far exceeded its paid subscriptions and reached far beyond its local distribution in Chicago:

The newspaper was read extensively in the South. Black Pullman porters and entertainers were used to distribute the paper across the Mason-Dixon line. The paper was smuggled into the south because white distributors refused to circulate *The Defender* and many groups such as the Ku Klux Klan tried to confiscate it or threatened its readers. The Defender was passed from person to person, and read aloud in barbershops and churches. It is estimated that at its height each paper sold was read by four to five African Americans, putting its readership at over 500,000 people each week. *The Chicago Defender* was the first black newspaper to have a circulation over 100,000, the first to have a health column, and the first to have a full page of comic strips.

www.pbs.org/blackpress/reslinks/index.html

The same can be said of all the black newspapers. African Americans hungry for news of the black community, found in the black press an authentic mirror of their lives, with all of the features so lacking in the general circulation press of the time. Here they were born, did get married, did graduate from college, did play baseball. In short, here they had well-rounded lives; a rich, dynamic culture of their own.

Because this site is so comprehensive, teachers will want to explore it themselves, but we would like to especially recommend two activities based on the site that will engage students in authentic inquiry and learning.

Activity One: Virtual Interviews

The website has transcripts of the conversations held with the people interviewed in the film.

www.pbs.org/blackpress/film/index.html

There is a good variety of people from whom students can choose to do their own interviews. Students can be prompted with this:

If you had the opportunity to talk with someone who lived during a time when black newspapers were the main source of information about the black community, what would you ask that person?

1. Have students prepare a of list of questions they would like to ask. Have them also leave room for any surprise information their subject may offer.

2. Have students choose two subjects to interview, so they get a range of views.

3. Have them take notes while conducting their interviews.

4. Then have them write a newspaper article about what the black press meant to the black community, based on their interviews.

Activity Two: Finding Similarities and Differences

Using the internet, teachers can locate the front page of two national newspapers published on the same day, or close. Distribute printed copies of the front pages for students to study and have students identify and note similarities and differences in the topics covered by each paper. Then have students offer explanations, based on their interviews from Activity 1, for the similarities and differences they find.

http://memory.loc.gov/ammem/today/jan05.html

http://learning.blogs.nytimes.com/on-this-day/

RIGHT

Sample pages from *The Chicago Defender* and *The New York Times* of July 26, 1948, available at http://learning.blogs.nytimes.com/on-this-day/july-26/

and at

www.loc.gov/exhibits/odyssey/archive/09/0902001r.jpg

Barnstorming into History

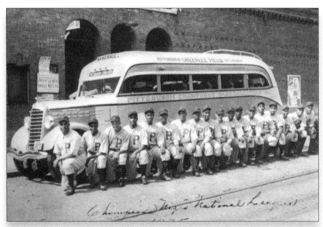

The champion Pittsburgh Crawfords, 1935
(National Baseball Hall of Fame Library, Cooperstown, NY)

They were saints and sinners, college professors and illiterates, serious men and clowns, teetotalers and Saturday night drunks. They were professional baseball players, some of them the equals of the great major-leaguers, with one other common tie: they were all Negroes.[1]

From about 1887 until 1946 an unwritten rule kept African-American baseball players out of the major leagues. As discussed in chapter one, it hadn't always been that way. But, as the exclusionary customs, traditions, and intimidations of a racially divided America ossified into law, ultimately confirmed by the *Plessy v. Ferguson* decision, what had been was no more. The iron fist of Jim Crow could and did officially extend its grip nationally to encompass all areas of public life. In that atmosphere, the more stridently racist players easily leveraged the unwritten agreement that African Americans be barred from all the teams and leagues nationwide. Following their lead and drawing on the pervasive and casual racism of the time, all of the teams across the country willingly joined in this collective agreement. The common "wisdom" of the time declared that African Americans were simply not capable of playing at the big league level. Nothing could have been further from the truth, but truth was not at the root of this exclusion, racism was.

Fortunately, African Americans were already beginning to organize. By the time their exclusion from the big leagues became firmly entrenched, there were already at least five all-black minor league teams. And what were then considered the major leagues, were in reality, much less organized arrangements than today's major leagues. The difference, therefore, between major and minor was much more fluid. And, leagues called major leagues were often simply state or regional leagues that came and went with astonishing speed. In July of 1887 when Cap Anson's threat that his

1. Robert Peterson, *Only the Ball Was White: A History of Legendary Black Players and All-Black Professional Teams*, (New York: Oxford University Press, 1970), p 3.

team wouldn't play any team with a black player on it and the baseball owners "gentlemen's agreement" merged, the stage was set for baseball to pursue its own version of separate but very unequal. Plessy simply confirmed what was already in place in the South and extended it to the rest of the nation.

Faced with what baseball historian, Roger Kahn, has called "the cotton curtain,"[2] black teams developed a parallel universe of all-black baseball over the late decades of the 19th century and the first half of the 20th century and began their journey into history. And journey it was: ". . . the black baseball player was nearly always a traveling man."[3] "Barnstorming and Negro baseball were practically synonymous in the minds of fans, and with good reason."[4] In an age before interstates and before public accommodations were open to black travelers, the teams criss-crossing the highways and by-ways of the United States, and are well-captured in the chapter title "Podunk Today, Hickory Switch Tomorrow" from Robert Peterson's, *Only the Ball Was White.*

Barnstorming?

The term "barnstorming" itself needs some attention. In common usage it conjures up images of adventurous, carefree young athletes and teams crossing and re-crossing the countryside in search of rollicking good times and the occasional ballgame. Indeed, that is the very image that the movie, *The Bingo Long Traveling All-Stars and Motor Kings* etched into the public mind with its release in 1976.[5] Although based in historical facts, the film plays fast and loose with them. It was, after all, meant to be entertainment. Unfortunately with so little else known about the Negro Leagues at the time, the movie became the public's image of the leagues. The actual world black baseball players were compelled to navigate was a landscape that required courage, ingenuity, and self-confidence. And, even though in the early years the teams did resort to some clowning on the fields in order to assuage white prejudices and to earn a living, that was not the whole of black baseball by any means.[6] Even the Indianapolis Clowns, like the Harlem Globetrotters of a later day, who replicated the Clowns' style of play for basketball crowds, were known as much for their baseball skills as they were for the entertainment that they brought to the game. The following offers a less flamboyant definition of the term and is more in keeping with what the term meant at the time.

1. To travel around the countryside making political speeches, giving lectures, or presenting theatrical performances.
2. To travel around an area appearing in exhibition sports events, especially baseball games.
   v.tr. To travel across while barnstorming.[7]

2. Roger Kahn, "We Never Called Them Bums," *Baseball as America: Seeing Ourselves Through Our National Game,* (Washington, D.C.: National Geographic Society, 2002), p. 160.

3. Peterson, p. 4.

4. *Ibid.,* p. 146.

5. In an interview on the *Star & Buc Wild* radio show, Buck O'Neil was confronted with the assertion that ". . . the Negro Leagues was made up of clowns, like in the Richard Pryor movie, *The Bingo Long Traveling All-Stars & Motor Kings.*" He responded, "It was *nothing* like that movie!" in Joe Posnanski, *The Soul of Baseball: A Road Trip Through Buck O'Neil's America,* (New York: Harper, 2007), p. 120-121.

6. The Indianapolis Clowns were a black touring baseball team that featured an entertaining mix of comedy, showmanship, and skill. Sometimes referred to as the Harlem Globetrotters of baseball—though the Globetrotters comedy evolved directly from the Clowns—they captured the affection of Americans of all ethnicities and classes. Allen J. Pollock, *Barnstorming to Heaven: Syd Pollock and His Great Black Teams,* (Tuscaloosa: U. of Alabama Press, 2006), jacket.

7. *The American Heritage Dictionary of the English Language,* 4th Edition, (Houghton Mifflin Co., 2000).

Questions that most Americans have never needed to ask were critical to travel in the United States for all persons of color for over one hundred years. Where can we get gas? Where can we use the rest room? Where can we eat breakfast, lunch, or dinner? Where can we stay overnight? If the car breaks down, are there service stations that we can use? Suppose someone gets sick, what hospitals or doctors can we go to? If I need a haircut, are there barbers available? What about showers and laundry on the road? These questions and more were of critical concern to the teams as they played their way around the country. "For a small-town baseball fan, white or black, barnstorming was [imagined to be] a glamorous trade, redolent of faraway places and the lure of the road. For the black barnstormer, it was grueling labor mixed with the constant threat—and often reality—of insult, rebut, and discrimination. But in Negro baseball, barnstorming was necessary for survival."[8]

8. Peterson, p. 157.

On the Road: Chronicling the Seasons

Perhaps the best way to begin to understand what the teams encountered is to let the players speak for themselves. Of course, it is always important to remember that memories, especially memories of the distant past can be faulty. Dates and events can merge, but, the essence of the memories will remain. Fortunately along with the growth of the leagues was the growth the black press, *The Chicago Defender, The Pittsburgh Courier, The Philadelphia Tribune, The Baltimore Afro-American,* and *The People's Voice* of Harlem, that covered black baseball while the general circulation press ignored it. These papers nurtured a cadre of elite sports reporters—Frank Albert Young, Dr. W. Rollo Wilson, Sam Lacy, Joe Bostic, and Wendell Smith—whose columns still survive and offer a day-to-day insider's view of the teams, the players, and the seasons of the Negro Leagues. And, they too, experienced the indignities of life on the road for African Americans. More important, they chronicled and published their experiences so we can step back in time to discover firsthand what being on the road in Jim Crow's America meant for African-American travelers.

Jim Reisler sums up the situation:

Covering the Negro leagues carried its own peculiar set of problems. Take the well-documented barnstorming aspect of the Negro league game, the scheduling of which made it impractical for the weekly papers to send writers with the teams. Relegated to the back alleys of the sports world, black teams played on—"every day in a different town, sometimes three games a day," said Buck Leonard. Crisscrossing the country in the trademark overcrowded buses; black teams took on all comers, from sandlot and mill teams to the professional black teams in their own loosely structured leagues. In 1938 alone, the Homestead

Grays played 210 games and traveled 30,000 miles. For their 80 or so home games, the Grays used Forbes Field, the Pittsburgh Pirates' ballpark. But they dressed at the local Y.M.C.A., with the ballpark locker rooms off limits. And, "When the writers traveled, they were subject to the same racial prejudices as the players."

Sam Lacey mirrors those words, with his story of how he was barred from press boxes all over the South. His columns of traveling with Jackie Robinson and the Brooklyn Dodgers tell of one rat-trap, flea-bag hotel after another, all, of course, across town from the hotel housing the white players.[9]

Jules Tygiel notes the irony of black sports writers' situation, "They too were victims of Jim Crow . . . segregation hid their considerable skills from the larger white audience and severely restricted their income. . . . Yet they rarely mentioned their own plight. Indeed the barriers for black journalists lasted long after those for athletes disappeared."[10] The life of anyone involved with the teams was daunting to be sure.

Hall of Famer Buck Leonard recalls his time playing outfield for the Brooklyn Royal Giants during the Depression, "We didn't have any home grounds. We played anywhere we could get a game. . . . Sometimes we would go up to New Hampshire and play around those county fairs for two or three weeks . . . sometimes getting $50 . . . sometimes passing the hat. . . . Fifty dollars was a lot of money for one whole team to get for a ballgame."[11]

Farm Wagons, Drays, Trains and Cars

William Julius "Judy" Johnson, clutch-hitting third baseman for the Pittsburgh Crawfords, recalls, "a non-stop bus ride from Chicago to Philadelphia after a doubleheader, 800 miles of catnaps and sandwiches and soda-pop for breakfast, lunch, and dinner . . . and we played a doubleheader that afternoon in Connie Mack Stadium."[12] Robert Peterson reports that the clubs "got around on the barnstorming trail any way they could . . . farm wagons and drays, trains and cars, . . . By the 1930s, most were traveling in their own buses, which ranged from broken-down, battered, creaking little vehicles to the best conveyances that era had to offer."[13] What needs to be remembered is that travel during this time meant mostly two-lane roads, climbing uphill and down, winding through cities and towns, with speed limits under 50 miles per hour most of the way. The superhighways of the Eisenhower years were still far into the future so a life on the road was often an endurance test. One "all-time record" comes from American Giants third baseman Gentleman Dave Malarcher. He remembers, "The team rode all the way from Monroe, Louisiana, to Winnepeg, Canada—a jaunt of some 1,700 miles—sleeping and eating in the bus all the way."[14] To be sure, at least

9. Jim Reisler, *Black Writers/Black Baseball: An Anthology of Articles from Black Sportswriters Who Covered the Negro Leagues,* (Jefferson, NC: McFarland & Company, 1994), p. 3-4.

10. *Ibid.,* p. 4.

11. Peterson, p. 151-2.

12. *Ibid.,* p. 155.

13. *Ibid.,* p. 155.

14. John Holway, *Voices from the Great Black Baseball Leagues,* (New York: Dodd, Mead & Company, 1975); and Jim Reisler, *Black Writers/Black Baseball.*

one notable white barnstorming team, the House of David club, experienced many of the same hardships barnstorming provided. The big difference was that they had no trouble finding places to stay or restaurants that would serve them.

For the players, survival depended on barnstorming, so any glamour it provided was incidental and short-lived. More often it was grueling labor [punctuated by] constant threat. For a black athlete it wasn't the only game in town, it was the best game in town.

Black Sportswriting

If Negro Leagues baseball was the great "unexplored continent . . . not a mere footnote to baseball history . . . fully *half* of baseball history!" much of what we know about that continent comes from another continent just beginning to be explored—the "Black Sportswriters Who Covered the Negro Leagues."[15] These were the men who often traveled with the teams and, beginning with Frank Young as early as 1914, kept up the drumbeat for integrating baseball. Their chronicles of the games and interviews with managers, players, and fans give us entrée into the America experienced by black ballplayers.

One of Frank Albert Young's most startling headlines appeared in *The Chicago Defender*, April 11, 1914: "Rube Foster's Team Starving in Oregon." After six paragraphs of asking and answering the question, "What place has the color line in professional baseball?" Young reports that, "On Wednesday, the 1st of April they [Foster's American Giants] arrived in Medford, Ore., and were turned down by every hotel and restaurant in town. . . Through a misunderstanding no arrangements were made for feeding the men, and at a Japanese restaurant, where no color line is drawn, it was announced there would be nothing served until noon. After considerable argument, the proprietor secured cheese and crackers and these comprised the Giants' breakfast."[16]

Throughout the article Young argues that:

[D]iscrimination in baseball is something for which the powers alone are responsible and which has no echo in the opinion of the general public. . . . willingness, not to say eagerness, is displayed by every semi-professional and collegiate manager to arrange games with the different Oriental clubs which visit this country from time to time, and this being the case, why should organized baseball seek to create opposition to a ball club whose only fault lies in the color of its members? . . . Organized baseball welcomes Cuban players . . . and the only reason for the refusal of the Coast league to accept the visitors as pre-season competitors seems to lie in the players' superior ability. If J. Cal Ewing and the Oakland management would

15. *Ibid.*
16. Frank Albert Young, *Chicago Defender*, April 11, 1914, p. 1, col. 1.

honestly and frankly state the causes for their disinclination to allow their respective ball clubs to meet with the Giants, the statements in effect would be as follows: "They are too fast for us."[17]

17. *Ibid.*
18. Reisler, p. 10.

Sam Lacy, sports editor for *The Baltimore Afro-American* continued Young's advocacy for integrating baseball and continued advocating for racial equality even after the teams were integrated. From a column, "Back in the Land of Make Believe," published on May 5, 1948, from St. Louis, where he was traveling with Jackie Robinson, he wrote:

> Only this is no fable or fairy tale, this is Dixie, U.S.A., where they sing the "Star-Spangled Banner" with their tongues in their cheeks, where they cry for constitutional rights, and cry when you ask for yours, where they send the white players of the Brooklyn Dodgers to one end of town and the colored players to the other. This is the Land of Make Believe, where they sing Democratic hymns from Hitler mouths.[18]

> *From Texarkana, Texas* And in keeping with practice in Texas, white taxicabs refuse to haul colored passengers. . . . Anyway, last week when the Cleveland Indians were in town with their three colored stars, Larry Doby, Satchel Paige, and Orestes Minoso, the taxicabs refused to haul them to the ballpark. Since there were no colored cabs available, and since the Indians were expecting them to play in the game against the New York Giants that afternoon, the players . . . walked. (Minoso later hit a two-run homer, "to thrill the taxi drivers who passed him up on their way to see the game.")

As if to underscore that mere integration of the teams did not mean that the black major leaguers could expect major league treatment, Lacy sprinkled his game reports with colorful stories from outside the ballparks. Although he saves his most scathing enmity for the South, he doesn't spare the brickbats when it comes to the North. Here are a few of his best:

> **Haines City, Florida, April 2, 1949** This town's colored fans are being admitted to spring training exhibition games for the first time in history. . . . When they turned out for the first games played by the Newark Bears, Yale Field workmen had to hurriedly construct a makeshift "colored" stand. . . . This reporter, looking for the "colored restroom" was directed to a tree about 35 yards off from where the right field foul line ended.

> **San Antonio, Texas, April 9, 1949** An interesting thing happened today . . . Robbie (Jackie Robinson) . . . told teammates: "I'm going to try my best in batting practice to hit one out of the park and watch the colored stands go wild. . . . Then, I'm going to swing like hell on the next pitch and miss . . . I

want to see what the whites reaction will be." He did just that . . . When his first hit bounced off the fence, the colored patrons broke into a wild demonstration. . . . When he whiffed on the next pitch, the white section became a bedlam of hoots and catcalls . . . during the game, the typical Dixie attitude prevailed again, and the closeness of the Bums . . . was revealed . . . Jackie stole second in the fourth and there was unrestrained whooping in one section of the park . . . later, he was thrown out trying to reach third on a fly to right, and happiness reigned supreme in the other part . . . Pee Wee Reese, a Southern boy from Kentucky, spoke up: "We can all go home now. *Everybody's happy!*"

Vero Beach, Florida, April 1, 1950 . . . Campanella was named as the lone colored player on a squad to play in West Palm Beach. En route back to Vero Beach, the team stopped for dinner at a roadside inn. . . . Several players who are on the squad for no more than tryouts and who will end up in Class A or B ball, went in, sat at the tables and ordered what they wished. Campanella, generally recognized as the best catcher in baseball, was forced to sit alone in the bus and eat what was brought out to him on a tray.

In Cincinnati, while the Netherlands-Plaza accepts the whole group, it is "suggested" that the colored members of the party stay out of the dining room. A special arrangement is made whereby their meals are served in their rooms.

The Dodgers' hotel in St. Louis is the Chase. Inferior ballplayers, some just up from the minors as low as Class B packed away to the exquisite Chase. Many of them couldn't carry Jackie's bat or Campanella's glove or Newk's rosin bag. But they went to their first class accommodations. The four of us squeezed into a third-class hotel in the colored section. . . . Newcombe, who was slated to pitch the next day, spent the night trying to sleep in a room located directly over a constantly screeching jukebox.

While Class B squirts lounged in luxury at the town's best hostelry, Robbie, the National League's Most Valuable Player; Newcombe, the 1949 Rookie of the Year; and Campy, the greatest catcher in the game were trying to find rest in a Jim Crow house in what many cities in Dixie call "Colored Town."

Uptown, in air-conditioned splendor, were three players on whom the Dodgers had asked waivers, meaning they could be had by any other club that wanted them for $10,000 each.

Downtown, in heat and noise and all-round discomfort, were three players whose combined value could conservatively be estimated at $1 million.

Beaumont, Texas, April 9, 1949 The usual "Jim Crow twist" was given reverse English Wednesday night when Brooklyn visited here. . . . Instead of barring the Dodgers' colored players from the clubhouse, Stuart Stadium officials "suggested" that Jackie Robinson and Roy Campanella use the players' quarters and the rest of the team dress in their hotel. . . . It so happened that the unfinished dressing room floor was covered with mud and water, shower facilities were incomplete and the place was entirely devoid of window covering.

Wendell Smith and *The Pittsburgh Courier*

Wendell Smith is acknowledged by all to be the best sportswriter of his generation. Smith began his career in 1937 with *The Pittsburgh Courier* following the Pittsburgh Crawfords. As Jim Reisler puts it, "Smith covered Negro league baseball like a blanket. His style could be folksy, but it turned direct when he was taking on both major league and black team owners. In addition to writing some of the very first interviews and player profiles of personalities in Pittsburgh's colorful baseball scene, he also fit the aggressive, sometimes angry style of *Courier* editor Robert L. Vann, who launched the paper on numerous crusades to benefit black America."[19] Tygiel called Smith, "the most talented and influential of the black journalists" of the era. "He could be bitterly sarcastic and vitriolic in his rage against Jim Crow, yet lyrical in his descriptive prose."[20]

The Courier itself was a lightning rod for the black community leading a nationwide petition drive protesting the misrepresentation of blacks in the popular daily radio comedy series *Amos 'n' Andy* and calling for it to be removed from the air.[21] As early as 1932, editor Robert L. Vann helped influence black voters to shift their political allegiance away from the Republican Party, which was often still thought of as the party of Lincoln, and to support the Democratic candidate Franklin D. Roosevelt. Under his guidance, Vann encouraged African Americans to support organizations advancing black causes and political equality such as The Urban League and the NAACP. It lent its support for improved housing, health and education, and counseled its readers on financial issues.

The Courier reached its widest circulation during WWII. "This was due in part to the successful "Double V" campaign spearheaded by *The Courier*. Beginning in the paper's February 7, 1942, edition and continuing weekly until 1943, the Double V campaign demanded that African Americans who were risking their lives abroad receive full citizenship rights at home. The newspaper printed articles, editorials, letters, Double V photographs, and drawings, and even designed a recognizable Double V sign to promote the campaign. Many other black newspapers endorsed the campaign as well, making it a nationwide effort."[22]

19. *Ibid.,* p. 33-4.
20. *Ibid,* p. 35.
21. Especially galling was the use of two white actors, Freeman Gosden and Charles Correll, out of the minstrel tradition, to play the leading roles.
22. www.pbs.org/ blackpress/news_bios/ courier.html

It is no surprise then to find *The Courier* and its sportswriter Wendell Smith leading the fight for major league baseball to end segregation. David Wiggins best summarized why integrating baseball was so important to African Americans and was so well argued by Wendell Smith:

Wendell Smith, of course, was the catalyst behind the newspaper's campaign effort. It is difficult to say with any degree of certainty just what influence Smith had on Rickey and the rest of the magnates in organized baseball. It seems safe to say, however, that without people such as Smith it might have been years before the men in organized baseball allowed Blacks in the National Game. What Smith did as effectively as anyone else was to point out that discrimination in organized baseball symbolized the dubious status of Blacks in American society. On several occasions, Smith expressed the feeling that until Blacks could participate fully in the national game, they could not lay claim to the rights of a full-fledged citizen. He made it clear that the campaign was not merely a fight to wear a baseball uniform. It was a struggle for status, a struggle to take democracy off of parchment and give it life. To Smith, the discrimination against Blacks in organized baseball cut deeper into his feelings than did other areas of employment discrimination. If baseball was indeed the National Pastime, the great leveler in society, then it naturally followed that black athletes deserved to participate in it.[23]

23. David K. Wiggins, "Wendell Smith, the *Pittsburgh Courier-Journal* and the Campaign to Include Blacks in Organized Baseball, 1933-1945," *Journal of Sport History*, Vol. 10, No. 2 (Summer 1983).

Joe Bostic and *The People's Voice*

The People's Voice of Harlem, owned by pastor and later congressman Adam Clayton Powell, Jr., and crusading sportswriter Joe Bostic were a perfect fit. Bostic earned his reputation in the black press through his relentless and aggressive style completely in keeping with the paper's masthead declaration, "A Militant Paper . . . Serving All People . . . The New Voice for the New Negro." He is best remembered for putting Branch Rickey on the spot in 1945 by arriving unannounced with two African-American ballplayers at the Bear Mountain spring training camp demanding tryouts for them. His aim was to prove that baseball's "pious pretense that baseball wasn't segregated, that the black players were perfectly welcome, and all they had to do was to try out," was a sham.

According to Bostic's retelling of his strategy to call baseball's bluff, Rickey exploded, "I don't appreciate being put in a position like this!" Dodger manager, Leo Durocher, however, stepped in and urged Rickey to "give the players a look." "You're pretty cute," Rickey told Joe. If I agree to try them out, it's the sports story of the century, and if I refuse to try them out, that's the sports story of the century." The players did get a look that day, thanks to Joe Bostic. But, according to Joe, "Rickey never forgave me. . . . He never spoke to me again as long as he lived."[24] Rickey, of course, ultimately forged ahead and signed Jackie Robinson two years later.

Interestingly enough, although integrating the major leagues was an important goal, it was also cause for concern. On August 12, 1939, Sam Lacy asked players what they thought about integrating the big leagues and got mixed responses. From Vic Harris, the soft-spoken captain of the Homestead Grays, he heard, "We do have some good ballplayers, but not nearly as many fit for the majors as seems to be the belief. But, if they start picking them up, what are the remaining players going to do to make a living? . . . Suppose our stars . . . are gobbled up by the big clubs, how could the other 75 or 80 percent survive." Jud Wilson, third baseman for the Philadelphia Stars, remarked, "It will never be, because the big league game, as it is now, is over-run with Southern blood. . . . The training camps are in the South, the majority of minor leagues are in the South and there's a strong Southern sentiment in the stands. When the teams are on the road, these fellows would have to stop at the same hotels, eat in the same dining rooms and sleep in the same train compartments with the colored players. There'd be trouble for sure. And, if we were sent to other hotels or otherwise separated, the colored fans and the colored players would get hotter than they are over the present arrangement."[25]

The same Joe Bostic that confronted Branch Rickey also voiced reservations. On July 11, 1942, he raised issues that demanded consideration. On the question of financial impact of integration he wrote, ". . . let's figure in the first season of the experiment [integration] that three Negro players went into the major leagues . . . and assume that they would get $15,000 each. . . . That item is covered by the East-West game alone, which gives you an idea of the immense financial return of Negro baseball in any given season. Make no mistake . . . the entry of even *one* player on a league team would serve completely to monopolize the attention of the Negro and white present followers of Negro baseball to the great injury of the Negro baseball exchequer."

Echoing Rube Foster's concern that African-American money stay in African-American hands, Bostic continued, "We control . . . the vast revenues and by products (he lists printers, Negro [news]papers and other advertising media, officials, scorekeepers, announcers, and secretaries among others) accruing from Negro baseball. And, I submit that it would evaporate with the diversion of interest and resultant diversions of patronage as the result of a few Negroes going into the other leagues."

He also asked, "Why subject any player to the humiliation and indignities associated with the problems of eating, sleeping and traveling in a layout dominated by prejudice-ridden Southern whites!" And as to the caliber of play he challenged the assumption that the major leagues were the actual holders of the best players. ". . . if

24. George L. Hiss, *Joe Bostic: The First Black American Radio Announcer*, (Bloomington, IN: Authorhouse: 2006), pp. 72-3.

25. Reisler, pp. 16-17.

26. *Ibid.*, pp. 80-81.

27. Washington and DuBois are often positioned as adversaries, but despite their different approaches, they often worked together and always had the same goal—improved conditions for African Americans. For example, Washington contributed significant financial support to DuBois's organization, the NAACP, for its voting rights campaign.

"[Washington] bowed and scraped … to white philanthropists and politicians, but he returned from these journeys into self-abasement with another classroom, science lab, dormitory, or teacher to place in service to our youth. The vision may have been limited … but Washington's was a pragmatism founded on an earned awareness of the potential violence of the racial resentments that surrounded his people. Even as he advocated restraint, he proclaimed self-reliance and organized our people along principles of mutual aid, 'lifting as ye climb.'"

"False, Fleeting, Perjured Clarence: Yale's Brightest and Blackest Go to Washington," in Toni Morrison, ed., *Race-ing Justice, En-Gendering Power: Essays on Anita Hill, Clarence Thomas, and the Construction of Social Reality* (New York: Pantheon Books, 1992), p. 93.

they think that they are really the world champions and have a right to the title, then I dare the winner of the World Series to meet the winner of a series between the Homestead Grays and the Kansas City Monarchs for the real undisputed title. Until that time, there is no proof that the white leagues' caliber of ball is superior over Negro ball."[26]

The terrible truth is that many of these concerns actually did, in fact, accompany integration and will be explored in the chapters to follow. What is important to remember is that in spite of these concerns, they were willing to take this very risky but necessary chance. There were no surprises. And, like the civil rights movement to follow, there would be a price to pay in order to make integration happen.

If students ask, as they are apt to do when confronted with injustice and the uncomfortable parts of the past, "Why didn't they do something?" and assert, "I would have never put up with that!" these stories, troubling as they are, are the answer.

They *did* do something—they organized, campaigned, argued, and spoke out on their own behalf. Why did they put up with this type of treatment? The answer is clear. They were the vanguard of a movement that would ultimately prevail. They laid the groundwork. They took it on the chin so that others to follow would have it easier. They were the front-line heroes.

Some years ago the document-based question on the Advanced Placement exam in United States History asked students to evaluate the extent to which Booker T. Washington and W.E.B. DuBois were successful advocates on behalf of African Americans. Only the best students recognized that evaluating the extent of the success of either required an understanding of the time and place from which and in which they each struggled.[27] So, too, the men and women of the Negro Leagues faced these same barriers yet soldiered on, firm in their belief that one day the full measure of America's best would be open, if not to them, for their children. That takes courage, and everyone was brave. It simply cannot be overemphasized that within the confines of Jim Crow America, there were both legal and customary limits that were necessary to navigate and dangerous to ignore. Incremental change required patience and persistence, less thrilling than more explosive alternatives, but ultimately more long-lived.

Introduction to
The Green Book Teaching Strategies

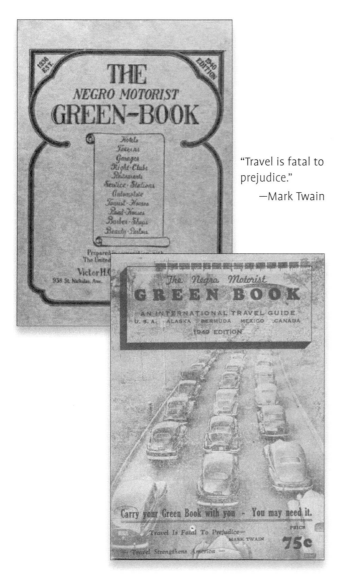

"Travel is fatal to prejudice."

—Mark Twain

The Negro Motorist Green-Book: An International Travel Guide
U.S.A. Alaska Bermuda Mexico Canada
1940 and 1949 editions

Background

The years between the end of Reconstruction and the early years of the Civil Rights era were by any estimation turbulent times. Textbooks have done an admirable job of illustrating the limitations and disabilities placed on African Americans and the efforts by some on their behalf during this time. What is less clearly described are the multiple ways African Americans resisted those disabilities and acted boldly on their own behalf. One way to explore these dimensions of African-American activism is through the lens of Negro League Baseball. In this way students will become acquainted with unfamiliar legends of the game, learn how their daily lives, in spite of their talent, were shaped to accommodate segregation by law in the South and through custom in the North, and enter the parallel world African Americans created for themselves during this time.

The time period between the end of Reconstruction and the post-WWII period was both, as Dickens would say, the best of times and the worst of times for African Americans in the United States. It was the best of times because freedom brought the chance to pursue the American dream; the worst, because, with the exception of actual slavery itself, it was the time period when African Americans experienced the worst that a country steeped in racism had to offer.

However, within that framework and in spite of the hideous constraints on every aspect of black life, black baseball players created a separate world of exceptional teams, players, and managers, denying by example the notion that they were incapable of playing with the best athletes of their time. And, the irony is that what passed for major league baseball at the end of the 19th century did not begin as a segregated sport. Like much else that became Jim Crow America, it took a concerted effort on the part of some players, latent racism on the part of others, and apathy by many.

One artifact of that time is *The Negro Motorist Green Book*. Between 1936 and 1964 Victor H. Green published *The Negro Motorist Green Book* in order to ease the problems of travel for black Americans. As he explained:

> With the introduction of this travel guide in 1936, it has been our idea to give the Negro traveler information that will keep him from running into difficulties, embarrassments and to make his trips more enjoyable.

He ends his introduction to the 1949 edition on this optimistic note:

> There will be a day sometime in the near future when this guide will not have to be published. That is when we as a race will have equal opportunities and privileges in the United States. It will be a great day for us to suspend this publication for then we can go wherever we please, and without embarrassment. But until that time comes we shall continue to publish this information for your convenience each year.

The Green Book itself is a treasure trove of fascinating ephemera that students will enjoy using and the mapping activities offer students a chance for a road trip in the Wayback Machine to relive Jim Crow America the way African Americans experienced it. Just the fact that this was published until 1964 will put a spin of currency on it. Most textbook narratives of the Jim Crow years place them almost exclusively during the later part of the 19th century, some extend them into the early years of the 20th century, but 1964 comes as a surprise.

Probably more than any other segment of the black community, Negro League ballplayers were, by definition, travelers, so who better to follow around the country to see what it was like.

Overview

The goal of this study guide is to suggest discussion questions, resources, and activities that will allow students to take a virtual road trip across America with a Negro League ball club during a typical baseball season.

In order to understand the full dimensions of what Jim Crow meant in terms of freedom of movement, freedom of association, personal safety, and personal well-being, students will recreate the routes from city to city and town to town that Negro League teams traveled over the course of the season. Questions that most Americans have never needed to ask were critical to travel in the United States for all persons of color for over one hundred years. Where can we get gas? Where can we use the rest room? Where can we eat breakfast, lunch, or dinner? Where can we stay overnight? If the car breaks down, are there service stations that we can use? Suppose someone gets sick, what hospitals or doctors can we go to? If I need a haircut, are there barbers available? What about showers and laundry on the road? These questions and more were of critical concern to the teams as they played their way around the country.

Materials

The Negro Motorist Green Book
Available in pdf at:
www.autolife.umd.umich.edu/Race/R_
Casestudy/87_135_1736_GreenBk.pdf
"The Open Road Wasn't Quite Open to All,"
Celia McGhee, *New York Times,* August 22, 2010
Available at: www.nytimes.com/2010/08/23/
books/23green.html?_r=1&pagewanted=all
Vintage maps of the United States
Internet access

Procedures

1. The first lesson in this sequence will focus on two vantage points. The first will be the portrayal of African Americans, especially African-American baseball players, in the popular press and other media at the turn of the last century. The second will be how African Americans portrayed themselves. Students will use vintage illustrations to compare and contrast the two points of view and draw conclusions about the relative accuracy of each to draw conclusions about the overall impact of each set of images.

2. The second lesson in this sequence will let students collaborate in pairs or groups to use a variety of mapping resources and *The Green Book* in order to plan a road trip for one of the Negro League teams. They will need to locate the places they will be playing, where they will be able to stay while they are on the road, what method of travel they will use, what back-up resources they would be able to rely on, etc. in order for them

to safely travel from their home field to the other cities and towns in the league and return home safely at the end of the trip.

3. Lesson three uses all the documents and artifacts from the first two lessons. Teachers can choose among a variety of assessment options to put students in the driver's seat in order for them to show what they've learned.

4. Lesson four focuses on literacy strategies using children's literature, *Ruth and the Green Book*. In this lesson students will read and respond to the story of Ruth and her family's trip from Chicago to her grandmother's home in Alabama. It is a gentle yet powerful story that illustrates the reality of what it was like for an African-American family to travel across the United States in 1949. Students will also have the opportunity to visualize the trip, listen to period music, select lunch choices from a vintage menu, and raise questions of their own about the world Ruth lived in.

Recommended Resources

There Was Always Sun Shining Somewhere: Life in the Negro Baseball Leagues, Refocus Films, produced and directed by Craig Davidson, written by Craig Davidson and Donn Rogosin, narrated by James Earl Jones, 1984 (58 minutes)

"Shadow Ball," Inning 5, *Baseball,* Ken Burns, PBS (120 minutes)

Only the Ball Was White, WTTW/Chicago, directed by Ken Solarz, narrated by Paul Winfield, 1992 (30 minutes)

Lesson 1: Image versus Reality

Elementary social studies teachers may be reluctant to approach the reality of Jim Crow America because so many of the images from this time period are too disturbing for younger students. In this lesson, however, students will study a series of common images of African Americans that were chosen specifically because they are ordinary rather than shocking. They include African-American baseball players and other African-American images that were published in magazines, on sheet music, commercial products, and in advertising at the end of the 19th century and the early years of the 20th century. Students will then compare those images with actual images drawn from African-American culture during the same time period in order to draw conclusions about the messages each set of images intended to convey. For this they will need to establish where the image was published, when it was published, who its intended audience was, and its intended message. Students should then be able to begin drawing conclusions about why there was such a difference between the two sets of images.

Materials

Image Gallery

Image analysis sheets

Procedure

Using the image analysis sheets, have students study and discuss the illustrations and draw conclusions about their use and meanings. The first group of images represents a small sampling of the kinds of images of African Americans that were common right up to the Civil Rights era. The second group of images of African Americans appeared in black newspapers and other black controlled venues during the same time period. Students should be able to explain how the message about African Americans sent by each set of images differs and explain why they differed.

GALLERY ONE

Image A:
Currier & Ives,
"A Baseball Hit"

Image B:
Currier & Ives,
"A Foul Tip"

Image C:
Sol Etyinge, 1878
"Baseball at
Blackville"

Image D:
Leslie's Weekly,
May 29, 1897, "Base-
ball at Possumville"

Image E:
"Little Puff of Smoke
Goodnight"
lyrics by
Ring Lardner

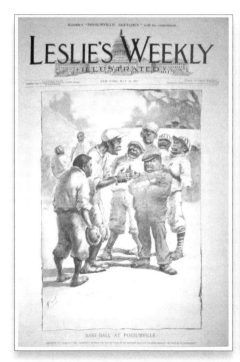

Image F:
Decorative trivet

Image G:
Junior Colored
Classics, 1931,
"Little Black
Sambo"

GALLERY TWO

Image A:
Andrew "Rube"
Foster, founder of
the Negro Leagues

Image B:
Negro Baseball
Pictorial Year Book
1944

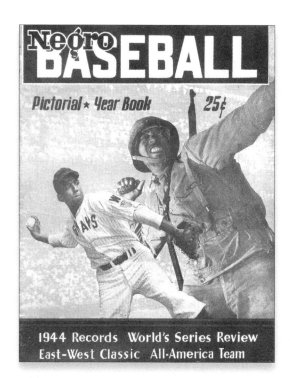

Image C:
Game day poster

Image D:
1934 East-West
All-Star Game,
Comiskey Park,
Chicago

Image E:
Newark Eagles fans sit in the stands enjoying a game.

Image F:
Future Hall of Famer Larry Doby, who would become the first African-American ballplayer in the American League, signs autographs for young Eagles fans at Ruppert Stadium in Newark.[1]

http://blog.nj.com/ledgerarchives/2009/02/the_africanamerican_newark_bas.html

Image Analysis Sheet

- What is the title of the painting or photograph? (if there is one)

  _____

- What time period does the painting or photograph represent? How can you tell?

  _____

- List the objects, person, or groups of people that can be identified.

  _____

- What describing words would you use to tell what emotions the person or group of people in the painting or photograph are feeling?

  _____

  _____

- How do you feel while you're looking at the painting or photograph? Why?

  _____

  _____

- What people or groups of people might especially like or not like what is shown in this painting or photograph? Why?

  _____

  _____

- What do you think the painter or photographer wanted people to think about the picture? Do you think the painter or photographer had a special audience in mind? Why?

  _____

  _____

- Write two questions you have about the scene or the person or groups of people in the painting or photograph.

  1. _____

  2. _____

- What title or caption would you give this painting or photograph?

  _____

Drawing Conclusions

After looking at the pictures in both galleries, what differences do you see between the way general circulation American magazines and advertisers saw African Americans and the way they saw themselves? How would you explain these differences?

Lesson 2: On the Road

For this lesson, students will use an outline map, road atlases or other maps of the Midwest and *The Green Book* to plan the itinerary for a road trip for the American Giants following the steps below. This would be a good activity for students to do with a partner or in groups.

Some of the places will have lots of the necessary amenities and be easy for students to locate, but some will be more challenging. Because some things like gas stations may not be available at some stops, students will need to plan ahead and get gas before heading to the next game. The cities and towns form a large loop through Wisconsin, Illinois, Iowa, Missouri, Kentucky, and Michigan.

They were chosen because some of the locations have a good variety of services, while some do not and will require students to think ahead in their planning. For example Fort Wayne, Indiana, has a barbershop, so they should plan to get haircuts while they are in Fort Wayne. They were also chosen because one of the themes we want to stress is the national scope of discrimination. By planning a team trip through the Midwest, students will get a firmer understanding that discrimination was not limited to the Southern states.

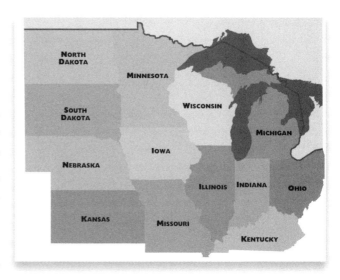

On an outline map of the Midwest:

1. Label all of the major cities in each state.

2. Label all of the state capitals.

3. Use a road atlas, or other available maps of the U.S., and the simulated schedule for July 1949 on the next page to locate the towns where games were played and add them to the map.

4. Use *The Green Book* to find:
   • Places to stay
   • Restaurants
   • Barbershops
   • Auto repair shops
   • Gas stations

Acting as scouts for the team, students will create the itinerary noting when and where the teams will stop, what items they will need to get ahead of time, before leaving, if those items wouldn't be available at the next stop, and what kinds of provisions (food, etc.) they should keep on the bus.

- While the team is on the road their bus will get a flat tire in Iowa, one of the players will break his leg in Indiana, and everyone will need a haircut.

- At many of the ballparks, players will not be allowed to use the locker rooms and showers. Where will they be able to suit up for the game and shower after? Will they have to wait until they reach the hotel at their next destination?

Drawing conclusions

After using the maps and *The Green Book,* students should be able to describe in a paragraph or three, what it would be like for the teams barnstorming through America's heartland.

Game Schedule Worksheet

Chicago American Giants July 1949						
SUNDAY	**MONDAY**	**TUESDAY**	**WEDNESDAY**	**THURSDAY**	**FRIDAY**	**SATURDAY**
Chicago, Illinois	Kenosha, Wisconsin	Rockford, Illinois	Peoria, Illinois		Waterloo, Iowa	
Des Moines, Iowa		St. Louis, Missouri	Carbondale, Illinois		Owensboro, Kentucky	
Louisville, Kentucky		Indianapolis, Indiana	Kokomo, Indiana	Fort Wayne, Indiana		South Bend, Indiana
Detroit, Michigan		Lansing, Michigan	Battle Creek, Michigan		Kalamazoo, Michigan	
Chicago, Illinois						

Teachers may also want to consider adding *Legends of the Game* to their classroom resources. Information can be found at www.tonydeesnegro league.com/catalog/item/1391517/8079643.htm

From the online description of the game:

This Collectors Edition board game showcases the history of the Negro and Latin leagues baseball. *Legends of the Game* is a tribute to players not allowed the opportunity to play baseball in the major leagues. Every baseball fan has dreamed of owning and running a baseball team. Well, now it's possible! Now you can buy, sell, and trade for legendary teams like the Detriot Stars, Chicago American Giants, New York Black Yankees, Memphis Red Sox, Pittsburgh Crawfords, St Louis Stars, Homestead Grays, and New York Cubans along with Hall of Fame players like Rube Foster, Buck Leonard, Josh Gibson, and Satchel Paige.

Ages 8+, 2-6 players

Lesson 3: Evaluating Evidence

After students have studied the images in Lesson 1, "Image versus Reality," and created the itinerary for the road trip in Lesson 2, "On the Road," they should be able to make judgments about the American scene during the late 19th and first half of the 20th century. In order for students to articulate their thoughts based on the evidence of the first two lessons, teachers can offer a variety of opportunities for students to show what they have learned and how they think about it.

Historic posters

Students can create posters that, to them, illustrate their understanding of the era. The posters should have a title and an explanation of why their illustration best represents what they understand about the era.

Historic bumper stickers

These are a good way to teach students to capture their ideas in a short but telling way. Just as the best bumper stickers say something important with few words, the students' bumper stickers should do the same. Students should be able to explain why their bumper stickers represent, to them, the essence of the American experience for African Americans during this time period.*

Historic heads

Using a silhouette of a baseball player's head, students will create a word cloud within the head of words that would show what the player thought about his world and his place in that world during this time period. You can use either generic silhouettes or create silhouettes of actual players. The word cloud should show, through size and shape, which thoughts were most important and which least important.

Historic baseball cards

Using the familiar format of baseball cards, students can research their favorite members of the Negro Leagues and create cards that, to them, best represent the talent and skills associated with their choices. They can do this for individual players, managers, or teams as a whole. They should be able to explain why they have made their choices and what the cards say about the choices they have made.

* Creating historic bumper stickers and historic heads exercise first appeared in James Percoco's, *Divided We Stand: Teaching About Conflict in U.S. History,* (Portsmouth, NH: Heinemann, 2001).

Lesson 4: *Ruth and The Green Book*

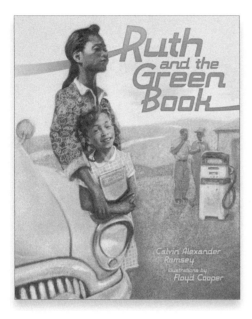

Ruth and the Green Book
Calvin Alexander Ramsey, Floyd Cooper, illustrator
Carolrhoda Books, 2010

Resources that would be helpful to teachers before imple-menting this lesson are linked below and include an in-terview with the author, an article by Celia McGee from *The New York Times,* "The Open Road Wasn't Open to All," and two websites devoted to the Memory Boxes created for the Dresser Trunk Project commemorating the places that welcomed traveling African Americans.

http://authorsontourlive.com/ruth-and-the-green-book/
www.nytimes.com/2010/08/23/books/23green.html
www.arch.umd.edu/news_and_events/?id=2561
www.architectmagazine.com/books/memory-boxes.aspx

The 1949 *Green Book* is available at:
www.autolife.umd.umich.edu/Race/R_Casestudy/Negro_motorist_green_bk.htm

During the years before the Civil Rights Act of 1964 opened public accommodations to all citizens, African Americans constructed a constellation of creative responses to the limitations imposed by segregated America. The nooks and crannies of these responses, as well as the larger, more readily identifiable responses, combine to create a picture of active resistance to imposed disabilities. For too many years, however, the reality of this struggle by African Americans was largely ignored. Historians wrote histories of slavery in which the voices of the enslaved made not a sound. Even now it remains tucked around the edges of American history. As James Loewen has persuasively argued, "both rac-ism and anti-racism are absent" from social studies textbooks written for students K-12.[1]

At the elementary level, the situation is exacer-bated by the inaccurate depiction of slavery when it is included. In a recent article, "A Closer Look: The Representation of Slavery in the *Dear America* Series," T. Lee Williams is troubled by the "soft-ened" portrayal of slavery in this series. Other prob-lems noted in the books include their focus on the experiences of those who worked in the house rather than the fields, a remarkable level of literacy, the "optimism" of the main characters, and the general over-simplification of slave life at every turn.[2]

True, the full reality of slavery would be disturbing for young students if it is presented in all its horror. However, casting these characters in the rosy glow of cheerful high hopes and expectations of freedom and casting slave families as whole and stable can convey to young learners that slavery itself wasn't so bad. Oddly, although the series glosses over the regular brutality that characterized slave life, "physical and emotional violence," when it does include a lynching, it's the lynching of a "minor white character initiated by slaves during a slave revolt."[3] Never mind that slave revolts were rare but rarer still, perhaps never, were lynchings of whites by slaves. So the one nod to the violence of slavery turns it on its head. Other issues such as presentism and exceptionalism further destroy the integrity of these narratives.[4] In short, any possible usefulness these books may offer an elementary educator, is nil and the damage inestimable. One might better tell fairy tales; at least they make no pretense of being history.

Fortunately, there are books that the elementary level social studies teacher can use that accurately depict the experience of African Americans in ways that advance understanding rather than wishful thinking. One such book is *Ruth and the Green Book*. Although it too is fiction, it is based firmly in the reality of African-Americans' lives during the years we call Jim Crow. As one reviewer writes, "Although the story is fictional, *The Green Book* and Jim Crow laws were not."[5] The story is set in the early 1950s and in it Ruth and her family travel from Chicago to visit her grandmother in Alabama. Along the way they encounter the daily discrimination that was Jim Crow America; gas stations where they were not allowed to use the restrooms, motels that would not allow them to stay, and restaurants where they were refused service. But, they also discover *The Green Book* and find a vibrant black community that

welcomed them with, literally, open arms. Along the way we discover that of all the gas stations in the country, only Esso stations gave them full service and sold *The Green Book*. For seventy-five cents they had a guide specifically designed for "black people who were traveling."[6]

The Negro Motorist Green-Book, commonly referred to as *The Green Book* was compiled in 1936 by New York City postman Victor Green. Originally he listed restaurants, gas stations, barber shops, and other kinds of services that would accommodate people in New York City. He soon began to expand its coverage to the entire United States and by 1949 it included Alaska, Bermuda, Mexico, and Canada as well. Several questions are suggested by both the book's distribution and its scope. If Jim Crow was a Southern phenomena, why was it necessary to include the whole of the United States and Canada? If Jim Crow, as it is commonly depicted, was a creature of the late 19th and early 20th century, why was *The Green Book* published until 1964? Why was Esso the only gas station chain willing to offer service to African-American travelers and sell the book? Students will have the opportunity to answer these and a host of other questions as they read Ruth's story and use the maps and *The Green Book* itself to map a journey across the country and back in time to the 1950s to join African-American travelers seeing "the U.S.A. in their Chevrolets."

1. James Loewen, *Lies My Teacher Told Me*, (New York: Touchstone Books, 1995).

2. T. Lee Williams, "A Closer Look: The Representation of Slavery in the *Dear America* Series," *Social Studies and the Young Learner*, January/February, 2009, 26-29. The books cited are *Freedom's Wings: Corey's Diary Kentucky to Ohio*, by Sharon Denis Wyeth; *A Picture of Freedom: The Diary of Clotee, a Slave Girl*, by Patricia McKissak; *I Thought My Soul Would Rise and Fly: The Diary of Patsy, a Freed Girl*, by Joyce Hansen; and *When Will This Cruel War Be Over? The Civil War Diary of Emma Simpson*, by Barry Denenberg.

3. *Ibid.*, p. 26.

4. *Ibid.*, p. 27.

5. www.midwestbookreview.com/cbw/dec_10.htm#AmericanHistory

6. Calvin Alexander Ramsey, *Ruth and the Green Book*, (Minneapolis: Carolrhoda Books, 2010).

Lesson 4, Part 1: Ruth's Story

For this project younger students will need to listen to the story of Ruth and her family and have time to enjoy the pictures. Older students will be able to read it themselves. Both the story and the illustrations offer important insights into the African-American experience of America in the 1950s. The hardcover version also includes a history of *The Green Book* that will demonstrate to students that the story is firmly based on factual information.

Vintage road maps will help students travel back to a time before interstate highways crisscrossed the country, when the average speed limit was fifty miles an hour, and main roads turned into Main Streets. This was a time before McDonald's dotted the landscape. It was a time when local restaurants were located on Main Street with only a few, if any, places to eat between towns. Although Americans had been tourists since the automobile became available, camping and motor courts were the norm, not Best Westerns or Holiday Inns. Vintage maps are cheap and easily available online, but are also readily available at places where antiques, junktiques, and collectibles are sold.

Copies of *The Green Book* should also be available for students to review. Young students will need help understanding it, but older students should find it readily accessible.

Materials

Ruth and the Green Book
The Green Book
Vintage maps

Procedures

For younger students: After listening to the story and stopping to look at and talk about the pictures, teachers can ask students the following questions. Older students can work together with a partner or in groups to answer the questions and complete the other activities.

- What parts of Ruth's story made you sad or angry?

- What parts of Ruth's story made you laugh or feel happy?

- Who were some of the people Ruth's family met on their trip that you liked? Why?

- Why did Ruth give Brown Bear to the little boy traveling with his mother?

- How would you have changed Ruth's story to make her trip better?

• Using a large map of the United States, teachers can trace Ruth's journey from Chicago to Alabama as they tell the story so that younger students can visualize the length of the journey.

- Ruth and her family sang as they traveled, probably listening to the popular songs of the day on their car radio. A number of online jukebox sites can help students hear what Ruth heard. Here is one:

  http://objflicks.com/TakeMeBackToTheFifties.htm

- Ruth's family ate as they traveled, from the picnic lunch Ruth's mother packed before they left Chicago, until they reached Tennessee and heard about *The Green Book*. Pass around copies of the Woolworth's menu and let students decide what they would have ordered. A larger image of the menu can be accessed by scrolling down the homepage at

  http://oldfortyfives.com.

  Have students figure out how much lunch would have cost. Ask them why they think Ruth and her family didn't stop at a Woolworth's, or someplace like a Woolworth's, for lunch.

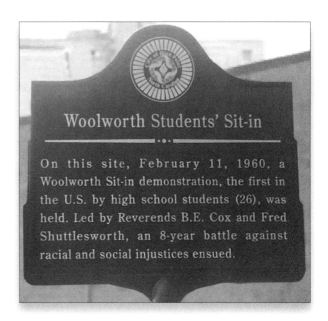

- Ask older students to read the historic marker and discuss what it says. Then ask them how it adds to their understanding of the choices Ruth's family made.

- It was Ruth's job to look for the sign below. What was special about this sign? What questions does it make you want to ask to discover why **Esso** gas stations were different from the one they stop at early in the story?

Geography skills are important for all students and *The Green Book* will let students follow in Ruth's footsteps to plot the journey from Chicago to Alabama and experience for themselves the challenges of finding places to eat and places to stay while they are "on the road."

Lesson 4, Part 2: Ruth's Road Trip with *The Green Book*

Using vintage maps and copies of *The Green Book,* have students work in groups or with a partner to trace the route they would take and note where they would stop and eat and where they would stay overnight. Remind students that speed limits in the early 1950s, before the interstate highway systems were built, were lower—50 mph between towns and cities, and 25 to 30 mph in town. Since most routes went through towns, they will have to take these slower speeds into account when they are looking for places they can stop.

Students can also use their math skills by using the maps to locate the miles between towns, as noted on the maps, and calculate how long it would take to get from place to place at 50 mph.

Wrapping up
Younger students

After reading the story and talking about the pictures and their own responses to the story, younger students can create their own illustrations to the story by drawing pictures that will help them remember Ruth and her family on their long trip to Grandmother's home in Alabama.

Older students

A good way to tie this lesson to the students' own area is to have the class work together to research the history of their town to find out whether or not Ruth and her family would have been welcome travelers in their town's restaurants, gas stations, or motels. They could start by looking for their town or the town closest to theirs in *The Green Book* to see if there are any services or places listed. If there are, that would indicate that restrictions were in place. They could then research town records that would indicate whether the restrictions were actual town or city ordinances, or the result of customs and traditions that didn't require ordinances in order to be effective and enforced. Students could also look in old yearbooks to see if there were African Americans living and going to school in their town or city prior to the Civil Rights Act of 1964. They can then compare their findings to their school and town today to see whether, and if so, how, real change has occurred.

South of the Border:
Winterball in Latin America

1946–47 "Album Caramelo Deportivo Felices" Cuban professional baseball card set

The 1930s and 40s witnessed a new opportunity for the black ballplayer—Latin America—where baseball, and not soccer, reigned supreme. As expressed by an official in the Dominican Republic government, "Baseball is spiritual in every aspect, as indulged in by Latin races."[1] The fans themselves typically underwrote their own local teams and helped to foster a sense of community identity and pride. Cuba was the first to recruit American ballplayers in 1929, followed by Venezuela in 1933 and the Dominican Republic in 1936; Mexico and Puerto Rico also were active in recruitment throughout those decades. Although it is unclear exactly why Negro League players were the primary recipients of the invitation to play while white major leaguers were not, there was some recognition that the best American talent available was black.[2] One other possible explanation is that the loosely enforced contracts in the Negro Leagues and the discrepancy in pay between them and the white players in the major leagues made Negro League players more receptive targets for recruitment. As sportswriter Ed Harris stated, "With some of the salaries paid the best players . . . the [Negro] Association would be better named the WPA League."[3] Josh Gibson also commented on the considerable financial incentives offered in Latin America: despite playing a lighter schedule, [I get] "twice as much salary, my room and board and transportation expenses."[4]

It's no surprise then that as soon as the regular season ended in the states, Negro League ballplayers headed for the sunshine, warmth, and baseball leagues of Latin

1. Larry Tye, *Satchel: The Life and Times of an American Legend,* (New York: Random House, 2009), p. 110.

2. *Ibid.,* p. 109.

3. Neil Lanctot, *Negro League Baseball: The Rise and Ruin of a Black Institution,* (Philadelphia: University of Philadelphia Press, 2004), 75.

4. *Ibid.,* p. 90.

America. In the days when even major league stars needed to supplement their incomes during the off-season, one of the better ways of doing that was playing baseball in Mexico, Cuba, Venezuela, and the Dominican Republic. For the men of the Negro Leagues, the freedom of the Latin countries gave them an "up close and personal" opportunity to experience baseball without Jim Crow on the team.

"Cool Papa" Bell remarked, "It was just real relaxing, something we weren't used to."[5] Satchel Paige was more specific, "I would be willing to go to South America and live in the jungles rather than go back to the league and play ball like I did for 10 years. The opportunities of a colored baseball player on these islands are the same or almost the same as those enjoyed by the white major leaguers in the States. That's something to think about."[6] Spec Roberts summarized his Mexican experience this way, "I had never been treated better or lived amid more hospitable surroundings anywhere."[7] The freedom to attend the best hotels, theaters, and restaurants without the specter of Jim Crow was such a contrast to what they had experienced in America that many players talked about staying, and some did.[8] One player who did was interviewed by Wendell Smith of the *Baltimore Afro-American,* in May 1944. Willie "El Diablo" Wells had just refused an offer from Effa Manley to play for the Newark Eagles, opting to stay in Mexico. Smith's interview offers the clearest articulation of what playing in Latin America offered American Negro League players.

> **Mexico City, Mexico** – Senor Willie Wells, late of Newark, New Jersey, and now of Vera Cruz, Mexico, was tilted far back in the barber's chair.
>
> "I understand that there is a lot of adverse talk about me in the States," Wells said, "because I quit the Newark Eagles and returned here to play ball. I hate that, but there's two sides to every story."
>
> "I came back here to play ball for Vera Cruz," Wells explained, "because I have a better future in Mexico than in the States. I wanted to stay and play with Newark because I consider Mr. and Mrs. Manley . . . [to be] fine people. But they couldn't offer me anything like I can get playing for Vera Cruz. Not only do I get more money playing here, but I live like a king."
>
> "Some people look at my situation simply from the standpoint of money," he said. "But there more to it than that. In the first place, I am not faced with the racial problem in Mexico. When I travel with the Vera Cruz team, we live in the best hotels, we eat in the best restaurants and can go any place we care to. You know as well as all other Negroes that we don't enjoy such privileges in the United States. We stay in any kind of hotels far from the best, and eat only where we know we will be accepted. Until recently, Negro players had to go all over the country in buses, while in Mexico, we've always traveled in trains."

5. Tye, p. 112.
6. *Ibid.,* p. 116.
7. *Ibid.,* p. 119.
8. *Ibid.,* p. 108.

In explaining the advantages of playing ball in Mexico, Wells pointed out that there is little difference between the life of a Mexican ballplayer and that of a big leaguer in the States.

"Players on teams in the Mexican league live just like big leaguers. . . . We have everything first class, plus the fact that the people here are much more considerate than the American baseball fan. I mean that we are heroes here, and not just ballplayers.

"One of the main reasons I came back to Mexico," he said, "is because I've found freedom and democracy here, something I never found in the United States. I was branded a Negro in the States, and had to act accordingly. Everything I did, including playing ball, was regulated by color. . . . Well, here in Mexico, I am a man. I can go as far in baseball as I am capable of going. I can live where I please and will encounter no restrictions of any kind because of my race. So, you see, that also has a lot to do with my decision to return here."[9]

Willie Wells's experiences reverberate throughout the interviews with former Negro League players. They found democracy and freedom in Latin America, the kind they didn't have in the United States. And it's important to remember that long after Jackie Robinson joined the Dodgers, African Americans continued to live in a deeply segregated society. So, why did they ever come back? Kadir Nelson's "Everyman" narrator speaks for all the former players when he says, "It was a lot of fun playing down there, but sometimes it would get lonely. They treated us nice and it was really beautiful, but after a while we'd get a little homesick. . . . Playing in Latin America was a great way to spend the winter; but ask anybody, it is tough going without a plate of greens, sweet candied yams, and some buttermilk biscuits for four months. There was always a language barrier, and their cultures were so different from ours."[10] Anyone who's ever traveled knows how good it feels to go home, no matter how much fun the traveling was. It was the same for these players. They were Americans.

A Different Kind of Culture

Before taking a closer look at the places where they played and the reactions of the Negro Leagues themselves to the opportunities playing south of the border, two questions need to be addressed. First, why, considering that Latin America and the Caribbean Islands had once been slave-holding societies, didn't they have the same restrictions on blacks that the United States had? And, second, how and why did Latin America and the Caribbean Islands become as crazy about baseball as the United States?

9. Jim Reisler, ed., *Black Writers/Black Baseball: An Anthology of Articles from Black Sportswriters Who Covered the Negro Leagues,* (Jefferson, NC: McFarland & Co., 1994) p. 44-45.

10. Kadir Nelson, *We Are the Ship: The Story of the Negro Leagues,* (New York: Jump at the Sun, 2008) p. 55.

We take for granted that Negro league players would not face the kind of discrimination Jim Crow America heaped upon them. But, why were South America and the Caribbean welcoming environments? In order to answer that question, students need to take a short journey into the history of slavery in South America and the Caribbean in order to see how the differences in the slave cultures and systems of North America and South America permanently determined the future trajectory of relationships between the races from the 16th century forward.

Social Organizations of Slave Societies

Slavery as practiced by the French and British was quite different from that practiced by the Spanish and Portuguese. Both systems were brutal, but in differing ways. Key to the difference in how slavery would impact former slave-holding countries lay in the conception of race understood in each area. "In Spanish and Portuguese America, an intricate system of racial classification emerged. Compared to the British and French, the Spanish and Portuguese were much more tolerant of racial mixing, an attitude encouraged by a shortage of European women, and recognized a wide range of racial gradations, including black, mestizo, quadroon, and octoroon. The American South, in contrast, adopted a two-category system of racial categorization in which any person with a black mother was automatically considered to be black."[11] What this meant was that in Latin America and the Caribbean, although sometimes attempted, no permanent racial barriers were erected between or among the variety of native, Spanish, Portuguese, and African backgrounds.

11. www.digitalhistory. uh.edu/database/ article_display. cfm?HHID=78

In his classic monograph on the topic, *Slave and Citizen,* Frank Tannenbaum, argued that the Catholicism of the Spanish and Portuguese was of critical importance, primarily because it granted the enslaved a moral life and personality. In the United States the enslaved were defined with the legal fiction that they were chattel property, not human beings. Slavery under the Spanish and Portuguese, although much harsher in many ways—"death rates among slaves in the Caribbean were one-third higher than in the South"—never attempted to perpetrate the fraud that the enslaved were any less a moral human being than they. For a slave in Brazil or Jamaica, freedom was, if one lived, inevitable. Add to this the high levels of intermarriage between slave and non-slave, and the possibility of rigid segregation similar to that practiced in the South becomes not only less likely, it becomes unthinkable.[12]

Since 1946, when Tannenbaum opened new and productive avenues for research, his work has been expanded and discrete studies have added texture and depth to his arguments. But none have overturned his essential assertions regarding the relative fluidity and social mobility present in Latin American and Caribbean societies. Herbert Klein's recent study, *African Slavery in Latin America and the Caribbean,* concludes that "relatively high rates of mobility and accommodation were achieved by the second or third generation after abolition. . . . By the last quarter of the 20th century the Afro-American presence had become an accustomed and accepted part of the culture and national self-identify of most of the ex-slave societies"[13] In short, for the players of the Negro Leagues, Latin America and the Caribbean offered a welcome respite from the daily racial disabilities of the United States.

Baseball Sweeps Across Latin America

How did our southern neighbors come to love baseball as much as we did in the states? Oddly enough, one of the few positive outcomes of United States' imperialistic incursions into Mexico, Central and South America and the Caribbean was the possible introduction of baseball. Baseball researcher and blogger Andrew G. Clem writes, "Wherever U.S. cultural influence has been the strongest, baseball has become popular in Latin America. Indeed, in many cases baseball was introduced during U.S. military occupations."[14] Conversely, the website *¡Viva Baseball!* argues that baseball was popular in Cuba long before American forces arrived in 1898. The evidence is clear that baseball was being played and enjoyed in Cuba before The War of 1898 but American interaction with Mexico and the Caribbean began long before 1898, so it is unclear how the American sport arrived in the area, but it also seems clear it was transplanted from the United States.

American interest in Central and South America and the Caribbean Islands began

12. Frank Tannenbaum, *Slave and Citizen: The Negro in the Americas,* (New York: A.A. Knopf, 1946).

13. Herbert S. Klein and Ben Vinson, *African Slavery in Latin America and the Caribbean,* (New York: Oxford University Press, 2007).

14. www.andrewclem.com/Baseball/LatinAmerican_Leagues.html

with the Monroe Doctrine in 1823 and has been the basis for United States intervention since. As early as 1846, with the Mexican American War, the United States has
pursued both benign and aggressive stances toward this area. A very brief timeline of
U.S. intervention between 1846 and 1933 would need to include the following:

1846	War with Mexico. U.S. acquires one-third of Mexico's territory
1850, 53, 54, 57	Interventions in Nicaragua
1898	War with Spain and occupation of Cuba, Puerto Rico, Guam and the Philippines
1903	Platt Amendment inserted into the Cuban constitution granting the United States the right to intervene in Cuban internal affairs
	U.S. supports Panamanian rebellion and acquires land for the Panama Canal
1904, 05, 06, 07	U.S. troops to Mexico, Honduras, and Cuba
1909	"Dollar Diplomacy": U.S. uses money, in the form of both aid and corporate investments to influence the internal affairs of these countries.
1910	U.S. Marines occupy Nicaragua
1915	U.S. Marines occupy Haiti
1916	Marines occupy the Dominican Republic
1917	U.S. troops enter Mexico to pursue Pancho Villa
1918–32	U.S. Marines occupy Panama, Nicaragua, the Dominican Republic, and El Salvador
1933	FDR announces the Good Neighbor Policy

This timeline could, of course, be extended right up to the present but from just this brief sketch it is easy to see that the on-going presence of the United States in this area accounts for the many ways that our culture has influenced the culture of Latin America. By far the most benign of these influences was the spread of baseball.

Latin American Baseball Threatens the Negro Leagues

By 1940, aggressive recruiting by Mexican teams provided a steady stream of the best black ballplayers and as a result, these losses to Mexico became a major issue facing black professional teams in the United States.[15] In a strange twist of fate, the owners of the Homestead Grays, Cumberland "Cum" Posey and Gus Greenlee, one-time owner of the Pittsburgh Crawfords, may have actually created the template for identifying the best players and then raiding other teams to get them, a technique then adopted by Mexican team owners. Posey and Greenlee regularly stocked their rosters by luring the best talent from other teams with offers of bonuses and higher pay. Better players meant more on-the-field success and bigger box office receipts. Greenlee, in particular, had his publicity department distribute worldwide an annual account of his team's achievements. Highlighted in the reports were accounts of the success of his star pitcher, Leroy "Satchel" Paige. The reports drew the attention of a Dominican Republic dentist-turned-political-crony, Dr. Jose Enrique Aybar, who was currently managing a team that was struggling in the standings. His team, the Dragones de Ciudad Trujillo was named after the Dominican dictator (who was also the honorary president of the team) and Trujillo hated to lose. Aybar took it upon himself to fly to New Orleans where the Crawfords were training and personally negotiated with Paige to play for the Dragones and to bring eight other players of his choosing with him. The year was 1937 and the record shows that the Dragones went on to win the Dominican league championship. Greenlee's Crawfords were decimated by the departures and within two years he was forced to sell the team. He cried "foul" long and hard, but it was a model of his own behavior that had led to his team's demise.[16]

The team owners and leagues in the states attempted to institute fines and threatened "lifetime bans" on deserting players, but neither stemmed the tide. Mexican officials vigorously undermined these types of efforts as they sought to elevate their league to the level of white major league baseball by providing players with amenities that were simply unavailable in the States. Columnist Eustace Gay of the *Philadelphia Tribune* reported that players traveled to games by rail, received decent housing, and medical care during the season.[17] The players valued playing in a "real" league where each team had its own park and where double-headers were characterized by the sec-

15. Lanctot, p. 100.
16. Tye, 109, p. 110.
17. Lanctot, p. 103.

18. Tye, p. 128.
19. Lanctot, p. 103.
20. Tye, p. 128.

ond game being a shortened informal exhibition, eliminating the pressure of another league game.[18] Effa Manley, co-owner with her husband of the Newark Eagles, remarked that although she did "not blame the ballplayers for going away where they can get more money," she felt that it would be "positively stupid for us to sit idly by and not make an effort to protect ourselves." She proposed working cooperatively with the Mexican League and in fact suggested that the Negro League become a "high class farm team," developing players for Mexico for which they would be financially well compensated. Her suggestion was predictably voted down by the other owners, but the perceived reality remained, expressed in the warning of Vic Harris, "we can't ignore the fact that all the good ballplayers are playing on foreign soil."[19] Subsequent attempts to address the issue through litigation, draft boards, continued threats of banishment from Negro League baseball, and even the involvement of the U.S. State Department were largely unsuccessful.

Puerto Rico

Baseball in Puerto Rico was central to the island's sense of identity. Baseball was what fishermen thought about when casting their lines and farmers when they harvested their crops. Fans developed personal relationships with the players and would frequently reward players for good play by handing coins and bills through the chicken-wire that separated stands from field. Double-headers were played every Sunday, one game in the morning and the second in the afternoon. Townspeople tried to find time for church before or after the games, "but if not, God would understand."[20] Into this environment stepped Negro League players in the 1930s, where they were met with immediate acceptance. Their presence was in fact marked by considerably more than acceptance, as they were viewed as heroes and assumed a larger-than-life status among the island's natives. Players were frequently invited into homes for a meal and conversation and nowhere on the island was there any presence of the segregation and oppression of Jim Crow. Decades after the last Negro player had gone home, older natives still talked about their exploits, still argued about umpires' calls, and debated who had been the best.

Cuba Imports Jim Crow

By 1942 the situation had changed, as far as the Cuban experience was concerned. Lured by the Caribbean sun, stunning mountain landscapes, beautiful white beaches and the emerald sea, white America began to discover what seemed to be an island paradise. The protection and safety offered, interestingly enough, by a totalitarian regime attracted wealthy Americans to invest in the Cuban economy and establish lucrative trading and business enterprises. More importantly though, the population of wealthy white Americans on the island grew and with it came the American influence of segregation. Whether as tourists or residents, Jim Crow was the traveling companion of these white Americans. As a consequence of this, black ballplayers no longer enjoyed the "freedom and democracy" referred to by Willie Wells just five years earlier. Players in Cuba suddenly found that the establishments and amenities they had previously enjoyed without a hint of discrimination were now off-limits to them. As pitcher Terris McDuffie stated: "Negroes are segregated at the decent eating places and hotels because so many American white people are taking over."[21] Puerto Rico and Venezuela remained popular for a longer period of time, McDuffie going on to state that the former was "everything Cuba is not."[22] The black ballplayer had once more been relegated to second-class citizenship as Jim Crow thinking began to influence the cultures of the Caribbean.

21. Lanctot, p. 163.
22. *Ibid.,* p. 163.

But, of course, when cultures meet, the influences move in two or more directions. So as much as the United States influenced Latin America by sending baseball to them, Latin America added its own style of play to the game. Melding Negro League ball with Latin American ball resulted in the Negro League players bringing back to the United States a hybrid style that would ultimately wow their own fans and, when the major leagues became re-integrated, thrill and amaze those crowds as well.

The teaching activities for this chapter highlight the resources of *¡Viva Baseball!,* located at http://exhibits.baseballhalloffame.org/viva/index.asp. This is a fabulous site that offers an avalanche of information, with the bonus option of being able to be read in either English or Spanish. Even if students know only a little Spanish, bilingual opportunities will enrich their experience of the site. By using the feature at the top of the site that allows the user to change the language, students will be able to easily switch from English to Spanish and see how similar the two languages are. And, for students whose first language is Spanish, they will be pleased to spend time in their own comfort zone.

Lesson 1: ¡Viva Baseball!
Four Strategies for Bilingual Learning

Although Negro League players enthusiastically joined Latin American teams during their off-seasons, they soon realized they would need to learn how to navigate in another language. *¡Viva Baseball!* located at http://exhibits.baseballhalloffame.org/viva.es/index.asp is equipped with a feature at the top of the page that allows the entire website to be read in either English or Spanish. This allows teachers to provide students with a bilingual learning experience.

Because of its bilingual capability, we've designed this series of lessons using this site in ways that will give students the opportunity to experience what the Negro League players experienced while playing in Cuba, Mexico, and other Latin American countries. They will also have a chance to see how closely English and Spanish are related, with many words being close to or the same as those in each language. These kinds of words are called cognates and can be important "beginnings" of learning another language.

FIRST

Have students read the opening paragraphs found on the home page of *¡Viva Baseball!* reproduced below. Then have them underline all the words that are the same or similar that they find in the Spanish version. Then let them guess the words that don't look familiar by seeing where the word is placed in the sentence or its proximity to a familiar word. Finally, with the English version covered up for this last part, have them translate the Spanish paragraphs into English so they can see how easy the first steps of learning another language can be.

For students whose first language is Spanish, just reverse the process. This strategy can be used with all parts of the website.

The Latin love affair with baseball is some 150 years old and still going strong. Followed, played and celebrated year-round in the Caribbean, baseball is so woven into local culture that it is as much Latin as it is American.

Latino ballplayers bring passion, excellence, and what Cuban ballplayer Octavio "Cookie" Rojas called "a special hunger" to the game, energizing and enriching our shared Inter-National Pastime. *¡Viva Baseball!*

SECOND

Another opportunity for students to become acquainted with the language of Latin America can be found at: *Would you make it in the major leagues?*

http://exhibits.baseballhalloffame.org/viva/history/barriers-makeit.asp

For this activity students must put themselves in the shoes of a Negro League player and answer questions requiring them to choose the correct word in Spanish to answer the questions. The result is shown immediately so they can continue choosing until they get it right.

THIRD

Interactive links for each country of the Caribbean and Mexico on the map site below lets students access larger maps of each of the countries, including demographic information, a short history of the game in that country, and information about the teams and the leagues that the Negro League players became part of. The countries include Cuba, the Dominican Republic, Mexico, Puerto Rico, Venezuela, and others. This site can also be used to remind students that although Puerto Rico is part of the Caribbean, it is also part of the United States.

http://exhibits.baseballhalloffame.org/viva/history/history.asp

El romance de los latinoamericanos con el béisbol se remonta unos 150 años atrás y aún sigue vigente. Seguido, jugado y celebrado todo el año en el Caribe, el béisbol está tan arraigado en la cultura local que es tan latino como estadounidense.

Los peloteros latinos aportan pasión, excelencia y lo que el jugador cubano Octavio "Cuqui" Rojas denominó "un hambre especial" por el juego, que energiza y enriquece nuestro Pasatiempo Inter-Nacional. *¡Viva Baseball!*

FOURTH

Many students will already be familiar with the names of players who came from the Caribbean and Mexico and became stars in the major leagues here in the States. This next link takes them to the National Baseball Hall of Fame plaques for them. Here students will be able to learn more about them. This link also has an expanding link on the left that lists many of the former and current players from Latin America that made it to the big leagues.

http://exhibits.baseballhalloffame.org/viva/roster/roster.asp

Because this website is rich with teachable materials, teachers will find many of their own ways to use the site creatively to bring bilingual teaching and learning into their classrooms.

Lesson 2: *No hablo inglés*
Empathy for the Bilingual Experience

Sugar, 2008
Written and directed by
Anna Boden and Ryan Fleck
Run time: 114 minutes

Sugar is the inspirational fictional story of Miguel Santos, a gifted pitcher struggling to make it to the big leagues of American baseball. Nicknamed "Azúcar" (Spanish for "sugar"), 19-year-old Miguel travels from his poor but tightly-knit community in the Dominican Republic to play minor league baseball in the United States—where anything is possible. He finds himself in a small Iowa town, where he struggles with the culture, the language, and the pressure of knowing that only his success can rescue his family.

The main character, Miguel "Sugar" Santos, gets his big chance to come to America and work his way up to the major leagues. He is sent to the Iowa Swings A-League Ball club and housed with a well-meaning farm family who does its best to make him welcome. It becomes clear that these folks have been housing newly-arrived Latino ballplayers for many years, yet they seem to have learned almost no Spanish, so communication is difficult and it's up to Sugar to learn English if he is going to survive. The film is full of sad, funny, and heart-breakingly real moments as Sugar learns to adjust to life in America and in American baseball.

One of the best features of the DVD is the extra feature: *Play Béisbol! The Dominican Dream.* In this,

Major League stars like Robinson Canó, Pedro Martinez, and David Ortiz recount their own memories and missteps as newcomers to the United States and to the major leagues. Their confirmation that the film accurately tells their story will help students see how difficult moving from one culture to another can be. This, coupled with the bilingual lessons will help build empathy for the players and their accomplishments.

N.B. **Because this is an R-rated film, I recommend getting permission from parents if you want to show the entire film.** It's certainly worth it, and there is nothing in the film that high school juniors and seniors would find shocking or unfamiliar. Its good qualities far outweigh its very brief sexual content and one scene of drugs being used; most scenes are completely suitable for younger students.

Scenes from the film.
Preview the trailer at:
http://www.imdb.com/title/tt0990413/?ref_=fn_al_tt_2

The Women of the Negro Leagues:
Effa Manley, Toni Stone,
Mamie "Peanut" Johnson, and Connie Morgan

Courtesy National Baseball Hall Of Fame

Effa Manley is the only woman honored by induction into the National Baseball Hall of Fame. As the owner and manager of the Newark Eagles, as a civil rights activist, and as an outspoken advocate on behalf of players, Manley earned her place in the Hall of Fame through her endless striving on behalf of her team and all of the Negro Leagues players. Hers is a story of overcoming the terrible odds against African Americans during the years of Jim Crow America and of overcoming the odds against women in order to use all of her powers to further the rights of not only African-American ballplayers, but all African Americans. As an organizer of the Citizens League for Fair Play, she led a successful effort to persuade the white owners of Harlem's largest department store, Blumstein's Department Store, to hire forty-five African Americans for clerical and sales positions. As the owner of the Eagles and a major player in the owners association, she consistently argued on behalf of respect for the league and fairness from the Major Leagues. At a time when it was not only a "white" world but a "man's" world, Effa Manley was a force to be reckoned with.

Second basemen Toni Stone and Connie Morgan, and pitcher "Peanut" Johnson were the only women to have ever played on Negro League teams. They played for the Indianapolis Clowns and the Kansas City Monarchs, two iconic teams of the Negro Leagues era, from 1953 to 1955. They too, like Effa Manley, struggled to use their talents when the odds were against them. And while it is true that at first they were considered novelties, signed to attract fans during the waning days of the Negro Leagues, they proved themselves to be skilled and talented athletes, comparable to everyone else on the teams, and better than some.

Recent interest in women in baseball was sparked with the 1988 release of the documentary *A League of Their Own*. The film chronicles a reunion of the members of the All American Girl's Professional Baseball League and weaves the story of the reunion around a history of the league by using home movies and old film clips from its 10-year existence. By the mid-1980s the story of the League had been largely forgotten except by the veterans who had played in it. That was when the members of the teams, led by Helen Callaghan, formerly of the Indianapolis Daisies, decided to film their annual reunion in Fort Wayne, Indiana. Fortunately, a local PBS television station showed interest in the story and agreed to lend a hand producing and funding the film. One happy result of its broadcast was that it gained the interest of producer/director Penny Marshall. As Marshall tells it in the filmed interview that runs in the "Diamond Dreams" exhibit at the National Baseball Hall of Fame and Museum, "I figured if I didn't know about this story, lots of other people didn't either." Of course, Marshall's film with the same title, *A League of Their Own*, released in 1992, became an instant classic, an "evergreen" in the lingo of the movie industry, a film that remains fresh forever.

Marshall's film chronicles the league over the course of its first season and is distinguished for, among other things, adding two important elements to the story. The first is what we all now know about the game, "There's no crying in baseball!" The second is a moment that leaps off the screen and sends an unspoken message of piercing clarity. In this scene the Rockford Peaches are playing against the Racine Belles. A player hits a dribbler into foul territory down the first base line. Standing behind the fence are three young African-American women and their dates. As the ball rolls toward them, one of the women steps through an opening in the fence, picks up the ball, and hurls a perfect stinging strike back to the Peaches' catcher, Dottie Hinson. There is a moment's pause as the women look at each other. Then, with a look of pleased confidence that says, "I'm your equal" she walks away. It's a powerful moment that can't help but remind us that even as we celebrate the All American Girl's Professional Baseball League, that the league would have been more aptly named the All American *White* Girl's Professional Baseball League. We've often wondered if the scene isn't there as Marshall's homage to the three women who played on the Negro Leagues teams. It's definitely there to acknowledge the racial divide, aptly captured by the literal fence between them.

The story of African-American women in baseball would have to wait until the next century for similar recognition. But, as interest grew in the Negro Leagues,

1. James Overmyer, *Queen of the Negro Leagues: Effa Manley and the Newark Eagles,* (Lanham, Maryland: Scarecrow Press, 1998) p. vii. Overmyer makes it clear, and testimony from former Newark Eagles players and other baseball luminaries confirms, that although Abe Manley bought the team and was co-owner with Effa, Effa ran the show—she simply was Newark Eagles baseball.

2. Ralph Crowder, "Don't Buy Where You Can't Work": An Investigation of the Political Forces and Social conflict Within the Harlem Boycott of 1934," *Afro-Americans in New York Life and History* 15.2 (July 31, 1991): 7. Other than the confusion about Effa Manley's name and position, this is an excellent article offering important insights into early direct action civil rights activities that are often overlooked in narratives about civil rights in the United States.

especially after Ted William's induction speech in 1966, and the first of the Negro Leagues players were inducted into the National Baseball Hall of Fame, sports fans, historians, and sports writers began excavating through the artifacts, ephemera, and records to recover this lost history of the game. Ultimately, this sifting though the past led to the stories of Effa Manley, Toni Stone, Connie Morgan, and Mamie "Peanut" Johnson and added a whole new perspective to the history of the re-integration of major league baseball.

Effa Manley, Owner

As recently as the early 1990s, Effa Manley, like much of the history of the Negro Leagues themselves, was largely unknown, even among baseball aficionados. James Overmyer relates his own "to a nearly perfect extent, ignorance of the Negro Leagues . . ." After a trip to Cooperstown for a meeting of the Society for American Baseball Research, his wife, who had toured the museum while he attended the meeting, asked him, "Who was Effa Manley?" Ultimately it became a question that led Overmyer to write his biography of her, *Queen of the Negro Leagues: Effa Manley and the Newark Eagles.* But at the time his answer to the question was, "Who?" To which his wife responded, "Well, her picture's in the museum. She did all sorts of progressive things to make Negro league baseball better, but the caption on her picture just calls her the 'glamour girl of the Negro leagues'."[1] He was not alone in his puzzlement about Effa Manley. In an article recounting one of the early 20th century civil rights battles, the "Don't Buy Where You Can't Work" Harlem boycott of stores held during the summer of 1934, in which Manley played a prominent role as an organizer and picketer, her name appears as "Etta" Manley. And, in spite of the fact that the call for the strike was made by Rev. Johnson and Manley, the researcher speculates that "Mrs. Manley may have been one of Johnson's parishioners or a member of the Harlem Women's Association. Adequate evidence does not exist to define her status clearly."[2] Had he had the correct spelling or broader knowledge of the Harlem activist scene, he would have, in fact, found a wealth of information about Effa Manley. Or, maybe not. Since even in knowledgeable baseball circles, she was relatively unknown until quite recently. But, as Overmyer demonstrates, there was a lot to know and admire about Effa Manley. The Hall of Fame display that Overmyer's wife found so disturbing has, along with the rest of the Hall's treatment of the Negro Leagues, been transformed. Overmyer reports, "The Hall of Fame and Museum's greatly expanded Negro Leagues exhibit, *Pride and Passion,* opened in June 1997 [and] the photo of Effa with its offending 'glamour girl' caption has been replaced by a segment of a computerized interactive photo exhibit which gives both her and the Eagles much more appropriate credit." And in the years since the latest edition of Overmyer's work was published in 1998, the Hall, in fact, has gone far beyond simply expanding the display; in 2006 Effa Manley, along with 16 more Negro League players, was inducted into the Hall of Fame itself. Today she remains the only woman to be so honored, all the more remarkable in a business where even today, women owners or managers are a rarity.

Effa came by her devotion to baseball and the Negro Leagues through the happy coincidence that her special devotion to Babe Ruth put her in the Yankee Stadium stands for the 1932 World Series where she met Abe Manley, a guy who loved everything about baseball. Soon their combined love of the game turned into love for each other. It was an odd pairing. Abe was fifteen years older than Effa and much darker, which, in some circles, even among African Americans, mattered. This takes us to the next unusual part of Effa's story. Although her mother was white and both of Effa's marriages were with black men, she was the child of a white stockbroker for whom her mother sewed. For Effa, growing up in a home with her black step-father and her half African-American brothers and sisters was normal. But it wasn't normal to everyone else. She tells the story about how, when she was in first grade, her teacher sent her to the principal who wanted to know why she was always playing with the "colored" children. It was her first encounter with the casual racism that was the order of the day. If anyone wanted to guess what motivated her activism, they would be on solid ground if they looked to her experiences growing up in a society where skin color was so very important. After graduating from high school, she moved to New York where she had no trouble shopping or eating in white stores and restaurants. But, she never felt comfortable being able to do things and go places where her family was unwelcome.

By the time Effa met Abe, she was ready to continue her life as a black woman and it wasn't until she was many years retired from baseball and Abe had died, that she admitted that she was actually white. It shouldn't have mattered, but it did. On the other hand, being accepted as black because she was Abe's wife gave her an entrée into the world of Negro League baseball she would never have had otherwise. And, of course, it helped that she and Abe owned the team!

Overmyer's biography of Effa and the Newark Eagles, tends to be more heavily weighted toward the fortunes of the Newark Eagles than toward Effa Manley's life, but in so many ways the two were inextricably intertwined.[3] Because of her experiences as a front-line civil rights activist and her position of power in Negro Leagues baseball circles, Effa Manley was particularly sensitive to the changes poised to begin after WWII. So it is no surprise to find her in Washington, D.C., in 1945 determined to "lift the 'iron curtain' that had fallen across baseball" over half a century earlier. She sensed that the time was ripe for integrating baseball and she wanted to find a way

3. Overmyer, p. ix. In one of those happy accidents of history, Overmyer recounts the story of how the abandoned files of the Newark Eagles were discovered in the basement of the former home of Effa and Abe Manley. The team files were apparently left behind when she moved to California in the mid-1950s. Instrumental to their recovery, Dr. Lawrence Hogan of Union Country College, arranged for the files to be housed in the Newark Public Library. As he put it, "The files open a door directly into the Eagles' office during those years—and those of us who do research into black baseball would be much poorer without them."

to bring her leagues into the system, "ideally as part of organized baseball's minor league system." This had been Andrew "Rube" Foster's goal as early as the 1920s when he organized the first Negro league. Now Effa Manley wanted to seize the day. As a "self-appointed emissary" for the Negro Leagues, she sought out George Trautman, president of the American Association, the highest ranking minor league association. Her mission was to convince Trautman to use his power to bring the Negro Leagues into the minor leagues as a legitimate part of organized baseball.

Integrating the Leagues

Trautman kept her waiting for hours and ultimately sent his wife to meet with her. As Effa described it, "It was his way of saying, 'I don't give a darn.'" She did eventually meet with him but nothing came of it. Unfortunately her attempt to broker a deal that would have positively changed the futures of hundreds of African-American players, owners, managers, and coaches, was one of the few times she failed in what she set out to accomplish. Had the Negro Leagues become part of the minor league system, hundreds of African-American players would have benefited. As it turned out, as we all know, the signing of Jackie Robinson, as wonderful as that was, ultimately was the beginning of the end for the Negro Leagues, players, managers, coaches, and other team-affiliated personnel.

In baseball, it's never good to strike out, but it's better to go down swinging than to watch the third strike sail past, to "go down looking." Effa wasn't the type of woman to go down looking. She had seen that integration of the major leagues was just a matter of time, and not much of it. So when her attempt to persuade the power brokers in the minor leagues to establish the Negro League teams as a legitimate part of the minor leagues failed, she set her sights on preserving the integrity of the contracts the Negro League teams had with their players, especially the players on her own Newark Eagles. This brought her toe to toe with Branch Rickey. At issue was the method by which Rickey began signing players. Rather than negotiating for players' contracts with the owners of the various Negro League teams, he instead negotiated with individual players as though they were free agents. At the time, all major league players were routinely bound by the standard reserve clause in their contracts. This meant that when their contracts expired they had two choices, negotiate with their current team or ask to be released or traded. In other words, management held all the aces. Players were not free to negotiate on their own. In contrast, some of the Negro League teams had operated under less formal contracts, sometimes nothing more binding than a handshake, as had been the case with Jackie Robinson and the Kansas City Monarchs. That would soon change.

The owners immediately realized that their existence was in real jeopardy. If the major league teams raided the Negro League teams of their best players without negotiating with the team owners and management and without compensating the teams, it would ruin the teams financially. No one, least of all Manley, wanted to stand in the way of African Americans playing in the major leagues, but she and the other team owners were not willing to let their rosters be raided and their contracts with their players ignored. They said as much in a letter to the commissioner of baseball, Albert B. Chandler: "We feel that the clubs of Organized Negro Baseball who have gone to so much expense to develop players and establish teams and leagues should be approached, and deals made with clubs involved." As J.B. Martin, owner of the Kansas City Monarchs put it while conceding that fair compensation for Jackie Robinson was a lost cause, ". . . BUT when they get other players, if they get them, we will place a reasonable price on them and demand it." In addition, all of the owners who had eschewed binding contracts, now adopted contracts that included "reserve clauses" in them.[4]

Manley, like the other owners who publicly cheered the success of their players as they entered one-by-one into the major leagues, privately resented being ignored by men like Branch Rickey. She got her chance to make sure he knew how she felt during the 1946 Fourth of July Gala in Yankee Stadium where her Newark Eagles were playing against the New York Black Barons. Hearing that Branch Rickey was in the stadium instead of across town where his own team was playing, she sought him out. As reported by Dan Parker, sports columnist for the New York *Daily Mirror*, she unleashed her considerable charm to deliver a very pointed message:

> Mr. Rickey, I hope you're not going to grab any more of our players," she cooed, as the Deacon turned purple. "You know that the contracts we have with our players would stand up better in court than those you have with the majors. You know, Mr. Rickey, we could make trouble for you on the Newcombe transaction if we wanted to," continued Mrs. Manley, enjoying the Deacon's discomfiture.[5]

Manley considered Rickey a life-long enemy and years later succinctly summarized his treatment of the Negro League owners this way: "He raped us."[6]

A Legacy of Activism

In the years following the demise of the Newark Eagles and the rest of the Negro Leagues, the death of her beloved husband, Abe, and having no ties left to Newark, Manley moved to Los Angeles. There, she turned her energy and attention to a new mission—that of gaining recognition for the hundreds of outstanding African-

4. *Ibid.,* p. 223.
5. *Ibid.,* p. 219
6. *Ibid.,* p. 219.

American players who had played during the Jim Crow era. She lent her name to fund-raising for projects to mark the contributions of former players like Chet Brewer, a leading Negro League pitcher in his day. Brewer was running a baseball program for boys at a city-owned park and through Manley's efforts the ballpark became "Chet Brewer Field." More important, she began a letter-writing campaign urging the National Baseball Hall of Fame to recognize the greats of the Negro Leagues by acknowledging them in some tangible way. Her letters also went out to Fred Claire, publicity director for the Dodgers, asking that former Negro League players be recognized at games of the newly relocated Los Angeles Dodgers. She then opened her voluminous scrapbook of memorabilia to collaborator Leon H. Hardwick, a retired sports editor, and produced, *Negro Baseball . . . Before Integration.*

Her dream to see former Negro League players honored in the Hall of Fame began to come true when, in 1971, Satchel Paige was inducted, followed by a half-dozen others over the next few years. But, those inducted were those who had been young enough at the time of the re-integration to make the transition into the major leagues and were inducted based on their play in the majors. And it should be noted that even with integration, the process of adding African-American players to major league teams was exceedingly slow. Many teams added only one or two players each season and many teams resisted integration well past the initial signing of Jackie Robinson. The Boston Red Sox were the last team to add an African-American player with the mid-season addition of Pumpsie Green in July of 1959, over a decade after Jackie Robinson's signing with the Dodgers. Pleased as she was by these first inductions, she still wanted the great players who never had the chance to play in the segregated majors to be honored and was "furious" according to C.C. Johnson Spink of the *Sporting News*, when the Hall's Special Committee on the Negro Leagues was disbanded in 1977 after choosing only nine players and leaving any further selections to the standing Veterans Committee.[7]

7.   *Ibid.,* p. 251-255.

Effa Manley died on April 16, 1981, leaving a legacy of courage and accomplishment as a civil rights activist, baseball legend, and dedicated advocate for the Negro Leagues she loved. She did not live long enough to see the founder of the first Negro League, Andrew "Rube" Foster or Ray Dandridge, Newark Eagle third baseman, inducted just a few months later in July of 1981. But, in 2006, a generous portion of her dream came true. Whenever she was asked who should be recognized by the Hall. She always answered, "I'd settle for thirty, but I could name a hundred." On July 30, 2006, the Hall inducted its largest class of new members, sixteen players from the Negro

Leagues and pre-Negro Leagues. And, what would have surprised and pleased her most of all was that she, herself, was so honored.[8]

8. Baseball Hall of Fame video link: http://baseballhall.org/hof/manley-effa

Her plaque in the Hall of Fame reads:

> A trailblazing owner and tireless crusader in the civil rights movement who earned the respect of her players and fellow owners. A business manager and co-owner of the Eagles, ensured team's financial success with creative promotions and advertising. Beloved by fans because she integrated her players into the community and fielded consistently competitive teams, highlighted by a 1946 Negro Leagues World Series championship. Represented team at league meetings and established a precedent of Negro Leagues clubs receiving fair compensation for players signed to major league contracts.

The Players: Toni Stone, Mamie "Peanut" Johnson, and Connie Morgan

In the same way that Effa Manley's story was lost for decades, so were the stories of Toni Stone, Mamie "Peanut" Johnson, and Connie Morgan. They were, in fact, so completely forgotten that when Ila Borders became the first white woman to play on a men's professional baseball team when she took the mound to pitch for the St. Paul, Minnesota Saints minor league team on May 31, 1997, newspapers and other media outlets across the country reported her as being the first woman to *ever* play with men on a professional level.

However, almost five decades earlier, in the early 1950s, three African-American women, Toni Stone, Mamie Johnson, and Connie Morgan, broke the gender barrier of professional baseball by playing in the Negro Leagues. A relatively minor and fleeting sensation at the time, much of the history and significance of their experiences has since been nearly completely lost or forgotten even in baseball circles. However, these three women were pioneers in the truest sense of the word and the story of their courage, passion, and pride can only serve to enhance and to inspire the cause of both civil rights and gender equality in America.

By the early years of the 1950s, after Jackie Robinson broke the color barrier in major league baseball, the Negro Leagues were struggling to stay afloat. Interest in and attendance at their ballgames had steadily declined since 1947. In the years immediately after the signing of Jackie Robinson, major league teams also began signing other African-American star players, taking a further toll on the Negro Leagues. The fans so essential to their existence began deserting them to watch their favorite players now

9. National Visionary Leadership Project, Oral History Archives at www.visionaryproject.org/johnsonmamie/

10. Martha Ackmann, *Curveball: The Remarkable Story of Toni Stone the First Woman to Play Professional Baseball in the Negro League,* (New York: Lawrence Hill Books, 2010), p. 155.

11. *Ibid.,* p. 156-157.

12. www.aolnews.com/wo10/09/16/mamie-johnson-peanut-who-stood-tall-in-negro-leagues

playing on major league teams. The few Negro League teams left by the early 1950s were barely solvent and owners had to look for new ways to shore up their sinking ship. Gimmick and novelty were two promising options and the ever-creative Syd Pollock, owner of the Indianapolis Clowns, hit upon the idea of signing female players to his team. By this time the All American Girls Professional League had proven that women could play a top-notch game of baseball. Like Branch Rickey of the Dodgers, Pollock endured ridicule and criticism for his decision, but was determined to test the waters. Initially viewed solely as a "novelty," perhaps even by Pollock, the move surprised everyone by its quick acceptance and the success with which his "experiment" was met. The earlier success of the Jackie Robinson experiment in large part rested upon the unique qualities of the individual chosen, a winning combination of character and ability. Likewise, Pollock's initial success with female players was largely influenced by the choices he made. Initially an admitted novelty, as were the three clowns who traveled with the team and entertained in the stands between innings and before and after the games, it immediately became clear that unlike the clowns, the women players took their roles very seriously, proving they belonged on the field. As Mamie Johnson emphatically stated it, "We didn't do any clowning—we played ball."[9]

Life on the road presented obvious challenges for a solitary female traveling with a group of men. The women made sure to quickly befriend a ballpark worker or attendant who could show her to a private spot under the stands where she could change into her uniform. Overnight accommodations proved to be a little more difficult. An occasional hotel room might be located but this option was limited even for the men, due to the Jim Crow laws of segregation that they regularly encountered. Johnson and Morgan met with particular success staying with African-American families and an unexpected benefit of such arrangements was that it provided a shelter, at least temporarily, from some of the discriminatory practices experienced by the men. However, Stone placed a very high value on her respect for and solidarity with her teammates. If a hotel or rooming house would accept her and not her teammates, she would refuse to stay there and retired to the bus with the men: "They're my brothers and we stick together."[10]

Stone eventually found a unique solution to the accommodation issue through both accident and ingenuity. Hotel proprietors would frequently mistake her for a prostitute traveling with the men to provide her "services" so they would direct her to the nearest brothel. There she was met with kindness, a clean bed, dinner, and breakfast in the morning. She developed an immediate camaraderie with the residents

Toni Stone

and they with her. "They took me in . . . they were nice girls." As Martha Ackmann writes in her biography of Stone. "Perhaps Toni saw something in the women that reminded her of her own outsider status, perhaps they saw the same in Toni's unconventional life." Stone developed an entire network of brothels throughout the South where she could stay when the team was in town or playing nearby. The relationships she developed with the women were warm, close, and supportive. There were mornings when she would awake to find a few dollars on her nightstand, lying next to her uniform which had been washed and folded while she slept. On one occasion when she mentioned some discomfort from having taken hard throws to the chest, one of the women sewed extra padding into the front of her uniform.[11] At times, they would even provide transportation and some would attend her games. These relationships helped Toni better endure her life on the road and provided strong emotional support from knowing she was not alone. Of course, for all three women, when arrangements could not be made, it was back to the bus with the men for a night of fitful and uncomfortable sleep.

Mamie "Peanut" Johnson

Taunts and Catcalls

Stone, Johnson, and Morgan, along with their teammates, were all forced to endure the usual taunts and catcalls from the grandstands and the opposing teams. As women however, they were frequently reminded that their place was at home and not on the ball field. Comments that they should be home making babies and baking for their husbands were common, and some even came from their own teammates. All three women were initially tested as to the possibility of "fooling around a little" and all made it clear that that was not what they were there for. Toni Stone made the most forceful statement in this regard, hitting a teammate over the head with a baseball bat "when he tried to get fresh" during one of their early bus rides and "damn near killed him." Needless to say, she made her point and was not bothered after that. Mamie Johnson recalls her experience in a calmer and more philosophic tone: "Like anything else, a lady being in a gentleman's field, there were one or two gents who were kind of ignorant, so you overlooked them. Then there were the gentlemen. So that's the way it was. And actually that didn't go on but for a couple of games and then they realized I was a ballplayer."[12]

Sportswriters of the day harbored some of the same assumptions about

Connie Morgan

Stone as did some of the hotel proprietors, and their questions were frequently focused on sleeping arrangements and the long bus rides, always with an undercurrent of implied sexual misbehavior. Opposing teams tried to intimidate with hard slides and inside pitches. These tactics, however, died down fairly quickly, probably for two reasons. For one, none of the three flinched or backed down from a challenge, physical or otherwise. The tough, competitive nature that had brought them to this level of play was practiced on the field and combined with their playing abilities, helped earn them, albeit slowly and perhaps begrudgingly, the respect of their peers. A second reason was one of simple economics. The presence of female players met Syd Pollock's goals of increased attendance and a renewed interest in the Negro League product. More people at the games meant more money for the players, particularly for exhibition and barnstorming games. It was in the players' best self-interest to support their presence and to avoid their absence from games due to injury.

Stone seems to be the one who had the most difficulty holding her tongue and corralling her temper. Her early "baseball bat episode" can readily attest to that. Her personality was fiery and, competitive by nature, she rightly possessed a strong self-confidence in her abilities. She had a forceful look in her eyes that said "do not stand in my way." Experiences with segregation were particularly maddening to her and she readily admitted that she initially "fought a lot" but credited her teammates with helping her change that: "They broke me of it—The fellas said they'd liable kill me." She found "a way of carrying [her]self" that brought a new honor and dignity to both herself as an individual and to her performance on the field. The other two women also had to find their way through this particular minefield and all three have talked of the strong influence the character of Jackie Robinson had on them. Mamie Johnson spoke for all of them when she said: "I call him the 'man among men.' A gentleman he was. That sticks out to me more than anything in the world."[13]

13. *Ibid.,* p. xiii and National Visionary Leadership Project, www.visionaryproject. org/johnsonmamie/

The Rondo Neighborhood

Marcenia Lyle "Toni" Stone was born in Bluefield, West Virginia, near the Kentucky border, on July 17, 1921. Her father, a veteran of WWI, served in the then strictly segregated ranks of the armed forces, and Toni was the second of four children that followed in close succession upon his return. As did many African-American families with roots in the South, her family moved north to St. Paul, Minnesota, when she was 11, joining the decades-old Great Migration to the industrial cities of the North. They settled in the Rondo neighborhood, an area where most of the St. Paul's small black population lived. Unique at the time, it was an integrated neighborhood. Although Minnesota was relatively safe, it was not completely without danger. Everyone in

Rondo could give a detailed account of an infamous lynching in the northern city of Duluth, even though it had occurred over ten years earlier in 1920. Despite its integrated status, Rondo was not immune to the possibility of racial tension and Toni encountered discrimination and the racial slurs and taunts that accompanied it. To her credit, she was quick to defend herself and her friends and often got into fights in doing so. Rondo had, nonetheless, been a stable and supportive neighborhood of hard-working families. Although hard hit by the Great Depression, the neighborhood survived through the mutual support of neighbors and a strong work ethic, and the Stone family fit right in. Her parents owned and operated a barbershop and beauty salon catering to a whites-only clientele, a common practice at the time. Whites would not patronize beauty parlors that were open to both races, so her parents found themselves forced into the difficult position of trying to strike a balance between self-respect and the need to make a living. They were a product of an older generation that tolerated segregation because their livelihoods depended on it. Their efforts left a deep impression on Stone. "I watched them work hard and I said to myself, 'If I can't be among the best [baseball players], then I'll just leave it alone.'" But, Toni Stone and her generation were about to become the face and the voice of a changing African-American community.[14]

In the Stone household, Marcenia was the athlete. She excelled at whatever sport she played, but baseball won her heart. "It was like a drug," she said, "Whenever summer would come around, the bats would start popping, I'd go crazy." She quickly earned the nickname "Tomboy Stone" and it was one she carried throughout her life. Her parents, however, were not at all supportive of their daughter playing baseball—"they thought it was sinful . . . [they would do] anything to discourage me." The conflicts over baseball escalated to the point that she was determined to run away from home, just to continue playing the sport she loved. It was only through the intervention of a local priest that a compromise was reached where Toni would be allowed to play, but only for the church team. If her parents couldn't stop her from playing, at least they could take some solace from the fact that she was playing for the church. Later they finally admitted that the priest's compromise was the right thing to do and began to delight in their daughter's growing self-confidence and ability. To her parents however, she was ever to remain "Marcenia," her given name, never "Tomboy or Toni."[15]

14. *Ibid.,* p. xii, 10.
15. *Ibid.,* p. x, 1-2.

"Cotton Pickers"

Stone's unwavering dream was to play professional baseball and she possessed the self-confidence and iron will to pursue that dream. It didn't hurt to also have a determined personality and a never-say-no, never-give-up attitude. Unfortunately, these qualities did not extend to her schoolwork. Playing for the church team had had a positive effect on her education—she was at least attending school regularly and was reading a lot more, but not her textbooks. Echoing a theme from today's African-American students, she said she especially disliked history classes. Her textbooks depicted African Americans only as subservient to whites and as victims, "as cotton pickers," with no significant mention of any black achievement. This contradicted her own experience and awareness of the contributions of African Americans she saw in her daily life, especially in the black music she loved. She knew there was more to discover. Her anger and frustration ultimately boiled down to referring to her history classes as "Captain John Smith and Pocahontas," [Even 50 years later, that phrase remained her shorthand for describing the intellectual impoverishment she experienced at school.][16] Boredom and disinterest made passing her classes at school an ongoing challenge, if not outright torment. She was instead a voracious reader of sports books, some of which she re-read many times. She devoured books that taught baseball strategy and ways to improve her game. She discovered newspapers, both local and national, where she could learn not only what was going on in the world of both white and black baseball, but also the world of African Americans, ". . . what the Negro was doing, what we were contributing."[17] Once again, however, Toni was frustrated by what she wasn't reading. There were few, if any, female African-American role models for her or others like her to look up to. Thus the seeds of her activism for both racial and gender equality were deeply sown.

16. *Ibid.,* p. 19.
17. *Ibid.,* p. 19-21.

Syd Pollock's Clowns

In 1952 the Indianapolis Clowns won the Negro League Championship but their prospects for a repeat performance the following year looked dim. They had lost their star outfielder, Henry Aaron, to the National League Boston Braves, and several other players had also left the team, either for the major leagues or for leagues in Canada or Latin America. The integration of the major leagues by black ballplayers was having an effect on all the teams. With interest and attendance in a slow but steady decline, two teams had already been forced to drop out of the league bringing the number of teams left in the league down to four. "Star power" was needed if the league was to survive, but while tryouts for the Clowns landed them several serviceable players, none was likely to draw fans in the required numbers. Fortunately, when owner Syd Pollock began searching for a solution, Toni Stone was ready.

Stone had spent much of the previous 15 years chasing her baseball dream across America. She had barnstormed in Minnesota, played on teams in San Francisco and New Orleans, and many cities and towns in-between, always with men. The Clowns were quite familiar with her, having played the New Orleans Creoles, Toni's latest team, on numerous occasions. Pollock was impressed with her ability but saw beyond simple performance to her box office potential. When he made her an offer during the off-season, Stone readily accepted, reporting to spring training in Norfolk, Virginia, the following April. As Ackmann reports, "Fate had handed Toni Stone one imperfect chance to live her dream and she stepped into it."[18]

Stone's pioneering career in the Negro Leagues lasted two seasons. Though initially viewed by the media, fans, and other players as a mere "novelty," she soon earned her place on the team and was able to garner the respect of her teammates through her ability, toughness, and knowledge of the game. Her play was solid and steady, especially at second base. Particularly impressive testimony about her came from one-time teammates and future Hall of Famers Ernie Banks and Henry Aaron. Both took note of her and were impressed with her game. Banks called her "smooth" and Aaron referred to her as "a very good baseball player."[19] Perhaps most important to the team's management, however, was that she met their goal of increased interest and attendance.

The *Ebony* "Puff Piece"

By July of 1953, Toni's first year with the Clowns, *Ebony* magazine drew attention to the rookie when it published a five-page feature about her. Accompanying photographs included a "glamour" shot complete with make-up, high heels, jewelry, and an elegant dress, all staged to show her going out on the town. Another, also staged, showed her washing windows at her home. One caption read: "Toni Stone is an attractive young lady who could be someone's secretary."[20] Details about her education were exaggerated. No one who knew Toni even casually would confuse her with a "secretary" or identify her with the woman implied by the staged photos. "Tomboy" Stone always dressed in jeans and baggy, loose-fitting tops and never wore a dress unless a special event such as a funeral or wedding forced her to. She was in fact, a jack-of-all-trades, accomplished in carpentry and construction, activities far removed from the "glamour girl and homemaker" in the article. More damaging, the article failed to report any of the real difficulties she faced as both an African-American traveling on the road and as a woman, the *first* woman, playing the man's game of professional baseball. The obvious intention of the feature was, of course, to enhance Toni's image as educated and feminine. As such, it was very much like the puff pieces staged for the same purpose about the young women of the All American Girls Professional Baseball League. Later she described the entire episode as a "mistake" and regretted having participated in it. "I was young," she said, "and they were capitalizing on me."[21] Ironically however, it was that very feature article that was to inspire Connie Morgan and prompt her to actively pursue her own professional career.

18. *Ibid.,* p. xiii.
19. *Ibid.,* p. x.
20. *Ibid.,* p. 142.
21. *Ibid.,* p. 142-3.

Contract Negotiations

While the Monarch's signing of Morgan initially posed a threat to Stone's playing status, it gave her the opportunity to represent herself in contract negotiations, another first for women in baseball. A common mis-perception is that Stone was traded to the Kansas City Monarchs halfway through the 1954 season, thus opening up the second base position for Connie Morgan. This, in fact, was not the case. Already upset that her playing time with the Clowns was always limited to three or four innings and two at-bats per game, the signing of Connie Morgan meant that her dream of playing professional major league baseball was being threatened. The spotlight was no longer going to be hers alone and the fact that Morgan played the same position—second base—combined to add to her concern. Then, when contracts were mailed out in February of 1954, she saw that she was being offered $350 per month, $50 less than her monthly salary the year before. When she next learned that the club intended to sign two more female players, Morgan and another rookie, Mamie "Peanut" Johnson, she also discovered Pollock had decided that only one woman at a time would be in the line-up. Stone's worst fears had been realized. Her playing time was going to be even further reduced and she was now in competition with two other women, both 14 years younger than she—Toni was 33 years old at this point and Johnson and Morgan both 19—how could she hope to compete? She knew that time was running out for her and her playing skills. She also knew that such skills only improved with practice and that she now faced the definite prospect of having less time and opportunity to hone those skills. Toni had a decision to make.

Clowns owner Syd Pollock knew his contract offer to Toni provided less than she had been earning the year before and he offered to contact the owner of the Kansas City Monarchs to see if they had any interest in her. They did, but their offer of $325 per month was even less than the Clowns. Should she remain with her current team, move to the Monarchs, or leave the game of professional baseball entirely? The answer came from correspondence with her closest friend and strongest advocate on the Clowns, Bunny Downs. Explaining her situation, she asked for his advice. His response was clear and direct. Already assuming her decision to continue playing, he wrote back to her, "Before you arrive at your salary terms, do a lot of thinking about YOUR future." This advice struck at the heart of Stone's assertive and competitive nature and she knew what she had to do. Playing for the Monarchs would offer her the best chance of playing and she had heard nothing but positive reports about the Monarch's manager, John "Buck" O'Neil. She agreed to meet with the owner of the Kansas City team, Tom Baird, and negotiated for herself a contract calling for a monthly salary of $400 with a possibility of a $200 bonus at the end of the season. She had not been traded and she had not retired. Recognizing her worth as both person and player, Toni Stone, the first woman to play professional baseball with men, now became the first woman to negotiate her own contract!

A New Beginning

The 1954 season, a difficult one for the Monarchs, turned out to be their last. Perhaps their bus catching fire that spring was a portent of things to come. It might have been saved when a passing sheriff stopped and offered to call for help. The call was anything but helpful. "Nothing serious," he was reported to have said, "Just a bus burning up with niggers on it." With no sense of urgency, help arrived too late to be of any use.[22] The players escaped unharmed but the bus and all their equipment was completely destroyed. Although the bus and equipment were quickly replaced and the schedule resumed, judging by the team's performance and morale that season, it appears that something had been lost. Players suddenly seemed old and tired. Crowds dwindled. Tensions grew and bickering among the players increased. Toni's enthusiasm for the Monarchs and Buck O'Neil suffered. As new players were added, Toni spent more time on the bench. When she was called upon to play, she was cold and out of practice and was not able to perform as before. Although O'Neil described her as "a pretty fair player," it became increasingly apparent as the season progressed that he had lost confidence in her, and tension between the two escalated into conflict. Nor were her teammates as supportive of her as they once had been. She turned in her uniform at the end of the season, returned to her home in Oakland, California, and made the decision not to return. Only thirty-four years old, even the trip home was an ordeal: "I got tired. I got so tired." The one thing that she thought would never abandon her was gone—she had lost her joy for the game.[23]

Satchel Paige once remarked that "we don't stop playing baseball because we get old. We get old because we stop playing baseball." This certainly applied to Stone upon her retirement from the Monarchs. "Not playing baseball hurt so damn bad I almost had a heart attack."[24] She felt lost and alone, aimless without her dreams of the game she loved. She knew she needed a purpose, but had no idea where to start. She continued to drift for a while but eventually found comfort and a solution through a return to the church that had helped her in her youth. With their guidance, she began to look outside herself, at ways she could reach out and help others. She began working at a local hospital, provided home health care, and began riding her bicycle around her Oakland neighborhood. "I kept active so I wouldn't lose my mind," she recalls. Her energy and optimism returned and she made many friends through her bicycle journeys. Never having developed cooking skills, neighbors would bring holiday meals to her. And, she always insisted that she pay for them, adamant that no one

22. *Ibid.,* p. 178.

23. *Ibid.,* p. 191-2.

24. Tracy Everbach, "Breaking Baseball Barriers: The 1953-1954 Negro League and Expansion of Women's Public Roles," *American Journalism,* Winter, 2005, 22 (1), 17; and Ron Thomas, "Baseball Pioneer Looks Back—Woman Played in the Negro Leagues."

should be exploited for their work. On this issue, she had had a lifetime of experience.

Finally, she began playing baseball again, playing with men's recreational teams as well as all-female teams. Her joy for life and for baseball had at last returned. She continued playing for the next thirty years—her last game was in 1986 at the age of sixty-five. By that time a resurgence of interest in Negro League baseball had begun and Toni's baseball history and significance were rediscovered. When the Negro Leagues Baseball Museum opened in Kansas City in 1990 it contained an exhibit of the three women who had played. She shared stories and memories with former league-mates at reunions. The National Baseball Hall of Fame in Cooperstown, New York, invited her to several commemorative events and St. Paul, Minnesota, proclaimed A "Toni Stone Day," where she renewed acquaintances with former friends and neighbors. Her life after baseball had given her a new humility and she approached each event with dignity, honor and pride. Toni Stone passed away on November 2, 1996, knowing that her life had made a difference. She had indeed come full circle.[25]

Mamie "Peanut" Johnson

Mamie Johnson was the second female player signed by the Indianapolis Clowns. Like Connie Morgan, who would follow Johnson to the Clowns one year later, she was also 19 years old when she joined the team. Like Stone, Johnson played with the boys as a kid. Unlike either Stone or Morgan however, Johnson received active support and encouragement, particularly from her grandmother, to pursue her interest in playing baseball.

Johnson was born Mamie Belton and raised in an all-black rural area outside of Ridgeway, South Carolina. Her mother moved to Washington, D.C., in search of employment when Mamie was still very young, leaving her in the care of her maternal grandmother on the family's eighty-acre farm. Her uncle, Leo "Bones" Belton, was a baseball fan and taught Mamie the game when she was just seven years old. Their relationship was a close one and since he was about the same age, Mamie considered him more a brother than an uncle.[26] They made their own baseballs by winding twine around a rock until it was about the size of a regular ball, and then sealing it with masking tape—"it would fly!" Enough space was available on the farm to create a makeshift baseball diamond and boys in the area would gather at her home to play baseball under the guidance of her uncle. Bats were made from tree limbs and the bases were pie plates. She would become angry if not included in the games, "If I didn't play I told my grandma and my grandma made them let me play." There were a couple of girls her age to play with "but they didn't like baseball and I did . . . so I played with the fellas." She developed her pitching skills by throwing at birds.

25. *Ibid.,* p. 194-99.

26. Alan Schwarz, "Breaking Gender Barriers in the Negro Leagues," *New York Times,* June 12, 2010; www.nytimes.com/2010/06/13/sports/baseball/13pitcher.html

"I learned to throw pretty hard like that [because] those birds could fly."

Mamie's passion for the game steadily grew along with her playing skills and she began to dream of playing professional baseball. "And then I used to think hey, I know I can't do this because they weren't even letting the white boys play with the black boys . . . and the black boys not even playin' so I know I'm not gonna make it . . . [but] you know, I just kept playin' and playin' and I say' one day I'm gonna play baseball."[27] It was shortly thereafter that her dream was renewed when Jackie Robinson broke into major league baseball—this event truly marked a turning point for her. Watching him play on television, "that gave me an idea within myself 'you can do this too . . . and it was all in my mind, I was gonna be the first girl to play major league baseball."[28] His demeanor both on and off the field was also an inspiration for her: "In order for you to endure and play the way you play, hey, you're good." It was with renewed pride and determination that she pursued her dream.

Johnson's grandmother passed away in 1945 and Mamie went to live with an aunt and uncle in New Jersey for a couple of years before moving to Washington, D.C., to live with her mother, who by this time was employed in a local hospital. In D.C., she got a job in an ice cream parlor and played baseball on the weekends, graduating to a semi-pro level with the all-black all-male Alexandria All-Stars and St. Cyprion teams. It was while playing for St. Cyprion that she heard about tryouts being offered by a new professional women's league and she decided to pursue this opportunity. It was in fact Mamie Johnson's experience at that tryout that reportedly inspired the African-American scene in the Hollywood film, *A League of Their Own.*[29]

Try-outs for the AAGPBL

Mamie and her teammate and friend, Rita Jones, were two of the hundreds who eagerly responded to a radio ad announcing that the All-American Girls Professional Baseball League was looking for players and would be holding tryouts in Alexandria, Virginia, near their Washington, D.C., homes. They drove there together and immediately noticed that everyone there was white, "but we didn't think anything of that." They got no farther than the sidelines of the field. As Johnson describes the experience, "They looked at us like we were crazy, as if to say, 'what do you want here?' We stood around for maybe 10 or 15 minutes. I didn't say anything. Rita didn't say anything. And they didn't say anything either. So I said to Rita 'I guess we better go. I don't think we're wanted here' So we left."[30] Remarkably, Johnson reports that this was her very first experience with segregation. She had grown up in an all-black area of South Carolina where "everything is there—you got a great big house, you got everything you wanted to eat, it's grown right on the farm, and you got room to run,

27. National Visionary Leadership Project, www.visionaryproject.org/johnsonmamie/

28. *Ibid.*

29. Alan Schwarz, *NYT,* June 12, 2010.

play, and do as you please." In addition, her own family was interracial, with a white grandfather on one side and a Native American grandfather on the other—"there was no bigotry in my family." Even when living in New Jersey, where she was the only African American in her school, she got along well—"they didn't know what I was or where I came from"—and did not knowingly experience active discrimination. "I was loved wherever I went . . . so [segregation] never took a toll on me that there was something different. . . . I didn't know anything about segregation until I went to try out for that girls' team. It dawned on me," she would later say, "they think we're not as good as they are."[31]

30. *Ibid.*

31. National Visionary Leadership Project and Ackmann, p. 158.

32. Mashberg, "'Peanut' a Big Deal—Was Negro Leagues Pioneer," in Everbach, p. 19. See also: James A. Ripley, *The Biographical Encyclopedia of the Negro Baseball Leagues,* (New York: Carroll & Graf Publishers, 1994).

Undaunted by her experience in Alexandria, Johnson returned to her home in Washington D.C., and resumed playing with the St. Cyprians recreational league team. It was there that she caught the eye of a scout for the Indianapolis Clowns and he recommended that she be given a tryout. Substantial risks regarding Johnson's potential participation with the team were noted. She lacked high level playing time and had never been on the road with a team, and her overall playing time was certainly not comparable to Toni Stone's. These issues notwithstanding, it was nonetheless arranged for Johnson to meet the Clowns during their September swing through Washington and to be evaluated by having her pitch against some of their players. Although her performance did not warrant an actual contract or commitment for the following season, she was invited to accompany the team on their two-month barnstorming tour that fall. So excited was Johnson at the prospect of pursuing her dream that she immediately quit her job in an ice cream parlor and simply "slipped away," a polite way of saying that she left without giving notice to friends or family. She left her nine month old son to the care of her mother and left her husband behind as well. Regarding his possible response to her decision, Johnson simply states: "It didn't make any difference because I was going to play anyway." She had achieved what she had thought to be an impossible dream and off she went to play "bus baseball" with the Indianapolis Clowns. There, she would have some female company in the presence of Toni Stone.

Mamie Johnson's stature on the pitching mound was considerably less than imposing. She stood 5'4" tall and her weight was variously reported as being anywhere from 98 to 120 pounds. She was deceptively strong however, stating that "I didn't come up off sandwiches, I came up off greens and cornbread and buttermilk."[32] Early in her first season with the Indianapolis Clowns, she faced second baseman Hank Bayliss of the Kansas City Monarchs and two of her first three pitches to him were strikes. He stepped out of the batters' box and called out to her: "How do you expect to strike anybody out? You're no bigger than a peanut." He proceeded to strike out on her next pitch and Mamie Johnson had earned herself a nickname.

Throughout the remainder of her career, she was known as "Peanut" Johnson.

Johnson's career spanned three full seasons, the longest tenure of the three. Yet, early in her first year, as excited as she was to be playing and with her dream of major league baseball still intact, she began thinking about a life after baseball and enrolled in college at the close of the season. By 1955, her third season with the Clowns, game attendance had declined, [the Clowns would in fact end up dropping out of the Negro League and become solely a barnstorming team soon thereafter] players' salaries had been reduced accordingly, and although she had met with success in her playing career, Johnson recognized that her hope of breaking into the major leagues had dwindled. She also wanted very much to be home raising her son. She retired from the Clowns and returned to college at New York University. She graduated with a nursing degree and returned to Washington, where she worked as a licensed practical nurse for over 30 years. She did not completely leave baseball however, as she was active in coaching youth baseball for many years.

For most Negro League players, both male and female, the statistical records of their performances offer but a brief glimpse into their identities and the role they played in making history. For Mamie Johnson however, her performance line—33 wins and 8 losses, appearing in 268 games—"not 270, 268," as she quickly corrected an interviewer—remains very important to both her identity and to the legacy she wishes to leave. "I was a ballplayer," she states emphatically, "this is what I was and this is the way I want to be known, a ballplayer."[33] Her legacy however, extends beyond the numbers and beyond the playing field. No one could fault her for having lingering feelings of anger or bitterness but Mamie Johnson harbors neither. The honor and dignity with which she approached the game and her life, is evident when she looks back at that experience, "I'm so glad to this day that they [The All American Girls Professional Baseball League] turned me down. To know that I was good enough to be with these gentlemen made me the proudest lady in the world. Now I can say that I've done something no other woman has done."[34] And her final advice reflects the same passion and pride: "Be the best you can be. And if there's anything, whatever it is, especially to the young ladies—if you want to play whatever, do it. And whatever else you want to do, you can do anything you want to do if you put your mind to it. Just work hard at it."[35]

Mamie is today the only surviving member of the trio who "played with the men." She lives in Washington, D.C., about a mile from the Capitol, enjoying a well-deserved retirement from her years of service to her community and to baseball. "A yellow and white candy-store type awning fronts her home, heralding the warm smile and lively personality visitors can expect within."[36] Her personality reflects that playful awning and she talks with nothing but warmth and affection about her three years in the

33. National Visionary Leadership Project, www.visionaryproject.org/johnsonmamie/
34. Swartz, Alan, *NYT*, June 12, 2010.
35. *Ibid.*
36. *Ibid.*

Negro League and her life on the road with the "fellas." Her strong sense of gratitude is but one more gift she has given to the game of baseball and to future generations of both old and young who are chasing a dream.

Connie Morgan

Connie Morgan joined the Indianapolis Clowns in the spring of 1954, about one month after Mamie Johnson reported. Like Johnson, she was 19 years old and had grown up playing baseball. Unlike Johnson, her childhood was spent in an urban and impoverished area of Philadelphia. Her talent became evident in high school. While playing softball at school, she was invited to play in a female recreational league. She proved her ability with a five year stint that saw her compile a composite batting average of approximately .370 while displaying exceptional fielding skills. By the end of high school she found herself alone as "the girls got to where they didn't want to play anymore." The concept of higher education, not to mention the possibility of obtaining a college athletic scholarship, was largely unknown within the impoverished predominantly African-American community in which Morgan had grown up. So, after graduating from high school she enrolled in a local business college to prepare for a secretarial career.

A Lucky Coincidence

It was while attending business school that Connie came across the article about Toni Stone in *Ebony* magazine. She was immediately inspired, announcing to her family her intention "to write to Toni Stone and see if I can get on a baseball team."[37] She proceeded to do exactly that and Toni forwarded her letter to the owner of the Clowns, Syd Pollock. He invited her to a tryout when the team would be playing near her home and on October 9, 1953, Morgan arrived in Baltimore for her evaluation. The Clowns were playing The Jackie Robinson All-Stars that day; Morgan holds the distinction of being one of the few ballplayers of any gender or color to tryout in front of an audience that included Peewee Reese, Luke Easter, Gil Hodges, and of course, Jackie Robinson. Following trials at several positions, second base appeared the best fit and Robinson noted her "good, strong arm." With the playing season about to conclude, Pollock told Connie that he would be in touch. The Clowns were definitely interested.

Morgan reported for spring training with the Clowns in the spring of 1954 and went on to play the entire season with the team. That was to be her one and only season as a professional player, and unfortunately for fans and future historians, little appears to have been recorded regarding her playing experiences. Perhaps the "novelty" of female players had run its course. Perhaps she was simply overshadowed by the celebrity of

37. Ackmann, p. 159.

Stone and Morgan, the first female player and the first female pitcher respectively, so that her third place status garnered less attention. Cursory information has survived but typically focuses on her appearance, "a petite and attractive gal-guardian of second base," and the usual, and in her case, modest statistical records. From what we do know from Toni Stone's experience, her play was probably limited to the first 3 or 4 innings, even less when Johnson pitched, owing to the Clowns' one-woman-at-a-time rule.

Connie Morgan completed business school following the 1954 season and returned to Philadelphia to work. She retired early at the age of 40 due to kidney disease and rarely talked of her time in the Negro Leagues, convinced that she did not really have an interesting story to tell. She spent her days alone, watching out her front window and was referred to by one neighbor as "the sentinel." None of her neighbors or even the next generation of her own family knew about her baseball history. However, with renewed interest in African-American and Negro League history in the early 1980s a researcher at the Afro-American Museum came across Morgan's name and set out to bring her story to light. It took months of searching, knocking on the doors of numerous homes and businesses, but Connie Morgan was at last "discovered" and her story celebrated. In 1995, the museum mounted a special exhibit to her and she was inducted into the Pennsylvania Sports Hall of Fame later that same year. She passed away in October of 1996 and the program at her funeral read, "She had a dream to play professional baseball and in 1954 that dream came true." The program also included a photograph taken with Jackie Robinson at her initial tryout with the Clowns. Then and now, fame was fleeting for Connie Morgan. Her grave at the Mount Lawn Cemetery in Sharon Hill, Pennsylvania, remains unmarked.[38]

Passion for the game, pride and identity, the hope and dream of success, and the strong determination and self-confidence to face adversity and pursue those dreams— these are the characteristics that link Toni Stone, Connie Morgan, and Mamie Johnson. They each faced the dual discrimination of being both African American and being a female playing a "man's game," at a time in America when asserting one's identity and one's civil rights presented significant challenges within both spheres. They faced these challenges with a dignity and honor not to be diminished with the passage of time. They played the game, they gained the respect and admiration of others, they made a statement—and they had fun doing so. Their contribution to both civil rights and to gender equality is a lesson in history not to be forgotten. Unfortunately, little at the National Baseball Hall of Fame and Museum commemorates their amazing contributions.

38. See chapter 7, "The Post-Game Show," for information about the project to honor the unmarked graves of Negro League players with headstones.

Lesson 1: The "Don't Buy Where You Can't Work" Campaigns

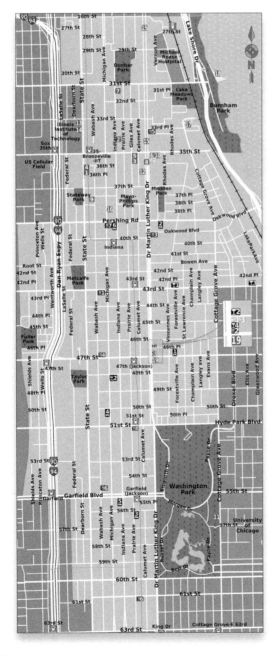

Bronzeville, Chicago

A common misconception among students is that between the end of Reconstruction and the beginning of the Civil Rights Movement, African Americans did little to resist the hardships of living in an America dominated by segregationist restrictions. Aside from the Harlem Renaissance, most students would be surprised to learn just how innovative and creative the African-American community was in pressing for economic, social, and political rights. In chapter 2, we discussed the "Red Summer of 1919" as one of the notable early examples of collective resistance and outright confrontation by African Americans to secure safety for themselves and their property from white violence.

Another kind of activism that also began in Chicago was the "Don't Buy Where You Can't Work" campaigns. Chicago was the home of Bronzeville, a thriving area of African-American homes, stores, hotels, nightclubs, restaurants, hospitals, and other services. But, in spite of the many features and attractions of this area, the fact remained that the majority of these businesses were white owned. Especially galling was that although African Americans were their main customers, African Americans were not hired to work in these stores except in menial positions away from the public eye. The one exception to this was in the case of elevator operators, a job traditionally held by African-American men at all the best downtown department stores where it was the custom for them to provide this service to the white clientele of these posh emporiums. This custom carried over to the department stores of Bronzeville and other black city neighborhoods, like Harlem. And, as in Chicago, the leaders of the African-American community of Harlem also were determined to do something about it. Beginning with the first boycott in 1929 in Chicago, the "Don't Buy Where You Can't Work" movement swept the large cities of the Midwest and Northeast. In Chicago, the first target was a "small chain of grocery stores" which "sparked a larger boycott against Woolworth stores." The news of the boycotts was carried by the fiery black newspaper, *The Chicago Whip*.

The Chicago Whip started in 1919. Run by Harvard trained lawyer Joseph Bibb until 1932, the *Whip* was considered a racially militant paper. Its "Don't Spend Your Money Where You Can't Work" campaign illustrates the black press's activism against injustice. The campaign advocated boycotting white store owners using discriminatory hiring practices in black neighborhoods. The campaign was instrumental in obtaining over 15,000 jobs in Chicago for blacks. The *Whip* survived until 1939.

The strategy spread like wildfire across large cities in the Midwest and Northeast, cities that had been part of the Great Migration after WWI.

PROCEDURES

One important component of the English Language Arts standards requires students to demonstrate their ability to listen and comprehend information that is delivered orally. For this lesson, students will connect to the link below from Gale Group: *U.S. History in Context*. It offers an excellent opportunity for students to practice this skill. The reading level of the content is high, but the text is highlighted word by word as the student listens to the article. After listening to the reading, students can then summarize the important goals of the participants, the strategies they used, and the extent to which they were successful.

http://ic.galegroup.com/ic/uhic/ReferenceDetailsPage/Reference
DetailsWindow?displayGroupName=Reference&prodId=UHIC&
action=e&windowstate=normal&catId=&documentId=GALE%
7CBT2338230739&mode=view&userGroupName=k12_histrc&
jsid=6e93a595e4759e7d683802951c98fb3d

Lesson 2: Women in Sports Before and After Title IX

Title IX, Education Amendments of 1972

No person in the United States shall, on the basis of sex, be excluded from participation in, be denied the benefits of, or be subjected to discrimination under any education program or activity receiving Federal financial assistance.

Introduction

Today's students would probably have a hard time believing that there was ever a time in America when girls and women athletes were not supported and applauded. Today our students see women competing in every type of sport, women as Olympic stars, and television and media coverage of women's sports. But, as we saw in the case of the women who were so much a part of the Negro Leagues, for most of our history, women on the playing field were rare. Indeed, much of the attention given to them was because they were so rare.

Most of us can name on one hand those women who gained fame as athletes before Title IX: Gertrude Ederle, Babe Didrikson Zaharias, Margaret Court, Althea Gibson, and Wilma Rudolph. Beyond these few is the great void. In fact, women in sports were so rare that Fact Monster's timeline of women in sport's first section is labeled, "BC to the 1950s" and includes entries for "events" such as Amelia Bloomer's recommendation of the pants subsequently named after her. Therefore, for most of human history girls and women were actively discouraged, if not actually forbidden, to participate in sports. Strenuous activity for women was thought to be at various times, evil, indelicate, unfeminine, a threat to the natural ordering of the sexes, and dangerous to their health and the well-being of the family. Besides, the common wisdom was that girls and women were simply incapable of high levels of accomplishment in sports; they weren't built for athletic competition. Referred to as the "gentler" sex, vigorous physical exercise would damage their delicate natures rendering them unfit for motherhood. These types of proscriptions did not, of course, apply to working-class women or women in slavery.

Prior to the 1972 passage of Title IX legislation, the situation for girls and women who had athletic ability was bleak. So a real appreciation for their achievements needs to be put into the context of the time during which they played. And, it is worth noting, that recent studies confirm that even today, "despite tremendous progress, sport continues to be a site where ideological beliefs about gender are deeply entrenched, specifically those regarding the inferiority of female athletes.[1]

Necessary Context

What we should see in the achievements of Toni Stone, Mamie Johnson, and Connie Morgan on the playing field and Effa Manley in the manager's office, is that in spite of a socio-cultural environment that militated against girls and women athletes and women in management roles, they were pioneers for change. It was the example of women like these that ultimately persuaded Congress to pass Title IX legislation, opening the door for today's women athletes.[2]

1. Joan Grassbaugh Forry, *Signs: Journal of Women in Culture & Society,* Spring 2009, Vol. 34 Issue 3, pp. 722-727. www.now.org/issues/title_ix/index.html

2. In the days before Title IX, only 1 in 27 girls played varsity high school sports. By 2001, that figure was up to 1 in 2.5, for a total of 2.8 million girls playing high school sports. Similarly, 32,000 women athletes played on intercollegiate teams prior to Title IX, compared with 150,000 today. Athletic scholarships for women were virtually non-existent prior to Title IX, but by 2003, there were more than $1 million in scholarships for women at Division I schools. *www.titleix.info/10-key-areas-of-title-ix/athletics.aspx*

PROCEDURES

For this lesson students will have the opportunity to use the websites for the Visionary Leadership Project at:

visionaryproject.org/

and Fact Monster's Timeline for Women in Sports at :

www.factmonster.com/spot/ womeninsportstimeline.html,

and

www.google.com

to research, read about, and report back on some of the most important and influential women in sports.

The format below allows students to focus on specific information, yet leaves room for them to explore other people and questions on their own. This would work equally well as individual, partnered, or group work.

Because we want to be sure that students learn about the women of the Negro Leagues as well as other women who have been pioneers in women's sports, all students will begin with reading about Effa Manley, Mamie Johnson, Connie Morgan, and Toni Stone.

Then they can select two or more other women from the list provided or others of their own choosing.

NAME	SPORT	WHAT SHE DID	WHY WE REMEMBER HER	HER LEGACY TO OTHER ATHLETES
Effa Manley				
Toni Stone				
Mamie Johnson				
Connie Morgan				

AMERICAN WOMEN IN SPORTS

Gertrude Ederle
Wilma Rudolph
Billie Jean King
Sonia O. Sullivan
Kate Taylor
Nancy Lopez
Serena and Venus Williams
Lisa Leslie
Bonnie Blair
Jackie Joyner-Kersee
Michelle Akers
Lisa Fernandez

Babe Didrikson Zaharias
Althea Gibson
Kelly Holmes
Pauline Cope
Margaret Court
Nancy Lieberman
Sheryl Swoopes
Mia Hamm
Florence Griffith-Joyner
Candace Parker
Cammi Granato
Abby Wambach

- What else did you find out about these women?

- What else would you like to know?

- Where do you think you can find the answers to your questions?

Jack Roosevelt Robinson
Part 1: The PLayer

The great accomplishment of Robinson in 1947 was not so much that he integrated baseball, but that he integrated those stands. Which is to say he started integrating his country, our country. And so when Robinson jittered off second base, upsetting the enemy pitcher, the number 42 sending signals of possible amazements, we all roared. Whites and blacks roaring for Robinson. And when he broke for third, the roar exploded to another level, and birds rose from the roofs of the ballpark and the stands shook so hard you thought they might fall.[1]

Like many New Yorkers leaving home for work on April 15, 1947, Jackie Robinson wore a suit, tie, and camel-hair coat as he headed for the subway. As he was leaving their apartment he turned to his wife, Rachel, and said, "Just in case you have trouble picking me out, I'll be wearing number 42."[2]

Neither Rachel nor any other observer would've had difficulty isolating Jackie Robinson at Brooklyn's Ebbets Field that afternoon. He was the one, the only African-American player to take the field in a major league baseball game in 60 years. A historian once remarked that he was "proudest of baseball when it led social change and innovation, rather than followed."[3] On that day in April, baseball had indeed led and became in truth what it had always claimed to be but never was: The National Pastime. What is more remarkable is that in 1947, in many places both in the North and South, East and West, African Americans couldn't stay at the same hotels as whites, eat in the same restaurants, or even drink from the same water fountains. It was a time when Robinson's older brother, Mack, second only to Jesse Owens in the 200-meter event in the 1936 Berlin Olympics, returned home only to wear his Olympic jacket to his street sweeping job. And, where Jackie, a five-sport national athletic star at UCLA was described by the *Los Angeles Times* as carrying a football "like it was a

1. www.petehamill.com/ ebbetsfield.html
2. George Will, "Taking a Bat to Prejudice," *Washington Post*, April 15, 2007.
3. Reference lost.

4. *Ibid.*

5. www.isteve.com/ JackieRobinson.htm

6. Will, April 15, 2007. A google search located over 100,000 hits for this reference.

watermelon and the guy who owned it was after him with a shotgun."[4] It was a time when schools and neighborhoods were segregated, in some places by law, in others by unwritten codes and traditions. It was a time when fifteen major league baseball owners voted to oppose the introduction of black players into the game. But, there were 16 major league teams, not 15, and, that made all the difference in the world.

Like Pete Hamill, sports writer Steve Sailer, credits Jackie Robinson for much more than any of his many accomplishments in baseball. In a cover article for the *National Review*, "How Jackie Robinson Desegregated America," he notes that Robinson's appearance in major league baseball is often "lumped in with the 1954 Brown decision . . . and the 1964 Civil Rights Act . . ." He argues instead:

> . . . two crucial differences stand out. 1) The integration of organized baseball preceded the civil-rights revolution, and in reality baseball helped make later reforms politically feasible by giving white Americans black heroes with whom to identify. 2) Government had almost nothing to do with this triumph of the competitive market. Baseball owners finally realized that the more they cared about the color of people's money, the less they could afford to care about the color of their skin.[5]

One can quibble about his analysis of the second distinguishing difference since there's no evidence that owners of an earlier era were less concerned with the gate than owners in 1947, but both he and Hamill recognized that what happened in the stands was critical to accelerating the changes to come.

An Unlikely Candidate

Jack Robinson was an unlikely candidate for the role he was asked to play in 1947. He possessed a short, sharp temper, was quick to take offense and quick to fight. In 1944, while serving as an officer in the still-segregated United States Army, he was court-martialed for refusing to move to the rear of an army bus. The Reverend Martin Luther King, Jr. later described him as a "sit-inner before sit-ins, a freedom rider before freedom rides."[6] Robinson expected and demanded treatment as a full American citizen and openly confronted those instances when equality was denied. The approaching storm of baseball integration did not appear to be a moment for which he was well suited.

However, he had other, equally important qualities that made him exactly the right man for the job. What attracted Branch Rickey, owner of the Brooklyn Dodgers was that, at 27, Robinson was significantly older than most first-year players, and he was married; factors that resonated with maturity and stability. As a star athlete in college, he already had experience playing on the national stage, he was comfortable in the limelight, and the media attention that accompanied exceptional play. Finally, he had served as an officer during WWII. His military experience forced a more disciplined attitude and behavior on Robinson and, as an officer, he had developed leadership skills. Discipline and leadership were going to be essential qualities if this effort to integrate baseball was to succeed. As a veteran, there was also the possibility of heightened popularity and with it greater acceptance among white fans of the game.

Do you think you can you take it?

Branch Rickey had chosen his man, but how could he be sure that Jackie Robinson could stand up to the pressure and abuse that he would surely experience? He needed to meet him. In the spring of 1945 Robinson was asked to Rickey's office in Brooklyn. The meeting would last for several hours as Rickey probed Robinson's temperament and character. He detailed for him the types of abuse and epithets he could depend on encountering as an unenlightened public responded to change with its usual cave-man behavior. The words and the music of discrimination punctuated the afternoon as Rickey and Robinson talked. Finally, the real question: "Do you think you can take it? Are you up to the job?"

Robinson hesitated and didn't answer, instead moved the conversation in another direction for awhile. This hesitation Rickey would later explain, impressed him. It was, in a sense, the final test of the afternoon. Had Robinson blurted out a hasty "Yes," Rickey would have looked further. He would have known Robinson wasn't fully aware of the magnitude of the moment and what it would mean to him personally as well as its impact on both the black and white communities. When he finally did say "yes," it  was measured and sincere—a mature and determined response to a difficult question.

Rickey structured one last condition into his offer—Robinson could not respond to any abuse or criticism directed his way for the first two years of his major league career. This applied to behavior on and off the field. It meant no retaliation of any kind—no arguing, no angry exchanges, no snappy one-line retorts or come-backs, no confrontations of any kind. Jackie was simply to take what came and walk away quietly. "Mr. Rickey, what do you want? Do you want a coward, a ballplayer who's afraid to fight back?" No, he answered, "I want a ballplayer with guts enough *not* to fight back!"[7]

Could anyone keep such a promise? Both must have had some doubts but the

7. Harvey Frommer, *Rickey and Robinson,* (New York: MacMillan, 1982), pp. 9-11.

Pittsburgh Courier,
Washington Edition,
Saturday, April 19, 1947

determined owner and the courageous young man shook hands and sealed a deal that guaranteed America would be forever changed from that moment on. In order to measure the power and importance of the moment, look no further than to Rev. King's remark to Jackie at dinner just two weeks before his assassination, "You made my job a lot easier."[8] Branch Rickey had indeed chosen the right man.

Being First Is Lonely

Jackie Robinson has been the subject of innumerable books and essays, newspaper columns, and magazine articles. He was rarely at a loss for words when interviewed, but he was just as likely to be an active participant in the era he was helping to create. He readily accepted most invitations to speak and wrote several books of his own. Reviewing one of his several autobiographies, *I Never Had It Made,* one is struck more by what is not included than in what he has chosen to discuss. The 287-page book does not contain a single reference to either Ebbets Field or to the Brooklyn Dodger fans. What makes this absence particularly notable is the fact that it is almost impossible to read accounts of other Dodger players—white Dodger players—and *not* encounter numerous references to both. The lack of such commentary and observation by Robinson, in his own autobiography in which he discusses in detail his struggles and successes, raises the question of whether the environment and the fans, famous and infamous for their emotional attachment to the team and its players, ever embraced the African-American players with the same open arms they clearly used for the rest of "dem bums." This question gains some momentum from a photograph taken outside Ebbets Field on what appears to be a cool autumn afternoon in 1947.

In the photograph, Robinson is seen walking up Bedford Avenue away from the stadium and he is completely alone. The area is not deserted—there are people nearby of varying ages and dress—but none appear to be paying much attention to him. This was someone who was not only a celebrity but also a very important part of the Dodgers' success on the playing field. The photograph captures but one small moment in time and is not accompanied with explanation or follow-up; any specific conclusion would be suspect. However, it simply appears out-of-place with the existing commentary of the time. So a search was launched for other photographs of Jackie Robinson. Hundreds are available for viewing and purchase on scores of websites. Images of Robinson in action on the baseball diamond predominate, and there are also many staged, portrait-like photographs. However, there are significantly fewer examples showing him with teammates and *not a single image* was found of Robinson posing with a Dodger fan.

Again, this observation is rendered more powerful when contrasted with the many photographs of white Dodger players—icons such as Gil Hodges, Duke Snider, Pee Wee Reese, and Carl Erskine—posing with the Ebbets Field faithful, young and old. Who was uncomfortable—the players or the fans, the photographers or their audience, the Dodger organization or the surrounding community? Or is the lack of just one image within a sample of over 400 images just a coincidence? These and other questions persist regarding the nature and the depth of African-American acceptance by the Brooklyn community. One final question is considered: was the acceptance by the community reserved for just the white players? If not, did acceptance of the African-American players ever extend beyond the playing field? And perhaps one last clue: of the hundreds of photographs reviewed, those of African-American players almost always showed them alone or in the company of *other* African-American players—very, very rarely does the photograph include a white teammate.

The Brooklyn Fans

Another insight into Jackie's relationship with the Dodger fans comes indirectly from a glimpse into the mores of the time provided by Doris Kearns Goodwin. In her remarkably personal and poignant portrait of growing up in the 1950s, and of growing up with the Brooklyn Dodgers, *Wait Till Next Year*, she talks about her neighborhood. She reports having been taught by her parents to always address all African-American adults with the title of "Mr." or "Mrs." A child addressing any adult by their first name would have been considered the height of rudeness at that time. But for many, that rule did not apply to children addressing adult African Americans by their first names. This breach of etiquette was allowed and was a way for white America to demean or to discount people, in an established and not too subtle form of disrespect. For the young Doris, however, the African-American shoe-shine man in her neighborhood was always "Mr. Johnson" and never "George," at least to the Kearns family.[9] Again, there are volumes of written and recorded material concerning Jackie Robinson. But even an exhaustive review of the literature yields no reference to him as "Mr. Robinson," or even to "Jack," his given name. This may in fact be

8. Cal Fussman, "I Was Allowed to Dream After That—Hank Aaron," *ESPN: The Magazine*, at http://sports.espn.go.com/espnmag/story?id=3629427 and in *After Jackie* (New York: ESPN Books, 2007).

9. Doris Kearns Goodwin, *Wait Till Next Year*, (New York: Simon & Schuster, 1998), p. 202.

an unfair observation. When someone receives a lot of media attention in America, a false sense of familiarity is assumed; in a sense, the person is brought into the public domain, and he or she now belongs to all of us. Given the symbolic nature of Robinson's quest for so many groups within American society, the likelihood of such familiarity is greatly enhanced even more. Thus the absence of a "Mr. Robinson" in the annals of major league history may not be significant. It may not even have been preferable to establish such an identity, given what his success or failure would come to mean for other groups who felt discriminated against and who needed to see him as "one of us" in order to experience the hope that he represented. Frankly, it is safe to assume that Jackie Robinson would have much preferred "Jackie" to many of the other names he was called during the course of his career. But the question remains. Everywhere he went, even in his first year with the Dodgers, he was almost always referred to as simply "Jackie." This implies an intimacy and familiarity that his presence was yet to justify. Ted Williams was always referred to as "Mr. Baseball," Stan Musial as "The Man," and even African-American Ernie Banks— "Mr. Cub"—and Reggie Jackson—"Mr. October"—were afforded respectful nicknames. A chapter in Ken Burns's *Baseball* is entitled "Mr. Mantle." In every interview, Mrs. Rachel Robinson always refers to her husband as "Jack," *never* "Jackie." Was there a subtle form of racial bias at work in even the most well-meaning and seemingly objective journalism that covered Mr. Jack Robinson? In 1947, how could there not have been?

Dodger Players React

Many authors and columnists praise the Brooklyn Dodger players of the 1940s and 1950s for their acceptance and tolerance of their fellow African-American teammates. Others assert that *only* the Brooklyn team, as constituted in the late 1940s, could have pioneered the integration of the major leagues. Some of these same authors are lavish in their praise of the close personal bonds that reportedly existed among the players. A closer review of the initial "adjustments," however, reveals conflicts and tensions in the clubhouse, on the playing field, and in the manager's office. These were just the conflicts Rickey expected and were the first opportunities for Robinson's presence to begin breaking down barriers in baseball that had taken over sixty years to build.

Major league baseball in the first half of the twentieth century was comprised of a disproportionate number of players from the southern United States. This was primarily due to the South's temperate climate which produced a longer baseball season. Half of the 1947 Brooklyn Dodgers team hailed from the South and most all were ambivalent, at best, about playing with Jackie Robinson.[10] They had grown up in a time and place where the secondary status of African Americans was a matter

10. Carl Prince, *Brooklyn's Dodgers: The Bums, the Borough, and the Best of Baseball, 1947-1957*, (New York: Oxford University Press, 1997) p. 4.

of course, segregation a way of life. Many had had very little experience even inter-acting with African Americans. Most players felt pressured, either by their friends in baseball or by their families and friends back home, to take a stand against the emerging African-American presence in baseball. Pee Wee Reese, a native of Lou-isville, Kentucky, a border city in a border state with a definite southern character, readily acknowledges some initial ambivalence: "What will my Louisville friends say about me playing with a colored guy? They probably won't like it, but I say to hell with anyone who doesn't like it."[11] This internal resolution was to prove significant in his subsequent relationship with Robinson. Preacher Roe, the pitcher from rural Arkansas, experienced similar hometown problems as Reese and chose to deal with them in the same way. For outfielder Dixie Walker, the problem was beyond his ability to resolve.

Dixie Walker's immense popularity with the Brooklyn fans had earned him the nickname "The People's Cherce" (*cherce* being Brooklynese for "choice"). Dodger President Branch Rickey knew that his response would be significant in helping to determine initial fan response to Robinson. Unfortunately for both Jackie and Mr. Rickey, Walker harbored some of the most racist sentiments on the team. When asked whether he would be able to accept Robinson's presence on the team, his reply was simple and direct: "I don't think I can, sir," and he requested a trade to another team.[12] Rickey promised to try to accommodate him and in return Walker assured him that the situation would not affect his play or competitive level. However, rumors soon surfaced that several Dodgers, Walker prominent among them, were circulating a petition stating that the team would refuse to play if Robinson remained on the roster. Years later, the existence of an actual petition remains contested but a team meeting called by the manager to confront it is not. Whatever action that may have been planned was effectively squelched and details were never released to the press. The fans and community remained unaware and the media were free to continue their rosy reports of Dodger camaraderie. For a number of Dodger players however, their days in Brooklyn were numbered.

Years later Walker sought to apologize for his attitude and his actions by explaining that he owned a successful hardware store in his hometown in Georgia and that he had been told by friends and associates there "that I would lose all my customers if I was playing with a black player—I couldn't chance losing my store."[13] While this account is probably accurate, it serves to neither explain nor excuse some of the cruel and harsh comments and behavior reportedly attributed to him during this era. And Walker is not alone—many discrepancies and contradictions are found in both sound and print between what a number of Dodger players said then and what they say now.

11. *Ibid.,* p. 4.
12. *Ibid.,* p. 8.
13. Roger Kahn, *Beyond the Boys of Summer* (New York: McGraw-Hill, 2005) p. 254.

Red Barber

It is difficult to imagine now, given Dodger broadcaster Red Barber's overwhelmingly positive national image and the close relationship he subsequently established with Jackie Robinson, but he too admits to some initial misgivings when he was told about the signing. "I have to be honest about it. I was born and raised in the Deep South and I had never even imagined that a Negro would play in the major leagues. The idea took me by surprise and I had to think about whether I could stay with the team."[14] It was a decision everyone in the Dodgers' organization would need to consider. Barber's ambivalence reveals that a southern heritage was one of the significant factors that determined one's response to Jackie Robinson's presence, but to his credit Barber's initial ambivalence was overcome. Ultimately he established a close personal relationship with Robinson, based on genuine respect and admiration. His is a story of courage and redemption and years later he states with conviction: "Jackie Robinson did much more for me than I ever did for him."[15] America was indeed capable of change and this represented new hope to millions—throughout America, and back home in Brooklyn.

Not everyone was able, or willing, to consider a path of similar enlightenment. Branch Rickey met with each of the Dodger players individually prior to the 1947 season to advise them of his plans to integrate the team with Jackie Robinson. He asked each of them if they would be able to accept this and play with him or if they wanted the team to pursue a trade to another organization. Several prominent and very popular and successful Dodger players, all of southern heritage, were subsequently traded, including Pete Reiser, Hugh Casey, and the three players linked to the alleged petition against Robinson—Ed Stanky, Bobby Bragan, and Dixie Walker. Over the course of Robinson's first two years with the Dodgers, Rickey quietly but efficiently "northern-ized" the Dodger team. To credit only the Dodger players for their tolerance and acceptance of integration and their African-American teammates is to ignore the human engineering efforts of Branch Rickey that helped to make possible the community and the camaraderie of the team that has since become the stuff of legend.[16]

Pee Wee Reese

Author Carl Prince asserts that the Brooklyn Dodgers always came together with remarkable cohesion when outsiders engaged in race-baiting. "Dodger unity in the face of outside prejudice remained a hallmark of the club to the end of its years in Brooklyn."[17] Two specific examples occurred early in Robinson's first year with the team. The first was an incident in Cincinnati when Pee Wee Reese walked over to Robinson and put his arm around him, an action that literally silenced both the crowd and

14. Ken Burns, *Baseball*, "The Fifth Inning"; www.youtube.com/watch?v=pJNNH2Rizt8
15. *Ibid.*
16. If the transition had been smooth, estimations of Robinson's courage could be justly diminished. It was not a smooth transition and Robinson and those who soon followed him showed enormous courage.
17. Prince, *Brooklyn's Dodgers*, p. 6.

the opposing team. Dodger short-stop, Pee Wee Reese, hailed from the border state of Kentucky and many wondered what his stance would be regarding Jackie Robinson. He recalls an initial reaction of disbelief—"no, that could never happen"—that was quickly overshadowed by worry—"I found out that he played shortstop." In a remarkably unbiased comment, particularly given the era and his own southern heritage, he added, "If he can take my job, he's entitled to it."[18] Reese always took the position that Jackie was a Dodger teammate. *You belong here … You're a full major-leaguer . . . I'll defend you to the hilt.*[19] His response to intensely abusive heckling from both players and fans one night in Cincinnati, early in Robinson's inaugural year has been called a pivotal moment in Robinson's career. In the midst of the heckling he walked across the infield to Robinson's spot at first base, stood next to him, and put his arm around him as if to announce, "this is my friend." There are reports from several in attendance of a collective "gasp" from the suddenly silent Cincinnati crowd but by the time their voices returned the heckling had stopped and the rest of the evening was relatively uneventful. And yet, Reese wasn't, as he put it, "some Great White Father." He wouldn't go to marches or carry the banner for civil rights. He was a product of his times and of his era. When

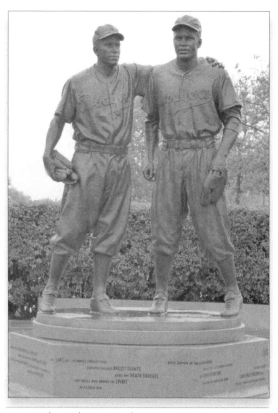

Jackie Robinson and Pee Wee Reese statue outside MCU Park

Courtesy National Baseball Hall Of Fame

18. www.nytimes.com/ specials/baseball/ bbo-reese-robinson. html

19. Roger Kahn, "The Jackie Robinson I Remember," *The Journal of Blacks in Higher Education*, Winter, 1996/1997, No. 14, p. 92. Reese's refusal to sign defused an effort among the players to present the petition threatening to quit if Robinson played. When Manager Leo Durocher heard about it he summoned a team meeting and explained: "And here's something else. He's only the first, boys, only the first. There's many more colored ballplayers coming right behind him, and they're hungry, boys. Unless you wake up, they're gonna run you right out of the park. I don't want to see your petition. I don't want to hear about it. Fuck your petition. The meeting's over. Go back to bed."

20. *Ibid.*
"...one day—it was probably in Cincinnati, Reese recalled, in 1947 or 1948—the attack was so nasty that Reese walked over to Robinson and put his hand on the black man's shoulder.

"Pee Wee kind of sensed the sort of hopeless, dead feeling in me and came over and stood beside me for a while," Robinson recalled, as quoted in the biography *Jackie Robinson,* by Arnold Rampersad (New York: Alfred A. Knopf, 1997). "He didn't say a word but he looked over at the chaps who were yelling at me through him and just stared. He was standing by me, I could tell you that." The hecklers ceased their attack. "I will never forget it," Robinson said.

Over the years, Reese became perhaps Robinson's best friend on the Dodgers, though there were others who were reasonably close to him as well, including the white players Carl Erskine, Gil Hodges and Ralph Branca, and, of his black teammates, Junior Gilliam in particular.

he retired he returned to his hometown of Louisville, Kentucky, where he invested in a bowling alley. Pee Wee Reese had supported Jackie fully, but the bowling alley was segregated.[20]

The second event occurred a few weeks later on the Dodgers' first visit to Philadelphia. The Phillies' dugout began their taunting during batting practice and continued a relentless assault through the first several innings, led by their manager. Ironically, it was Ed Stanky, one of the Dodger players allegedly involved in starting a team petition against Robinson at the start of the year, who now came to his defense. He left the Dodger dugout and yelled a challenge to the Philadelphia manager: "Why don't you pick on someone who can fight back?" The rest of the Dodgers stood up as if to follow and the Philadelphia dugout suddenly became quiet and it remained so for the rest of the game. It was said that Branch Rickey actually enjoyed these kinds of incidents because of the unifying effect they appeared to have on the team.[21]

A Growing Sense of Community

Over six years into the "The Great Experiment" of integration, the Brooklyn Dodgers, and Jackie Robinson, were still fighting some of the same battles, but they were now fighting them together. The Dodgers were in Milwaukee in August 1953 to play the Braves in an important series with pennant implications. An incident occurred in the first game that illustrates the internal sense of community that had developed on the Dodger team by that time. The Braves were known to be one of the National League's most vocally racist teams. Hall of Fame–pitcher Warren Spahn and his all-star teammate Lew Burdette consistently threw more beanballs at black players than white ones, with the usual justification that blacks lacked courage and could be intimidated. Milwaukee fans echoed their players' sentiments and the apprehensive Dodgers always knew that a visit to the Wisconsin city would be filled with tension amid the specter of conflict. Midway through the first contest, Roy Campanella came to the plate and Lew Burdette started him off by calling him a "black mother-fucker." He got two quick strikes on the furious Dodger catcher then followed with two pitches at Campanella's head, both of which sent him diving to the dirt. After the second, Burdette shouted from the mound, "Nigger, get up and hit." Campanella struck out on the next pitch and then took off for the mound and for Burdette, bat in hand. When the Braves catcher grabbed him from behind, the Dodger team "swarmed out of the dugout" and a "melee" ensued.[22] This was a defining public moment for the team. It demonstrated that while internal racial unrest might afflict the team from time to time, this Dodger team would strenuously protect its own when threatened by others.

Jackie Robinson remained at the center of many racial episodes the Dodger team encountered throughout his ten year career. Perhaps it was the symbolism he embodied for so many Americans of different backgrounds that served as a constant reminder to his teammates to do the right thing. Or perhaps it was a growing respect for his ability as a player, or an up-close appreciation of the pain that race-baiting inflicted on him on a daily basis. And the money didn't hurt either, as Robinson and his teammates cashed World Series checks in 6 of his 10 years with the team.[23]

Pitcher Don Newcombe's account of the African-American ballplayer's experience in St. Louis in the early 1950s is graphic in its portrayal of the segregation and discrimination of the era; it is also significant for its veiled condemnation of his white Dodger teammates and indicates the presence of internal racial tension.

> Every time we'd arrive in St. Louis on the train, me and Jackie and Roy would have to get our suitcases and carry them through Union Station and stand on the curb trying to find a cab. Sometimes we had to wait 30 to 45 minutes, because white drivers wouldn't pick up black guys. They'd just drive by us in that St. Louis heat—and only God knows how hot it gets in St. Louis.
>
> We'd finally get a cab that would take us to a substandard hotel with no air-conditioning, while the white players went on their air-conditioned bus from Union Station to the Chase Hotel and didn't have to even so much as touch their shaving kits until they got to their rooms. Not one of them—not *one* of the white guys on the Brooklyn Dodgers—ever got off that bus and said, 'I'm going to go with Jackie, Don, and Roy just to see how they have to live, just to find out.[24]

Whether from a sense of defensiveness, an expression of anger or guilt, or just making some conversation, at least one Dodger player answered Newcombe's challenge. "We later heard that one of our teammates, who will remain nameless, was sitting on the bus in St. Louis and said to nobody in particular, 'Fuck them black sonsabitches. Let them go for themselves. We didn't ask them to be here. They asked to be here.' *Our* teammate."[25]

"Our Teammate"

Carl Erskine, another of Robinson's close friends on the Dodgers possessed a remarkable sense of self-awareness. A review of numerous interviews with the former pitcher, both verbal and written, reveal a presence of mind, a keen sense of time and place, while in the midst of some of the most historic and exciting times in Dodger history. Yet even he was unable to recognize and appreciate the magnitude of the impact of the African-American integration that the Dodgers helped to lead. "Looking back,

But Reese's attitude, including that defining gesture of solidarity on the field that they were, in the end, teammates and brothers under the skin, did not come from a save-the-world mentality.

"Something in my gut reacted to the moment," Reese said. "Something about—what?—the unfairness of it? The injustice of it? I don't know."

21. Burns, "The Fifth Inning," *Baseball.*

22. *Brooklyn Eagle,* August 4, 1953.

23. Jack Robinson's many accomplishments on the playing field are well documented and require no retelling here.

24. Fussman, Carl, *After Jackie* (New York: ESPN Books, 2007), p. 61.

25. *Ibid.,* p. 63.

maybe I should have taken the lead in talking to the Chase Hotel in St. Louis. I was the player representative of the Dodgers for eight years or so, and I could've gone to the Chase management and said, 'Hey, why are you the only hotel in the league that won't allow our black players to stay?' I don't think we saw the civil rights picture quite the same way people looking back today see it. Plus, we all had our own pressures at the time, and we all reacted in our own individual ways."[26] From another observer, such a comment might be construed as naïve or simplistic or perhaps more than a little insensitive, comparing the death threats received by Robinson with "our own pressures at the time." The fact that it came from a man with Erskine's considerable insight and close friendship with Robinson speaks more to a simple reflection of the general pervasiveness and cultural acceptance of the physical and psychic distance between the races that was characteristic of the era.

Don Newcombe is actually able to offer some empathy and support for the white players: "Sometimes the white guys wondered why we were so bitter. Black guys experienced it. White guys tried to interpret it. But how can somebody else interpret what I feel inside my skin? Can you know how I feel just because *you think* it's the way I'm supposed to feel?"[27]

Not all behavior could be so easily excused. The Dodgers were on their way North by train to open the season and several of the players were playing cards together in the club car; Jackie Robinson sat alone nearby, reading a newspaper. Pitcher Hugh Casey, a Southern native, was not doing well in the game that evening, losing each and every hand without offering much competition. Without saying a word, he suddenly stood up, walked over to where Robinson sat, and reached down and rubbed his head several times—and then returned to his seat at the table. No one said a word.[28]

Pitcher Preacher Roe, a native of rural Arkansas, provides a final answer to Don Newcombe's challenge: "Why didn't we do something? We did. We played with him."[29] Roe's comment may in fact be the wisest and most direct. For many players throughout the league and throughout the era, simple tolerance and participation may have been the most powerful and most profound statement they were capable of making.

Leading the Way

Baseball has a history of leading social change and innovation and the Brooklyn Dodgers' decision to integrate major league baseball in 1945 is perhaps the brightest example of such leadership. As such, it is difficult to tell their story without some examination of the results of their decision. It came with a price tag that should not be overlooked or dismissed.

26. *Ibid.,* p. 73.
27. *Ibid.,* p. 62.
28. *Ibid.,* p. 78.
29. *The Boys of Summer,* VHS (New York: Vid America, 2002).

Buck O'Neil and Sammy Haynes, both veterans of and recognized spokesmen for the Negro Leagues, unequivocally endorse Jackie Robinson's integration of major league baseball. O'Neil enthused, "We had finally made it," and Haynes, "Oh yes, it was worth it," despite the fact that the action effectively ended both of their Negro League careers.[30] Even though the integration of African Americans transformed the game into what it had always professed to be—but what in reality it never was, "the national pastime"—it also sounded the death knell for black baseball in America. Effa Manley, the owner of the Newark Eagles, the team that sent Monte Irvin, Larry Doby, Roy Campanella, and Don Newcombe to the major leagues, put a more personal face on the results: "The livelihood, the careers, the families of four hundred Negro ballplayers are in jeopardy because four players were successful in getting to the major leagues."[31] For decades the Negro Leagues were the second largest black business in the country, but by 1955 there were fewer African Americans making their living in professional baseball than at any time in the twentieth century. Black teams still operating were no longer supported by ticket receipts but by selling their best players to the major leagues. The "Great Experiment" was to be a sword that cut both ways.[32]

The Cost of Integration

Bob Kendrick, the director of marketing for the Negro Leagues Baseball Museum in Kansas City offers his observations on the impact of Jackie Robinson. "Be careful what you wish for because you just might get it. There's always a cost for progress. Many in the black community saw the words "integration' and 'equality' as synonymous. They felt that if they got access that they would be treated equally. This wasn't the case and in the process of change, a great deal was lost." Cal Fussman agrees but also presents another side to the celebratory attitude that has come to embrace the integration of baseball. Drawing on the support from former players, newspaper writers, and historians, he asserts that "The passing of the Negro Leagues was as catastrophic for the African-American community as it was, on another level, beautiful."[33]

Bob Veale, former major-league pitcher and veteran of the Negro National League, traces the demise of black baseball and its immediate economic impact: "Instead of playing four times a week, it got to be only on the weekends. Then it wasn't at all. You know, the Negro Leagues meant a lot of money for a lot of people. How many years did it take before the Negro Leagues folded for good? How many mouths weren't fed during that time?" Teammate Buck Leonard is more direct: "After Jackie, we couldn't draw flies."[34]

Negro League veteran and historian John "Buck" O'Neil was introduced to much

30. Burns, "The Fifth Inning", *Baseball.*

31. *Ibid.*

32. Robert Peterson, "And the Walls Came Tumbling Down," *Only the Ball Was White,* (New York: Oxford University Press, 1970), p. 194-205.

33. Fussman, p. 118.

34. *Ibid.,* p. 120, 125.

of America through Ken Burns' 1994 documentary entitled simply *Baseball*. His smooth voice, gentle demeanor, and a remarkably forgiving and accepting attitude earned him the title, "Ambassador of Baseball," that he carried until his passing in 2007. His description of the era and of the black community, while somewhat lengthy, provides an important summary of the effects of baseball's integration:

> Anybody who was black who was somebody who came to Kansas City stayed in the Streets Hotel. Ballplayers, jazz musicians—we all traveled in the same circuit and we all stayed in the same hotels because they were the black hotels. Louis Armstrong . . . Duke Ellington . . . the best food in the country—the Streets was the place to be. After big league baseball integrated, things got a whole lot tougher for hotels, restaurants, and other businesses in the black community. The musicians who were performing at the big hotels downtown now began to stay in them. The Streets lost all that business and it became hard to compete. Fans from out of town weren't making the trip into Kansas City to see the Negro League games anymore, so they weren't staying in the Streets. It was quite a change. Before, money made by the black community had always been spent in the black community because it was just about the only place we could spend it. When integration started, we started to spend it somewhere else. In Kansas City, blacks began moving farther south where they hadn't used to be able to live before. All the doctors and lawyers started moving out with their clientele. In truth, the death of the Negro Leagues just about killed the center of the black community."[35]

Fussman emphasizes this effect on the African-American community: "Black businesses, black-owned hotels, black-owned sports teams, and black-owned businesses of all sorts had benefited from segregation because it gave them a clientele. In an integrated society, they couldn't compete. The small black pharmacy just didn't have the capital to compete with the large white one downtown. So once there was integration, a lot of these black-owned businesses went under."[36]

The effect on African-American media was particularly profound; a cruel irony. The black press had for years led the call for the major leagues to integrate.[37] Now that they were, their own professional lives were in jeopardy. There was a symbiotic relationship between the black newspapers and the Negro Leagues, the same way there is for all sporting teams and the press. Quite simply, sports sell newspapers and newspapers promote sports. Historian Larry Lester points to the immediate effect of Robinson's presence in Brooklyn and on the road: "There was usually just one big sportswriter on a black newspaper, and now he was divided. Was he going to cover

35. *Ibid.,* p. 128 and Joe Posnanski, *The Soul of Baseball: A Road Trip Through Buck O'Neil's America,* (New York: Harper, 2007).

36. Fussman, p. 128.

37. Chris Lamb, "What's Wrong With Baseball," *Western Journal of Black Studies; The Pittsburgh Courier* and the Beginning of Its Campaign to Integrate the National Pastime," Vol. 26, No. 4, 2002; and Brian Carroll, "From Fraternity to Fracture: Black Press Coverage of and Involvement in Negro League Baseball in the 1920s," *American Journalism,* Vol. 23, No. 2, 2006.

the Negro Leagues or was he going to follow Jackie Robinson?" Rob Ruck, author and senior lecturer in the Department of History at the University of Pittsburgh states that for most black newspaper writers, this was not really a decision at all: "If you were a black sportswriter and you placed a value on being part of an integrated America, you felt beholden, morally obligated, to take part in that integration once the walls began to fall." The effect was two-fold: newspaper coverage of the Negro Leagues steadily declined, hastening the demise of that institution, and African-American writers left their papers and took many of their black readers with them. The black newspaper also became a casualty.[38]

There was another significant effect on the African-American community initiated by these changes in the black media. Train travel was still the dominant mode of long-distance and interstate transportation in America through the middle of the twentieth century. Porters on the trains were predominantly African American and they served an important function within the black community. Black newspapers were distributed to them and they became primary disseminators of information for African Americans living all across the southern United States. Newspapers such as the black *Pittsburgh Courier* helped African Americans learn about opportunities in the North and make decisions about where they might want to migrate. With a decline in the institution of the African-American newspaper, an important network of communication was affected and the flow of accurate and timely information was disrupted.

Ruck summarizes it this way, "Integration brought the best young black players to major league teams. It brought the black fans into major league stadiums. But it did not bring black institutions or black leadership into society."[39] For Fussman, integration did more than exclude some institutions, it actually hastened their demise.

38. Robert Ruck, *Sandlot Seasons: Sport in Black Pittsburgh* (Champaign: Univ. of Illinois Press, 1993).

39. *Ibid.*

The End of an Era

Nothing lasts forever. The Dodgers finally won the World Series in 1955 only to learn on October 9, 1957, that the team's owner, Walter O'Malley, was moving the team; the Brooklyn Dodgers were leaving Brooklyn for Los Angeles, California. The grand arena where this story began, the cathedral of baseball, Ebetts Field, was soon reduced to rubble. On February 20, 1960, the wrecking ball came to Ebbets Field. A ceremony was held at home plate and the longtime public address announcer called the event; several former Dodger players were in attendance. The two-ton wrecking ball was painted to resemble a baseball and the two hundred fans that had assembled watched as the first blow was struck against the visitors' dugout.

40. According to an article in the March, 22, 1951, *Reading Eagle,* "Robinson Offered Managerial Berth." Walter O'Malley offered him a job managing the Dodger farm team, the Montreal Royals, "when his playing days are over." The story ran a few days later in the *Pittsburgh Press,* "Robinson Linked to Montreal Job, Jackie May Become Manager of Royals." In the article O'Malley emphasized that "no formal offer" had been made. At the time of the "offer" Branch Rickey had parted company with Walter O'Malley and was managing the Pittsburgh Pirates. The offer may have been a plant. Whether it was or not we may never know. What we do know is that it never came to fruition.

He did, however, serve as an analyst for ABC's *Major League Baseball Game of the Week* and as a part-time commentator for the Montreal Expos, and was the manager of the Brooklyn Dodgers football team. http://en.wikipedia.org/wiki/Jackie_Robinson

41. Roger Kahn, "The Jackie Robinson I Remember," *The Journal of Blacks in Higher Education,* Winter, 1996/1997, No. 14, p. 92.

42. *Ibid.,* p. 93.

43. http://en.wikipedia.org/wiki/Jackie_Robinson

Jackie Robinson died on October 24, 1972, at the age of 53. Many believe the stress and abuse he endured in his groundbreaking role aged him well before his time. For all his determination, patience, courage, and accomplishments, he was never offered a major league job of any kind at the end of his playing career, not even by the Dodger organization.[40] His close friend Roger Kahn sums up his thoughts on it this way: "'Manager?' He was a profound student of the game and clearly inspirational. . . . With his intelligence and his great capacity for growth, Jackie Robinson should have been made Commissioner of baseball."[41]

After Baseball

Some say there are no second acts in American's lives. Had Jackie Robinson's gift to America consisted only of literally "stepping up to the plate" to integrate the major leagues, it would have been more than enough, in fact it would have been a lavish legacy and in many ways an unearned gift. His presence, his great success, and his dignity were a daily rebuke to the segregationist heart of America and a symbol of hope for countless African-American kids. But his ten years on the field were just a prelude to the legacy he crafted after baseball. Dr. King wasn't simply flattering Robinson when he said his work had made King's work easier. In Robinson's own words he was "a pressure group for civil rights."[42] Upon leaving baseball he took the position of vice president of personnel for Chock full o'Nuts Coffee, becoming the first African American to serve as a vice president of a major corporation. He also helped found The Freedom National Bank, a Harlem-based, black-owned, commercial bank to advance black entrepreneurship; chaired the NAACP Freedom Fund Drive and served on its board until 1967; and in 1970 started the Jackie Robinson Construction Company to build low-income housing.[43]

In addition to his public positions, however, Robinson was one of the most prolific writers and fund raisers on behalf of civil rights. In letters to Presidents

Eisenhower, Nixon, Kennedy, and Johnson, Robinson consistently advocated for "equal rights for all." In 1957 when proposed civil rights legislation did not go far enough, he telegraphed the White House saying, ". . . we disagree that half loaf better than none."

His 1958 letter to President Eisenhower during the integration of Central High School in Little Rock, Arkansas, written on Chock full o'Nuts corporate stationery calls for action, not further counsel for patience on the part of African Americans. When "legalized hatchet men" were attacking and beating people in Selma, Alabama, he wired Johnson insisting "[he] take immediate action . . . to avoid open warfare by aroused Negroes. America cannot afford this in 1965."

Throughout the turbulence of the early civil rights movement, Robinson could be counted on to speak up, write, and march on behalf of the cause. When his failing health would have been reason enough to leave the fight to others, he instead used his fame and influence to continue a life-long battle for full participation in the American Dream for himself and others. It is this side of the Jackie Robinson story that we turn to in *Part 2: The Civil Rights Years*.

Part 2

"Dear Mr. President . . ."
The Civil Right Years

Commemorating a watershed moment in American history.
March on Washington, 1963

In the process of what James Loewen calls "herofication," when telling the stories of people who have made a difference, we tend to lose important personal qualities and telling details about them as fully-rounded people. Because we admire them and hope their stories will inspire young people, we often feel compelled to turn them into plaster saints. This often takes the form of "sins of omission," i.e., excising inconvenient truths—such as the fact that the writer of the Declaration of Independence and most of our other founders were slave owners, or failing to note that Woodrow Wilson's political positions had a dark side, notably his adventuring into Russia, South America, and Mexico, and that his virulent racism resulted in his wholesale segregation of the federal bureaucracy. In the case of Helen Keller, whom Loewen discusses in some detail, her socialist activism on behalf of worker safety in order to prevent work-related blindness has been lost. Her *entire adult* life has been lost in favor of the story of her early years. She's become a children's story. And, of course, Loewen's point is that all these "cherry tree" myths do nothing but bore kids to tears.[1]

A similar fate has befallen Jackie Robinson. The "children's story" version of his re-integration of the major leagues that is clearly meant to inspire, has instead lead some, even in the African-American community, to distort the courage it required for him to place himself in the eye of the storm into "selling out."[2] As Paul Harvey used to say, it's time to tell "the rest of the story." This is particularly important in the case of Jackie Robinson because the broad outlines of his story are familiar; therefore, the inherent probability of a high degree of interest already exists. Kids should know that he did much more than simply take it on the chin and smile. He was a fighter, he was dedicated to improving the lives of African Americans, and he was willing to use his celebrity to gain any advantage it might accrue toward their civil rights. Between the end of his playing career in 1957 and his death in 1972, Jackie Robinson was one of the foremost activists on the civil rights scene. His letters to the rich and powerful were themselves a powerful voice as well as persuasive fundraisers. He was sometimes the quiet voice of conscience and at other times the stentorian bugle of righteous outrage.

Michael G. Long, the editor of *First Class Citizenship: The Civil Rights Letters of Jackie Robinson,* happily admits he happened upon the letters of Jackie Robinson while doing researching on Richard Nixon at the National Archives. As he tells it, archivist Paul Wormser, approached him and asked him, "Have you seen the Jackie Robinson file?" He credits "that beautiful question" for starting him on an odyssey into a side of Jackie Robinson he would not have otherwise pursued. The result was a journey through the correspondence of Jackie Robinson with all of the important players of the Civil Rights era: Richard Nixon, Dwight D. Eisenhower, Nelson Rockefeller, John F. Kennedy, Martin Luther King, Jr., Malcolm X, and many more. The result is a compelling and vivid portrait of Robinson's activism that had been either forgotten or overlooked. Long says it best:

> Perhaps it has been safe and convenient for us to picture Robinson as the tolerant, clean-cut ballplayer who gently helped to integrate professional sports for the United States. But however comfortable it may be, our collective focus on the first part of his baseball career is utterly unfair to the Jackie Robinson who loudly criticized the practices and policies of racist America, devoted countless hours to civil rights fund-raising and rallies, twisted the arms of politicians hungry for black votes and yet fearful of a white backlash, and encouraged young African Americans who have since become well-known veterans in the ongoing battle for civil rights.[3]

For our purposes here it would be impractical and probably impossible to attempt to replicate the full scope of Robinson's civil rights agenda. For that, Long's work is best and we recommend it as required reading for anyone who wants a complete picture of the man. What we have done, instead, is excerpt, chronologically, a sampling of the correspondence to give teachers a good sense of Robinson's activism during, but mostly after, his baseball career, between 1946 and his death in 1972.[4] Robinson's political perspective may surprise some, but his early political association

1. James Loewen, "Handicapped by History: The Process of Hero-making," *Lies My Teacher Told Me,* (New York: Touchstone Books, 1995), pp. 18-36.

2. Joe Posnanski, *The Soul of Baseball, A Road Trip Through Buck O'Neil's America,* (New York: Harper, 2007), p. 119. Buck O'Neil upon being confronted by a "shock jock" radio interviewer with this, "Jackie Robinson was a sellout, am I right?" replied, "No, sir, you are not right." The interviewer continued, "He turned on his own people and went to play for the white leagues." Again, Buck emphasized, "No, sir. Jackie Robinson was a hero. He was an American hero."

3. Michael G. Long, ed., "Editor's Introduction," *First Class Citizenship, The Civil Rights Letters of Jackie Robinson,* (Henry Holt: New York, 2007), p. xv. James Loewen, *Lies My Teacher Told Me,* pointed out this same phenomenon as it relates to Helen Keller in his chapter one, "Handicapped By History."

4. All excerpts are from Michael Long's edited compilation cited above.

with some members of the Republican Party, like that of many African Americans at the time, was in flux. The Republicans had been the party of Lincoln and many, including Robinson, believed they would be allies in the struggle for civil rights. That, ultimately, would change over time.

Early Republican Allies

Between 1957 and 1972, the bulk of the modern era of the civil rights movement, the country was forced to confront its past and contemplate its future. It was also a time when the political alignments of the past hundred years were dramatically shifting as well. The party of Lincoln that Robinson was drawn to was on its way to becoming a party in which Barry Goldwater could feel comfortable. It was a time when Richard Nixon seemed a more active advocate for civil rights than Dwight Eisenhower. The John F. Kennedy best remembered today for his stance on civil rights was then still a cautious follower. Rockefeller Republicans were giving ground to a more southern brand of Republicanism and the Democrats still carried the lingering odor of Strom Thurmond and the Dixiecrats. As Robinson and others navigated these ever-changing political currents, his steady focus remained on his primary goal: improvement in every aspect of American life for African Americans. For Jackie, party loyalty or loyalty to a politician, however powerful, was never as important to him as was loyalty to the cause of improving the civil rights of African Americans. He supported those who supported his cause and he wasn't opposed to telling them so.

The letters allow us to see his political position in transition. As Long explains, ". . . he lavished praise on those who sought to overcome racial segregation (for example, Lyndon Johnson and the Freedom Riders of the 1960s) . . . [but] also wrote scorching letters to those who dared to differ with his vision of fair play for African Americans (for example, Barry Goldwater and Adam Clayton Powell, Jr.). . . It is not always easy to understand this prophet with pen in hand. Robinson's passion for civil rights was complicated and nuanced . . . offering his support to Democrats and Republicans, questioning the tactics of civil rights leaders . . . and challenging the nation's leaders to fulfill the promises of democracy and capitalism."[5] And, surprisingly enough, even he, like other civil rights activists, earned an FBI file at the direction of J. Edgar Hoover.

5. *Ibid.*, p. xv.

The Power of His Pen

Robinson attracted admirers from a cross section of Americans including the head of the Socialist Party, Norman Thomas. On September 23, 1947, he wrote: Now that the Dodgers have won the pennant, it is very appropriate, I think, to thank you not only for what you did in the pennant race but for what you have done for the colored race. . . . You have performed a real service to our country and in general to a world which must learn to honor men for what they are and do regardless of race."

Sometimes admirers overstepped their bounds, however, like one star-struck young lady who wrote of her love. To her he reminded her, "When I married Mrs. Robinson, I exchanged vows to love, honor, and cherish her for the rest of my life . . . any sneaking, skulking escapade would destroy the very thing that lets me hold my head up high." And, in a brilliant, yet subtle, finish he adds, "Just in case you might want to write me again, I must inform you that all my mail is opened at the Brooklyn baseball club offices and then forwarded to me." And closes: "Yours in reproof."

After attending an anniversary dinner for the Anti-Defamation League of B'nai B'rith, and meeting President Eisenhower he wrote to him, "It was a great privilege for me to appear on a program in which the President of the United States took part. It was equally great for me to experience the warmth and sincerity of your handshake in the midst of such an illustrious group of Americans." (November 25, 1953)

In this letter to Maxwell Rabb, secretary to the Eisenhower cabinet, he seeks help securing a federal mortgage for a New York City housing project for minorities: "I was very interested in Mr. Alan Paton's[6] story in the *Saturday Evening Post*, where he said, 'The Negroes today are no longer saying let my people go, but let my people in.' He was referring to the tremendous need there is for minority housing. . . . I do hope I can get a favorable reaction from you on this matter."

6. Author of *Cry the Beloved Country.*

In a letter to sports writer, Bill Keefe, Robinson responds to an editorial suggesting that he (Robinson) was the catalyst for a new Louisiana law criminalizing interracial sports: "We (African-American athletes) ask for nothing special. We ask only that we be permitted to live as you live, and as our nation's constitution provides. We ask only, in sports, that we be permitted to compete on an even basis and, if we are not worthy, then the competition shall, per se, eliminate us. Certainly you, and the people of Louisiana, should be capable of facing such competition." He ends with, "I am happy for you, that you were born white. It would have been extremely difficult for you had it been otherwise."

In 1956 at the Democratic National Convention, the convention rejected a platform plank affirming a commitment to implementing Supreme Court decisions prohibiting segregation . . . including *Brown v. Board of Education of Topeka, Kansas.* Afterward, Herbert Lehman (former New York State Governor, and in 1956, a New York State Senator) responded to a wire Robinson sent to him at the convention expressing his regret that the minority report on civil rights had been rejected.

A measure of how celebrated he was comes from this letter to him from Harold

Howland at the State Department asking him to undertake a good will tour abroad. The letter doesn't indicate where they wanted him to tour, but mentions some of the athletes who had accepted the invitation: "Bob Mathias, Sammy Lee, Jesse Owens, and Bob Richards." During the Cold War Era, the United States tried to bolster its image in the world by sending black athletes to nations in Africa and India. As the United States and the Soviet Union competed for allies in the emerging nations of

Africa, the Soviet Union took advantage of racial confrontations here in the United States to persuade African nations that the United States was a racist society unworthy of their support.

The newsreels and newspaper headlines of the scenes around Central High in Little Rock, Arkansas after *Brown v. Board* showed a side of the United States we hoped to minimize. With both the United Nations in New York City and ambassadors from these new African nations arriving in Washington, D.C., racial barriers in hotels, taxis, and restaurants fell, but much of America was not New York City or Washington, D.C.

The Robinson–King Collaboration

The first evidence of Robinson and Martin Luther King, Jr. collaborating dates from an exchange of letters in February of 1957. At the time Robinson had just been elected as National Chairman of the 1957 National Association for the Advancement of Colored People Freedom Fund Campaign. King was the new president of the Southern Christian Leadership Conference (SCLC). King's role in the Montgomery bus boycott had earned high praise from Robinson. To his wife Rachel he wrote, "The more I read about the Montgomery situation, the more respect I have for the job they are doing." Likewise, King admired Robinson. When Robinson asked for his assistance as a member of the National Advisory Committee to raise funds, King wrote, "I will do all within my power to make time for such a magnificent task." Although the NAACP and SCLC found issues to scrap about during the 1950s and 60s, the relationship between King and Robinson was strong and mutually respectful.

Losing Confidence in Eisenhower and Nixon

Long notes the beginning of Robinson's frustration with Republican leaders he had once supported because of their support, however lukewarm, of civil rights. "Unlike other civil rights leaders at the time, Robinson publicly supported Eisenhower as a proponent of the civil rights movement . . . [that] enthusiastic support of Eisenhower began to soften, however, when the president refused to make a public statement following the January 10 [1957] bombing of several homes and churches of civil rights activists in Montgomery, Alabama."[7] In an April 24, 1957, letter to Martin Luther King, Jr., Robinson offers regret that he can't be in Montgomery but, "later chaired a campaign [that raised $50,000] to rebuild black churches that were bombed in 1962."[8] By May, he again asks Eisenhower by way of a letter to Maxwell Rabb, to "get an expression from President Eisenhower condemning violence. Such a statement would give us a great deal of encouragement and would certainly give me the necessary material for my comments about the President when I'm at my NAACP meetings." In return he received this vague response from Eisenhower, "As you know, problems which touch upon human values present deep-seated emotional difficulties. It is our hope that we can continue to foster a moral climate within which the forces of informed good will operate effectively in an atmosphere of democracy."

His enthusiasm for Richard Nixon also begins to waver. During the 1956 presidential race, New York Senator Lehman criticized Nixon's anti-civil rights record pointing to the stark contrast between his recent public speeches and the votes he cast in both the House and Senate. Robinson wrote to Nixon, "[Friends] ask, "How can you support Nixon after the poor civil rights record he had in the Senate? Can't you see he's making these speeches now with his eyes on the presidency in 1960?" Nixon reassured him of his support by saying, "The matter of assuring equal opportunities for all is one of the most important and far-reaching problems facing this nation. Not only is our position a concern domestically, but the decisions made and steps taken are under constant scrutiny abroad."

Even as Robinson continued to nurture confidence in Eisenhower, it is clear that he was becoming increasingly frustrated by him. "At his [Eisenhower's] press conference on July 17, 1957, he says, "I personally believe if you try to go too far too fast in laws in this delicate field, that has involved the emotions of so many millions of Americans, you are making a mistake. I believe we have got to have laws that go along with education and understanding. And I believe that if you go beyond that at any time, you cause trouble rather than benefit."[9] For people who had waited a hundred years, the message to go slow and wait was hard to swallow. In response, on July 19, Robinson wrote to Maxwell Rabb, "The President, all the senators and everyone else must know that we are not asking for any special favors. . . . All over the world oppressed people are crying for and getting their freedom, yet in what is supposed to be the world's greatest Democracy, many of our responsible leaders appear to be unduly influenced by the few bigots who fear the universal acceptance of civil rights."

His position is especially clear in this telegram sent in reference to a watered-down civil rights bill containing a voting rights provision gutted "by segregationist senators."

7. *Ibid.,* p. 28.

8. *Ibid.,* p. 28, 154.

9. Eisenhower quoted in Long, p. 34.

The bill passed, however, and was signed into law September 9, 1957, making it the first civil rights law in over eighty years.

During the crisis in Little Rock, Robinson turned to New York Governor Averell Harriman. Harriman sent this in response, September 8, 1957:

Thank you for your letter. I fully share your concern over recent events in Arkansas. They not only violate the constitutional rights of American citizens, but are damaging to our prestige around the world. This seriously weakens our leadership in the fight against communism. I earnestly hope that Governor Faubus now realizes that he has been badly advised. . . . The use of the National Guard, which is largely supported by federal funds, to defy, rather than uphold, our federal constitution is a precedent which must not be permitted to stand.

September 13, 1957, he again wrote to Eisenhower expressing his frustration with Eisenhower's handling of the crisis in Little Rock: ". . . I read your statement in the papers advising patience. We are wondering to whom you are referring when you say we must be patient. It is easy for those who haven't felt the evils of a prejudiced society to urge it, but for us who as Americans have patiently waited all these years for the rights supposedly guaranteed us under our Constitution; it is not an easy task. Nevertheless, we have done it. . . . In my opinion, people the world over would hail you if you made a statement that would clearly put your office behind the efforts for civil rights. As it is now, you see what the Communist nations are doing with the material we have given them. I am aware, Mr. President, this letter expresses a mood of frustration. It is a mood generally found among Negro Americans today and should be a matter of concern to you as it is to us."

Robinson's concerns were broad and deep, encompassing all areas of discrimination. On November 4, 1957, he wrote to Louis Seaton, vice president of personnel at General Motors in response to an article in the *Wall Street Journal*. In the article the General Manager of the plant is quoted as saying, "When we moved into the South, we agreed to abide by local custom and not hire Negroes for production work. This is no time for social reforming in that area, and we're not about to try it." Robinson wrote: "There is a great deal of concern in the Negro community over this remark. . . . We have heard of the trouble in Cleveland, in Tarrytown, New York, and in Michigan, where like the Southern Negro worker, employment is limited to menial jobs. . . . I, like my friends, are General Motors users now, but it appears to me I can't continue to buy the product of a prejudiced company . . ." He then followed up his letter to Seaton with one to Walter Reuther, president of the United Auto Workers, "It is my opinion, Negroes should not buy any of this product unless some action is taken by them [General Motors Management]. With this market as competitive as it is, we don't have to spend our dollars where we can't earn them."

The events of the 1960s accelerated at an astonishing pace in the realm of the civil rights struggle. Our bookshelves sag from the weight of the avalanche of research devoted to this most pivotal of times in American history. Throughout these years, Robinson lent his considerable celebrity and voice to both the SCLC and the NAACP, wrote on behalf of civil rights legislation, raised funds to rebuild churches reduced to ashes by southern mobs, spoke at endless numbers of conferences and conventions, marched with Dr. King in Washington, and continued writing to those in power on behalf of civil rights in all arenas. Though he supported Nixon for the presidency in 1960, he came to appreciate the work of the Kennedy administration on behalf of civil rights.

Neither a Republican nor a Democrat

Robinson frequently stated that he was neither a Republican nor a Democrat but was always ready to support those who supported civil rights. And he was not easily persuaded by "talk." He is quoted in an article about a major civil rights speech delivered by Robert Kennedy at the University of Georgia by Peter Lisagor of the Washington Bureau of the *Chicago Daily News* as saying, "They've said so many wonderful things, but we've been hearing that for a long time. Now we're waiting to see if there is going to be follow through." Lisagor began the piece saying, "Jackie Robinson, the former baseball star who campaigned for Republican presidential candidate Richard Nixon, has changed his mind about the Kennedy boys." Robinson was quick to correct that assumption, "Not so fast . . . I just feel when anyone does the right thing it must be recognized." It wasn't until after President Kennedy arranged for the Alabama National Guard, the Alabama State Police, the FBI, and the U.S. Border Patrol to provide protection for the Freedom Riders, that he becomes more enthusiastic. In a letter thanking Attorney General Robert Kennedy, he ends with, "You have earned our respect. We are proud of the job you are doing."[10]

10. Peter Lisagor, in Long, p. 127-9.

However supportive he was to his fellow civil rights leaders, he was sharply critical of extremism. In a letter in response to criticism of him from Malcolm X, published in the *New York Amsterdam News,* he writes, "Frankly your letter to me is one of the things I will cherish. Coming from you, an attack is a tribute. I am also honored to have been placed in the distinguished company of Dr. Ralph Bunch, whom you also attacked. . . . I do not hide behind any coat-tails as you do when caught in one of your numerous outlandish statements. Your usual 'out' is to duck responsibility by stating: 'The Honorable Elijah Muhammad says . . .' Personally, I reject your racist views. I reject your dream of a separate state. I believe that many Americans black and white, are committed to fighting for those freedoms for which Medgar Evers, William Moore, the Birmingham children and President John F. Kennedy died. You say that I have never shown my appreciation to the Negro masses. I assume that is why the NAACP branches all over the country constantly invite me to address them. . . . Thank God for our Dr. Bunche, our Roy Wilkins, our Dr. King, and Mr. Randolph. I am also grateful for those people you consider 'white bosses.' I hate to think where we would be if we followed your leadership."

And after decades of support for New York's Governor Nelson Rockefeller, his actions in ordering the assault on Attica Prison in which 23 or the 39 inmates killed were African American and his "defensive testimony before the investigating state commission . . . and changes in welfare policy, . . . and Rockefeller's support for Nixon's proposed one-year moratorium on busing" prompted this rebuke: "I believe you have lost the sensitivity and understanding I felt was yours when I worked with you. Somehow, it seems to me, getting ahead politically is more important to you than what is right. Perhaps you honestly feel you are doing what is right but it certainly is not the way Governor Rockefeller used to function."

Jackie Robinson's last public appearance was on October 15, 1972. "Robinson threw out the ceremonial first ball of the second game of the 1972 World Series, marking the twenty-fifth anniversary of his role in shattering Major League Baseball's color barrier. In his televised speech, he stated: I am extremely proud and pleased to be here this afternoon but must admit I'm going to be tremendously more pleased and more proud when I look at that third base coaching line one day and see a black face managing in baseball." Nine days later he was gone. Only 53 years old, white-haired, unsteady on his feet, and nearly blind from diabetes, his last public moment was another moment to urge baseball to open its doors again.[11]

Today he lies in Cypress Hills Cemetery in Queens, New York, 16 miles from the former site of Ebbets Field. It is there that his legacy is best defined with the words he asked to have inscribed on his gravestone, "A life is not important except in the impact it has on other lives."

What remains are the memories. Pete Hamill remembers. Retracing the steps he had walked so many years earlier, he writes, "I started walking home, the way I did as a boy, through Prospect Park, and all around me I could hear a roar, and there in my mind, as it will be forever, was the image of Robinson, dancing off third."[12]

11. Long, p. 318.

12. www.petehamill.com/ ebbetsfield.html

13. Robert Frost, "Reluctance" *A Boy's Will* (London: D. Nutt, 1913).

Ah, when to the heart of man
  Was it ever less than a treason
To go with the drift of things,
  To yield with a grace to reason,
And bow and accept the end
  Of a love or a season?[13]

Lesson 1: Learning with Primary Sources: Valises, Scrapbooks, FaKeBooks, and Posters

Using primary sources is one of the niftier ways to start teaching elementary students to look carefully, compare sources, become comfortable with chronological order, and interpret historical materials. For younger students an emphasis on visual literacy will let students interpret pictures, graphs, and maps. To these types of materials, teachers can add excerpts from letters, speeches, and other types of written materials for older students. Students of all ages like adding musical literacy to their skills and are often surprised by what they can learn about people, events, and time periods when they become familiar with that era's "sound track."

The selection of documents in this DBQ (document based question) spans the full range of types of primary sources so that teachers can select those most appropriate for their classroom.

Some of the criteria we used for this DBQ were

- **Interest**   We looked for documents that would pique students' interest—easy to interpret, but not too easy.

- **Reading Level**   For young students, we chose mostly pictures, music, and other visual materials, but added a few written documents that are appropriate for young learners. For older students the reading level of the materials is either at grade level or slightly above, in order to challenge them and add to their vocabulary. Those that are slightly above have been augmented with side-by-side vocabulary help. Teachers can chose which documents are most appropriate for their students.

- **Length**   Teachers sometimes make the mistake of including primary sources that are too long, especially if the students will be working with the documents within a single class period. The Advanced Placement Exam is a good example to follow. The documents they use for high school students rarely exceed a short paragraph. The trick is to do good editing; keep it short but be sure the excerpt is able to convey the main point of the writer's argument. Ours are short.

- **Points of View**   All appropriate points of view have been included.

- **Variety of Sources**   We looked for a wide variety of sources and have included photographs, baseball cards, letters, and music lyrics. The sources also offer a representative sampling of the various roles that Jackie Robinson played during his lifetime: U.S. Army officer, player for the

Kansas City Monarchs, rookie with the Dodger's Montreal farm team, as a member of the Dodgers, and later as a Hall of Famer and civil rights activist. As much as possible we have included copies of original letters and telegrams so that students can get a sense of the real artifact. Reading someone else's mail is so much more enjoyable than a typed copy of it!

- **Location**   Many of the primary sources can be found on-line, but we have included them here to make sure that the lesson can be done in class even if computers are not available. Our sources included the National Archives, the Library of Congress, and the National Baseball Hall of Fame and Museum.

We recommend the tools for analyzing documents and other features for teaching with documents that can be found at the website for the National Archives.

www.archives.gov/education/research/

Using primary sources opens up dozens of ways to organize teaching. They can be used as bell-ringer activities to introduce a lesson, they can be used for inquiry-based group work, they can be part of "learning to look" or "learning to listen" activities, and including artifacts offers even more possibilities. A "learning valise" filled with artifacts lets students be history detectives figuring out who the "owner" of the valise is. If the valise seems to have items that don't immediately seem connected, students can work together checking dates, where the items came from, what they are used for, for written documents like letters and who their recipients were, to figure out how the items are related.

Students can demonstrate their understanding in standard formats, like essays, but another option that students can use to show their understanding is creating a FaKebook page. Directions and the start-up link can be found at:

http://classtools.net/fb/home/page.

Collages, posters and scrapbooks are also terrific ways for students to show what they've learned as they gather pictures and other artifacts to organize a pictorial representation of Jackie's life and legacy. The photographs and other materials gathered here will give students a head start on their projects.

Lt. Jack Robinson, 1942

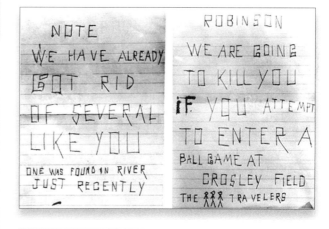

Brooklyn Dodger, 1947
Fan mail

Kansas City Monarch, 1945
Montreal Dodger, 1946

The Library of Congress received four music related requests in their Copyright Office in 1947—the year Jackie Robinson made his Major League debut.

"Did You See Jackie Robinson Hit That Ball?" was easily the most famous of those four honorary songs and an instant classic. The song was originally written and performed by Buddy Johnson, who recorded it in 1949 and saw it peak on the charts at number 13. That same year Count Basie recorded the song on the Victor label with vocalist Taps Miller, and this version became a true baseball standard.

Additional details about the life and times of Jackie Robinson can be found on the Baseball Almanac website. Other important details for those looking for additional data about this music include the original recording (Decca 24675), the original words and music (LOC EU 169446), and the Count Basie recording (Victor 20-3514).

www.baseball-almanac.com/poetry/po_jackier.shtml

Did You See Jackie Robinson Hit That Ball? (1949 Version)

"Did You See Jackie Robinson Hit That Ball?" www.youtube.com/watch?v=r-7Ac2LVVYU

Excellent YouTube video with images from Jackie's years with the Dodgers.

"Did You See Jackie Robinson Hit That Ball?" written and recorded by Woodrow Buddy Johnson and recorded by Count Basie (1949)

Did you see Jackie Robinson hit that ball?
It went zoomin cross the left field wall.
Yeah boy, yes, yes. Jackie hit that ball.

And when he swung his bat,
the crowd went wild,
because he knocked that ball a solid mile.
Yeah boy, yes, yes. Jackie hit that ball.

Satchel Paige is mellow,
so is Campanella,
Newcombe and Doby, too.
But it's a natural fact,
when Jackie comes to bat,
the other team is through.

Did you see Jackie Robinson hit that ball?
Did he hit it? Yeah, and that ain't all.
He stole home.
Yes, yes, Jackie's real gone.

Did you see Jackie Robinson hit that ball?
Did he hit it? Yeah, and that ain't all.
He stole home.
Yes, yes, Jackie's real gone.
Jackie's a real
gone guy.

Lesson 2: Cap, Jackie, and Ted—
The Rise and Fall of Jim Crow Baseball*

All the world's a stage,
And all the men and women merely players:
They have their exits and their entrances;
And one man in his time plays, many parts . . .
—As You Like It: Act 2, Scene 7, William Shakespeare

Adrian Constantine "Cap" Anson left a mixed legacy. Clearly the most well known and popular baseball player of his era, he can also lay claim to the title of baseball's first superstar. He strode onto the stage of major league baseball in 1875 and played for a record-setting twenty-eight seasons, twenty with a batting average over .300. He was the first player to amass 3,000 hits and he held numerous other records at his retirement in the early 1900s. His success was celebrated with his induction into the National Baseball Hall of Fame in 1939. Without question he was adored by his teammates and the fans.

There was, however, another, darker side to Cap Anson. He was an avowed and outspoken racist. Given his prominence on the playing field and popularity with fans, his vehement, vocal, and profane refusal to share the playing field with "niggers" earned him another title, "The Father of Segregated Baseball." His successful leadership of the efforts to eliminate all African-American players from the game meant sixty years of segregated baseball in America.

Jackie Robinson was an unlikely candidate for the role he was asked to play in 1947. He possessed a short, sharp temper, was quick to take offense, quick to fight. In 1944, while serving in the still-segregated United States Army, he was court-martialed for refusing to move to the rear of an army bus. Martin Luther King would later describe him as a, "sit-inner before sit-ins, a freedom rider before freedom rides." But, he had other qualities that made him the likeliest candidate to begin the modern integration of major league baseball. He was married, knew the limelight from his days as a star

*This teaching strategy first appeared in the April 2010 issue of the Organization of American Historians' *Magazine of History*.

ADRIAN C. ANSON.
ALLEN & GINTER'S
RICHMOND. Cigarettes. VIRGINIA

athlete at UCLA, and had served his country. When challenged by Branch Rickey, owner of the Brooklyn Dodgers, to show the courage to resist fighting back in the face of the worst kinds of racist taunts he was sure to face, he accepted that challenge and never failed in the task.

Like Anson, his legacy was two-fold. His prowess on the playing field led to his induction into the Baseball Hall of Fame in 1962, "on the same terms as everyone else." In the years since 1962, however, his legacy of civil rights activism both on and off the field led to the 2008 rededication of his place in the Hall. His plaque now includes, "Displayed tremendous courage and poise in 1947 when he integrated the modern major leagues in the face of intense adversity."

Ted Williams' legacy is no less mixed. A prominent figure in any debate regarding the best hitter to ever play the game, he is the last to have hit for a .400 average, a record now almost 70 years old. A six-time batting champion, his prodigious hit and home run totals are all the more impressive considering that his 19-year career with the Boston Red Sox was interrupted twice by military service, causing him to miss nearly five full seasons. Unlike Anson, Williams' career was characterized by an uneasy relationship with the Boston fans and a frequently contentious relationship with the media.

But Williams had another side too. Behind the scenes he worked tirelessly, and anonymously, visiting hospitals and contributing to a variety of charitable endeavors. On the field he was completely unselfish about giving advice to teammates and opponents alike. He, too, was elected to the National Baseball Hall of Fame and inducted into it in 1966. Although seemingly out of character, yet completely in character, he stunned the audience when he used his induction speech to speak on behalf of the Negro League players he admired. "I've been a very lucky guy to have worn a baseball uniform, and I hope some day the names of Satchel Paige and Josh Gibson in some way can be added as a symbol of the great Negro players who are not here only because they weren't given a chance."

Anson, Robinson, and Williams have become iconic symbols in the history of the African-American ballplayer's experience. Anson used his stage to help usher in 60 years of segregated baseball. Robinson stepped up to the plate and by so doing became the public face of a changing America. Williams drew attention to the reality of the continued exclusion from recognition of some of the best baseball players ever to play the game. When Williams spoke of Josh Gibson and Satchel Paige, baseball had already been desegregated but much of American life rigidly adhered to the color line. In 1966 African Americans still rarely appeared on network television, and when they did they were usually cast in the roles of domestics. The civil rights movement itself was still new and resistance to it still strong.

Time Frame: Two 50-minute class periods
National Standards with performance indicators:

Era 5: Civil War and Reconstruction

Standard 3A, The student understands the political controversy over Reconstruction.

Performance: Analyze how shared values of the North and South limited support for social and racial democratization.

Standard 3B, The student understands the Reconstruction programs to transform social relations in the South.

Performance: Explain the economic and social problems facing the South and appraise their impact on different social groups.

Performance: Assess how the political and economic position of African Americans in the northern and western states changed during Reconstruction.

Era 9: Postwar United States 1945 to the early 1970s

Standard 3A, The student understands the debates of the post-World War II era [especially those related to civil rights].

Performance: Assess the importance of the individual in history.

Standard 4A, The student understands the "Second Reconstruction" and its advancement of civil rights.

Performance: Explain the origins of the postwar civil rights movement and the role of the NAACP in the legal assault on segregation.

Performance: Evaluate the agendas, strategies, and effectiveness of various Americans in the quest for civil rights and equal opportunities.

Student Objectives: Students will be able to

- Interpret primary documents

- Evaluate the role of the individual in history

- Explain and discuss important elements of the times in which each man lived

- Determine to what extent individuals both led and reflected their era

- Synthesize evidence in order to write a well-organized essay

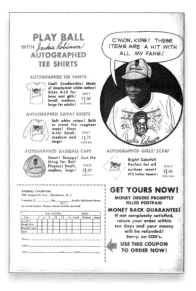

Background/Preparation

Cap Anson grew up during the Jim Crow era. His values and life experiences were not atypical of whites during that time. In order to teach about his role in segregating baseball, it's important to contextualize his life. He was a man of his times. This is not to excuse him, but to understand him. Beyond that, however, is the issue of individual choice. Even during an era when racism was so common as to be unremarkable, just the way things were, Anson's vehement racism was notable.

His actions offer a rich opportunity for students to wrestle with issues of individual responsibility and American ideals. The question could be asked, "Based on your understanding of the Declaration of Independence and the Constitution, was Cap Anson a good citizen?" Certainly the decision in *Plessy* would support Anson. However, John Marshall Harlan's Dissent to *Plessy* ultimately overturned it giving students support to argue that he was not a good citizen. Informed debates on issues like these are the substance of any number of Supreme Court cases, and students will benefit from the opportunity to engage in the complexity of these issues.

Jackie Robinson did not begin the civil rights movement. But when he stoically faced daily race-baiting taunts, beanballs, and sharpened cleats, he forced Americans to see racism on a national stage in its beloved sport, its great American pastime. As Scott Simon explains it, "With Vernon Johns, Thurgood Marshall, A. Philip Randolph, and many more, it had already produced heroes. But Robinson's courage put a familiar face on the kind of bravery that it took . . . the civil rights marchers who [later] faced down stinging water sprays, sharp rocks, and snapping police dogs."

Ted Williams's role in calling for justice for African-American players who were shut out of the major leagues will introduce someone to the conversation about the civil rights movement of the 1960s to show that people from all walks of life can have an impact on the course of history.

Anson, Robinson, and Williams used the stages their athletic abilities provided to influence others. Each chose what their influence would be.

Procedures

Background reading: As a homework assignment the night before the lesson, assign students the three short articles listed below. Together they will provide an overview of the men who are central to the lesson. In addition teachers could consider doing a short review of the 14th Amendment, the pertinent sections of the decision in *Plessy v Ferguson*, and John Marshall Harlan's dissent. These will remind students of the issues that framed the mores of the time period. It is critical that teachers frame this as a national issue. Racism may have been etched into the stones of the South, but it was alive and well in the North as well.

Cap's Great Shame by Howard W. Rosenberg
www.capanson.com/chapter4.html

Hub Bids Kid Adieu by John Updike
www.newyorker.com/archive/1960/10/22/1960_10_22_109_TNY_CARDS_000266305?printable=true

Jim Crow, Meet Lieutenant Robinson: A 1944 Court Martial by John Vernon
www.archives.gov/publications/prologue/2008/spring/robinson.html

Class discussion: The readings can be used as a springboard for class discussion to introduce students to the connection between the world of baseball and civil rights. All three of the readings offer opportunities to draw connections between the promises of the 14th Amendment, the conflicting interpretations of the Plessy decision, and the backgrounds and motives of Anson, Robinson, and Williams.

Group work: Divide the class into groups to review a portion of the documents, answer questions, and draw conclusions. Have each member of the group present one of the group's answers to their document's questions. References to the documents should be included in each presentation. During presentations students should take notes on the documents that were analyzed by the other groups in order to be prepared for the individual assignment.

Individual work: Have students each write a 200–300 word essay that addresses the academic prompt for the DBQ as a whole.

Lesson Extension: The Negro Leagues Baseball Museum offers packages of baseball cards that could be used for an individual or group project researching Negro League players and their teams. www.nlbm.com/

Documents

Directions

The following question requires you to construct a coherent essay that integrates your interpretation of the documents and your knowledge of the period referred to in the question. High scores will be earned only by essays that both cite key pieces of evidence from the documents and draw on outside knowledge of the period.

Prompt

From the end of Reconstruction until the Civil Rights era of the 1960s, America restricted the lives of African Americans both legally and through custom and tradition. In what ways and to what extent were the actions and behaviors of Cap Anson, Jackie Robinson, and Ted Williams reflections of the times in which they lived, reflections of their personal values, and instruments of change in American life?

Use the documents and your knowledge of the time period, 1880–1970, to construct your answer.

DOCUMENT A

Source: Philadelphia Winter Meeting of the National Assoc. of Base Ball Players, December 12, 1867

[The Nominating Committee of the National Association of Base Ball Players] . . . unanimously agrees to: the exclusion of any club which may be composed of one or more colored persons.

Quoted in Robert Peterson, *Only the Ball Was White* (New York: Oxford University Press, 1970), 16-17.

DOCUMENT B

Source: 14th Amendment of the U.S. Constitution, 1868

Section. 1. All persons born or naturalized in the United States and subject to the jurisdiction thereof, are citizens of the United States and of the State wherein they reside. No State shall make or enforce any law which shall abridge the privileges or immunities of citizens of the United States; nor shall any State deprive any person of life, liberty, or property, without due process of law; nor deny to any person within its jurisdiction the equal protection of the laws.

DOCUMENT C

Source: Message given to St. Louis Browns owner on the eve of an exhibition game between the Browns and the all-Negro Cuban Giants at West Farms, N.Y., 1887

We, the undersigned members of the St. Louis Base Ball Club, do not agree to play against negroes tomorrow. We will cheerfully play against white people at any time, and think, by refusing to play, we are only doing what is right, taking everything into consideration and the shape the team is in at present.

DOCUMENT D

Source: *The Sporting News*, July 11, 1887

A new trouble has just arisen in the affairs of certain baseball associations [which] has done more damage to the International League than to any other we know of. We refer to the importation of colored players into the ranks of that body.

DOCUMENT E

Source: A member of the Buffalo Bisons quoted in the *Buffalo Courier,* April 14, 1889

The feeling is pretty general among professional ball-players that colored men should not play with white men.

DOCUMENT F

Source: Sol White, *Sol White's History of Colored Baseball* (1889)
White was a Negro leagues player and historian

His [Anson's] repugnant feeling, shown at every opportunity, toward colored players, was a source of comment throughout every league in the country, and his opposition, with his great popularity and power in base ball circles, hastened the exclusion of the black man from white leagues.

DOCUMENT G

Source: Justice Henry Brown on behalf of the Supreme Court in *Plessy v. Ferguson,* 1896

That the Separate Car Act does not conflict with the Thirteenth Amendment, which abolished slavery . . . is too clear for argument. . . . A statute which implies merely a legal distinction between the white and colored races — a distinction which is founded in the color of the two races, and which must always exist so long as white men are distinguished from the other race by color — has no tendency to destroy the legal equality of the two races. . . . The object of the Fourteenth Amendment was undoubtedly to enforce the absolute equality of the two races before the law, but in the nature of things it could not have been intended to abolish distinctions based upon color, or to enforce social, as distinguished from political equality, or a commingling of the two races upon terms unsatisfactory to either.

DOCUMENT H

Source: John Marshall Harlan, Dissent in *Plessy v. Ferguson*, 1896

Our Constitution is color-blind, and neither knows nor tolerates classes among citizens. In respect of civil rights, all citizens are equal before the law...In my opinion, the judgment this day rendered will, in time, prove to be quite as pernicious as the decision made by this tribunal in the **Dred Scott** case. . . . The present decision, it may well be apprehended, will not only stimulate aggressions, more or less brutal and irritating, upon the admitted rights of colored citizens, but will encourage the belief that it is possible, by means of state enactments, to defeat the beneficent purposes which the people of the United States had in view when they adopted the recent amendments of the Constitution.

For the reasons stated, I am constrained to withhold my assent from the opinion and judgment of the majority.

DOCUMENT I

Source: *Adrian Constantine Anson, A ball player's career: being the personal experiences and reminiscences of Adrian C. Anson*
(Chicago: Era Publishing Co., 1900)

Clarence was a little darky that I had met some time before while in Philadelphia, a singer and dancer of no mean ability, and a little coon whose skill in handling the baton would have put to blush many a bandmaster of national reputation. . . . Outside of his dancing and his power of mimicry he was, however, a "no account nigger" . . . a chocolate-covered coon . . . and more than once did I wish that he'd been left behind.

DOCUMENT J

Source: Lyrics by sportswriter Ring Lardner and music by professional baseball player "Doc White" (1910)
E. Azalia Hackley Col., Detroit Public Library

DOCUMENT K

Source: Sports writer Harvey Frommer, *Rickey and Robinson: The Men Who Broke Baseball's Color Line*
(New York: Macmillan, 1982)

Jackie Robinson and Branch Rickey met and set in motion what was known as "the noble experiment." Rickey said, "I want to beg two things of you, Jackie. Give it all you have as a ballplayer. As a man, give continuing loyalty to your race and to the critical cause you are going to symbolize. And above all, do not fight. No matter how vile the abuse, you must ignore it. You are carrying the reputation of a race on your shoulders. Bear it well, and the day will come when every team in baseball will open its doors to Negroes.

DOCUMENT L

**Source: Group portrait of players from the Monarch and
Hillsdale baseball teams in front of the grandstands
before opening game of 1924 Colored World Series**
Library of Congress

DOCUMENT M

**Source: Scott Simon, *Jackie Robinson
and the Integration of Baseball***
(Hoboken, NJ: John Wiley & Sons, Inc., 2002)

"I know you're a good ballplayer," said Rickey. "I've got to know if you've got the guts."

"Do you want a player who doesn't have the guts to fight back?" said Robinson.

"I'm looking for a ballplayer," Rickey thundered, "with the guts *not* to fight back!"

DOCUMENT N

**Source: Telegram to the White House from
Jackie Robinson, August 13, 1957**

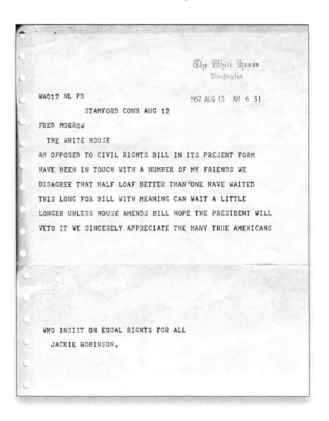

DOCUMENT O

March on Washington, 1963

DOCUMENT P

Source: Telegram to the White House from Jackie Robinson, March 9, 1965

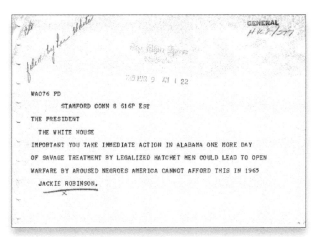

DOCUMENT Q

Source: *Jackie Robinson: I Never Had it Made*
(New York: Harper Collins Publishers, 1995)

A life is not important except in the impact it has on other lives.

I'm not concerned with your liking or disliking me . . . All I ask is that you respect me as a human being.

Life is not a spectator sport. If you're going to spend your whole life in the grandstand just watching what goes on, in my opinion you're wasting your life.

There's not an American in this country free until every one of us is free.

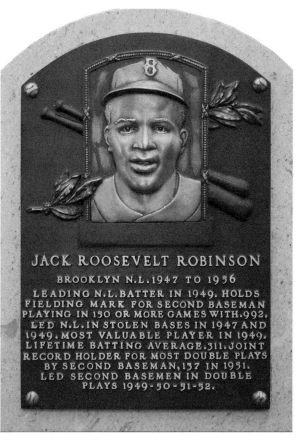

Courtesy National Baseball Hall Of Fame

DOCUMENT R

Source: National Baseball Hall of Fame Induction Speech, Ted Williams, 1966

Ballplayers are not born great. They're not born great hitters or pitchers or managers, and luck isn't a big factor. No one has come up with a substitute for hard work. I've never met a great player who didn't have to work harder at learning to play ball than anything else he ever did. To me it was the greatest fun I ever had, which probably explains why today I feel both humility and pride, because God let me play the game and learn to be good at it. He has gone past me, and he's pushing, and I say to him, "go get 'em Willie." Baseball gives every American boy a chance to excel. Not just to be as good as anybody else, but to be better. This is the nature of man and the name of the game. I hope someday Satchel Paige and Josh Gibson will be voted into the Hall of Fame as symbols of the great Negro players who are not here only because they weren't given the chance.

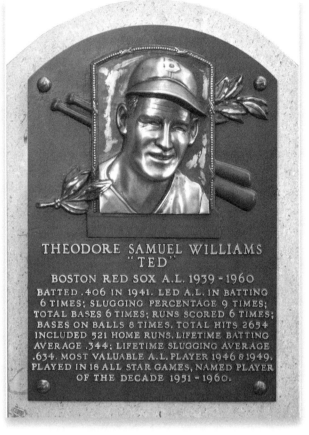

Courtesy National Baseball Hall Of Fame

DOCUMENT S

Source: *My Turn at Bat*, Ted Williams and John Underwood, 1969

I don't know how a man wants to be remembered, other than for his achievements. I just haven't thought about it.

I believe I am a compassionate man. I believe I'm concerned with people. I don't think I was ever as concerned or as compassionate in those early days as I am now. Why the hell should I have been. I was worried about Theodore Samuel Williams. I was worried about hitting, I was worried about my career, I was worried about money.

I know what has been right in my life and what has been wrong. If you put it all down, I feel in my heart I would have been more on the right side than on the wrong.

DOCUMENT T

Source: Ted Williams accepting a brotherhood award at Howard University, 1971

As I look back on my career—and it was wonderful to me, and I'm thankful that I was given the chance to play baseball; it's about the only thing I could do—and I've thought many a time, what would have happened to me if I hadn't had a chance to play baseball? A chill goes up my back when I think I might have been denied this if I had been black.

DOCUMENT U

Source: *The Storytellers: From Mel Allen to Bob Costas, Sixty Years of Baseball Tales from the Broadcast Booth*
Curt Smith, (Macmillan General Reference; 1997)

[References to Ted Williams]

He threw tantrums, spit at fans, reviled the press, and was a dazzling interview . . . the most volcanic athlete since [Babe] Ruth.   —Curt Smith

Every time he got a chance he'd visit hospitals and take autographed baseballs. As he finished, he told the nuns, "God bless you ladies in your love for kids. Don't tell anybody, especially a news writer, that I was here.

—Jimmy Dudley

For further reading

Cal Fussman, *After Jackie: Pride, Prejudice, and Baseball's Forgotten Heroes,* ESPN, 2007

Lawrence D. Hogan, ed., *Shades of Glory: The Negro Leagues and the Story of African-American Baseball,* National Geographic Society, 2006

Robert Peterson, *Only the Ball Was White,* Oxford University Press, 1970

Joe Posnanski, *The Soul of Baseball: A Road Trip Through Buck O'Neil's America,* Harper Paperbacks, 2008

Mark Ribowsky, *The Complete History of the Negro Leagues, 1884 to 1955,* Citadel Press, 2002

Scott Simon, *Jackie Robinson and the Integration of Baseball,* Wiley, 2002

For young adults

David A. Adler, *Campy: The Story of Roy Campanella,* Viking, 2007

Mark Chiarello and Jack Morelli, *Heroes of the Negro Leagues,* Abrama Books, 2007

Barry Denenberg, *Stealing Home: The Story of Jackie Robinson,* Scholastic, 1990

Laura Driscoll, *Negro Leagues All-Black Baseball,* Grosset & Dunlap, 2002

Dn Gutman, *Jackie and Me,* Avon Books, 1999

Bette Bao Lord, *In the Year of the Boar and Jackie Robinson,* Harper, 1984

Patricia C. and Fredrick McKissack, *Black Diamond,* Scholastic, 2008

Kadir Nelson, *We Are the Ship, The Story of Negro Leagues Baseball,* Jump at the Sun, 2008

James Strum, *Satchel Paige: Striking Out Jim Crow,* Hyperion, 2007

Myron Uhlberg, *Dad, Jackie and Me,* Peachtree, 2005

Lesson 3: Using Text Sets
Children's and YA Literature for Teachers and Students

Well—it's our game; that's the chief fact in connection with it; America's game; it has the snap, go, fling of the American atmosphere; it belongs as much to our institutions; fits into them as significantly as our Constitution's laws; is just as important in the sum total of our historic life.

—Walt Whitman

Text sets offer teachers an engaging way for students to expand their understandings of a topic, improve literacy and vocabulary skills, and work within a setting of choice.

A text set is a collection of resources often from different genres, media, and levels of reading difficulty that are designed to be supportive of the learning of readers with a range of experiences and interests. A text set collection focuses on one concept or topic and can include multiple genres such as books, charts and maps, informational pamphlets, poetry and songs, photographs, non-fiction books, almanacs, encyclopedias, videos, DVDs, or CD-ROMs.

Typically, text sets are unified by the topic they explore. While at the same time, they are differentiated by their genres and format. The collection might include a range of kinds of texts all on the same topic. "Flight" for example, can be a text set focal topic for a collection of texts that range from books on Charles Lindbergh to how birds fly. Text sets might also be built around:

A unit in the curriculum. Text sets lend themselves to unit studies. If the class is studying the Civil War, teachers and students can compile text sets around different aspects of the period: a military text set, a Lincoln text set, a text set focused on slavery. Kids can then easily put their fingers on Civil War information.

A topic with general and lasting appeal. Baskets of texts grouped around global subjects of interest such as the environment can occupy a permanent place in a classroom.

An author. These text sets contain examples of the author's work as well as biographical information about the author.

Social issues. Text sets grouped around issues such as disabilities, diversity, sibling rivalry, and divorce can be particularly supportive and helpful for kids at times.

The text set below has been compiled around the topic of Negro League baseball and its impact on civil rights. The purpose is to demonstrate a clear connection between wins and losses on the playing field and those in the larger arena of civil rights advocacy in the United States. The time frame for the collection spans materials from about the late 19th century to the far side of the mid-20th century. The selections reflect a wide range of reading levels in order to allow students with varying reading ability levels to be fully involved in the materials.

Also included are a number of picture books. Wilkins, Sheffield, Ford, and Cruz's research, (May/June 2008, "Images of Struggle and Triumph: Using Picture Books to Teach about Civil Rights in the Secondary Classroom," *Social Education*, National Council for the Social Studies) offer critical insights into the powerful social studies learning that can accompany ". . . rich illustration[s]. . . . This connection of picture and text creates a rich portrait of the period" for students of all reading levels. "The use of selected images also enables the author to emphasize themes, emotions, and significant details that might otherwise be lost in a conventional text-only medium."[1] In this way the pictures themselves *are* the text to be read and interpreted.

1. Diana Mitchell, "Using Children's Literature to Spark Learning," *English Journal*, 87, No. 2, 1998.

Text sets can be used in any number of ways in the classroom.

- Free reading is a strategy that many schools are reconnecting with because of the real gains in reading skills when students are offered opportunities to make their own choices about what to read and given reading time. (*This We Believe in Action*, National Middle Schools Association)

- Reading circles

- Jigsaw group work—each group chooses a book and collaborates on a presentation to teach the other students about their selection.

- Collaboration with English Language Arts colleagues on student book reviews

- Students themselves can contribute to the text sets by reading and presenting persuasive arguments on behalf of their choices.

- Myra Zarnowski's, "Powerful Pairs, Triplets, Quads, and More: Looking at Historical Interpretation," (*History Makers: A Questioning Approach to Reading and Writing Biographies*), demonstrates how pairing texts on the same topic helps students to become adept at discerning the role of historical interpretation and the value of illustrations in furthering the arguments of the authors.

However text sets are used, the advantage of encouraging students to make their own reading choices tends to raise their interest level and improve their reading skills in an enjoyable way.

Sample Text Set:
The Negro Leagues' Contributions to Civil Rights

This set contains biography, fiction, film, and music to engage and inspire readers of all ages and at all levels of reading skill.

The books and other materials chosen for this sample text set have been selected from reading lists provided by the National Council for the Social Studies, "Notable Social Studies Trade Books for Young People," The Coretta Scott King Award winners, and Newbury and Caldecott Award winners.

Black Diamond
Authors: Patricia C. and Fredrick McKissack

From Booklist—

GR. 6–10. This book goes far beyond the few familiar photographs and names most readers associate with the Negro Baseball Leagues, and it makes the trip in style. We discover, for example, that George Washington's troops were "batting balls and running bases" and that the nineteenth-century relationship between baseball and race was more diverse than many young readers may realize. The McKissacks carefully record the differences of opinion about some events and the difficulty of finding source material. Oral histories from surviving players add startling depth to descriptions of conditions of play and travel, and Jackie Robinson's entry into major league ball becomes a richer and more complicated moment because the authors show where Robinson came from (and how) in addition to where he went. A player roster will be helpful to students, and a time line carefully weaves together the sports world and the world of lynchings, race riots, the Civil War, and the incandescent electric lamp.   —*Mary Harris Veeder*

Negro Leagues All-Black Baseball
Author: Laura Driscoll
Illustrator: Tracy Mitchell

From Booklist—

Gr. 3–5. "I love baseball. I know a lot about it. But before last fall, I had never heard of the Negro Leagues," begins Emily Brooks, who, as Driscoll's narrator, relates what she learned in Cooperstown in a report for class. The enthusiastic, clear delivery makes this entry in the *Smart about History* series a solid choice for middle-graders. Emily takes readers back to the late 1800s when Bud Fowler (credited with inventing shin guards because white players kept spiking him) played on a pro team and then follows the history through the creation of the Negro Leagues in the 1920s to the 1969 election of Satchel Paige to the Baseball Hall of Fame. There's nothing about current black players, but Emily certainly gives kids a clear view of the racism that marked the past and introduces them to a few of the great African American players of their day. The vintage black-and-white photos are fascinating, and the lively artwork keeps to the spirit of the game without trivializing the racial inequity. Too bad there is no bibliography so kids can read on.

—*Stephanie Zvirin,*
Copyright © American Library Association

A Negro League Scrapbook

Author: Carole Boston Weatherford

GR. 2-4. Buck O'Neil, Chairman of the Negro Leagues Baseball Museum and former player and manager, leads off with a sprightly introduction to pages of sepia, black-and-white, and color photographs and images laid out in this attractive scrapbook presentation. Each spread begins with a rhyming, almost rap-style couplet, which is effective if occasionally clunky. Set against backgrounds that range from plain matte white to textured and colored papers, short running text, sidebars, quotes, and backgrounds survey the Negro Leagues from 1887, when the owners of major league ball agreed not to hire any more black players, to Jackie Robinson's signing with the Brooklyn Dodgers in 1947. Hall of Famers who came from the Negro Leagues and the first blacks on major league teams are just two of the topics covered in the many informational boxes. A lively presentation; give it credit for at least a triple.

—GraceAnne DeCandido
Copyright © American Library Association

Campy, The Story of Roy Campanella

Author: David A. Adler

From Booklist—

GR. 2–4. Roy Campanella, one of the greatest catchers in baseball history, was the second African American signed by Branch Rickey to play for the Brooklyn Dodgers. He joined the team in 1948, one year after his teammate, Jackie Robinson, broke the color line. Adler, author of the Cam Jansen mystery series as well as numerous historical biographies for young readers, capably reprises Campy's on-field triumphs (three-time National League Most Valuable Player) and off-field tragedy (he was paralyzed in a car accident in 1958), while James delivers evocative illustrations in the soft-focus, pastel-heavy style that has become standard for baseball nostalgia. There is no shortage of picture books about the Brooklyn Dodgers, but Campy's inspirational life story, less well known among today's children than Robinson's, deserves to be

heard, and baseball-loving baby-boomer grandparents, who came of age in the 1950s, will relish the chance to tell it.

—Bill Ott

Heroes of the Negro Leagues

Author: Jack Morelli
Illustrator: Mark Chiarello

GR. 5-12. First published as trading cards in 1990, these out-of-print watercolor images by award-winning artist Mark Chiarello are now collected for the first time in book form, along with incisive text by Jack Morelli and 39 brand-new images created especially for this book, including portraits of Satchel Paige, Hank Aaron, and Jackie Robinson. The legendary Negro Leagues are regarded with reverence and awe, and play a vital role in black history. The publication of these cards marked the first time most of these players ever appeared on baseball cards.

The book comes with a free DVD of the film: *Only the Ball Was White.*

Dad, Jackie and Me

Author: Myron Uhlberg
Illustrator: Colin Bootman

From Booklist—

Gr. 2-4, younger for reading aloud. Following in the tradition of Bette Bao Lord's *In the Year of the Boar and Jackie Robinson* (1984), about a young Chinese immigrant to Brooklyn in 1947 who identifies with the travails of the rookie Dodger first baseman, Uhlberg tells another story of an outsider who feels a bond with Robinson. This outsider, though, is a real-life figure, the author's deaf father, who saw in the African American Robinson's stoic endurance of prejudice on and off the field a parallel to his own experience as a deaf man. It takes the young Uhlberg, narrator of the story, a while to overcome his embarrassment at his father's attempts to cheer for Robinson ("AH-GEE, AH-GEE," the deaf man yells from the Ebbets Field grandstand, attempting to say "Jackie"), but eventually Dad's devotion wins the day in a moving finale. Colin Bootman, who earned a Coretta Scott Honor Award for *Almost to Freedom* (2003), uses evocative watercolors rich in soft browns and lush greens to capture both the feel of the 1940s (fedora-wearing fans) and the electricity of Robinson's play.

—*Bill Ott*

In the Year of the Boar and Jackie Robinson

Author: Bette Bao Lord
Illustrator: Marc Simont

Gr. 4. Young Chinese immigrant Shirley Temple Wong (a name she picked out for herself) becomes a Dodger fan, learning about America and rooting for Jackie Robinson. She begins to feel at home, and yet deep within herself, Shirley discovers that she wants to hold on to her memories of China, and the knowledge that she is Chinese inside, as well as American. She can be both—a "double happiness."

—*Scholastic Press*

We Are the Ship, The Story of Negro Leagues Baseball

Author and illustrator: Kadir Nelson

"We are the ship; all else the sea." —Rube Foster, founder of the Negro National League
Gr. 5–8. The story of Negro League baseball is the story of gifted athletes and determined owners; of racial discrimination and international sportsmanship; of fortunes won and lost; of triumphs and defeats on and off the field. It is a perfect mirror for the social and political history of black America in the first half of the twentieth century. But most of all, the story of the Negro Leagues is about hundreds of unsung heroes who overcame segregation, hatred, terrible conditions, and low pay to do the one thing they loved more than anything else in the world: play ball. Using an "Everyman" player as his narrator, Kadir Nelson tells the story of Negro League baseball from its beginnings in the 1920s through its decline after Jackie Robinson crossed over to the majors in 1947. The voice is so authentic, you will feel as if you are sitting on dusty bleachers listening intently to the memories of a man who has known the great ballplayers of that time and shared their experiences. But what makes this book so outstanding are the dozens of full-page and double-page oil paintings—breathtaking in their perspectives, rich in emotion, and created with understanding and affection for these lost heroes of our national game.

Satchel Paige, Striking Out Jim Crow

Author: James Strum
Illustrator: Rich Tommaso

Gr. 5–8. Baseball Hall of Famer Leroy "Satchel" Paige (1905? –1982) changed the face of the game in a career that spanned five decades. Much has been written about this larger-than-life pitcher, but when it comes to Paige, fact does not easily separate from fiction. He made a point of writing his own history . . . and then re-writing it. A tall, lanky fireballer, he was arguably the Negro League's hardest thrower, most entertaining storyteller and greatest gate attraction. Now the Center for Cartoon Studies turns a graphic novelist's eye to Paige's story. Told from the point of view of a sharecropper, this compelling narrative follows Paige from game to game as he travels throughout the segregated South.

In stark prose and powerful graphics, author and artist share the story of a sports hero, role model, consummate showman, and era-defining American.

A Whole New Ball Game: The Story of the All-American Girls Professional Baseball League

Author: Sue Macy

From Publishers Weekly—
Gr. 6–up. Macy offers an excellent introduction to one of the least explored areas of baseball history (recently popularized in the film *A League of Their Own*). Established by Chicago Cubs owner and chewing-gum magnate Phil Wrigley in 1943 as an entertainment alternative to the war-depleted major leagues, the AAGPBL lasted until 1954—and until very recently was all but forgotten. Macy has wisely chosen to focus not on the trivia of games

past (although the appendix offers enough statistics to satisfy the most rabid baseball addict) but on the social history that produced the league and on the experiences of its players. She writes frankly about such problems as alcoholism and unwanted sexual advances from team officials, fans and sportswriters. The book is particularly astute in its observations on the league as a forum for female bonding, something that few women of the time had at their disposal. Perhaps the most affecting passages concern the reluctance of AAGPBL veterans to discuss their experiences until the rise of the women's movement gave them a renewed sense of self-worth. These tough and funny women emerge as heroic figures worthy of admiration and emulation. Archival photographs add to the book's historical value and its sense of fun. A worthy addition to the library of any baseball fan.

Copyright 1993 Reed Business Information, Inc.

HEY Batta Batta SWING!

Authors: Sally Cook & James Charlton

Illustrator: Ross MacDonald

From Publishers Weekly—

Starred Review. Gr. 2–5. With a catchy, conversational style, the authors present a potpourri of anecdotes and facts that reveal the many ways baseball has changed over the years. One of the many entertaining aspects of the book is the way the writers weave insider slang into the narrative, highlighted in bold and defined in the margin (e.g., "gappers: hits between outfielders"; "tweeners: hits between infielders"). Fans will lap up details of the evolving style of the players' uniforms, the evolution of the jerseys' numbering system, the genesis of some of the stars' nicknames, and the ways that teammates have "doctored" balls and bats to enhance their performance. Among the kid-pleasing bits of trivia are the facts that, with only one umpire in the field in professional baseball's early days (rather than the current total of four), incidents of cheating regularly occurred, including players running directly from first to third base, and fielders tripping base runners. The book provides dates for

events and incidents on a spotty basis, rendering some of the comparisons between yesteryear and the present murky. With a signature style that recalls vintage cartoons, MacDonald's (*Another Perfect Day*) watercolor and pencil crayon illustrations pleasingly convey the text's lighthearted tone. Baseball buffs will find this a diverting—and occasionally wild—outing indeed.

Copyright © Reed Business Information

Jackie Robinson and the Integration of Baseball

Author: Scott Simon

"An extraordinary book . . . invitingly written and brisk."
—*Chicago Tribune*

"Perhaps no one has ever told the tale [of Robinson's arrival in the major leagues] so well as [Simon] does in this extended essay."
—*The Washington Post Book World*

"Scott Simon tells a compelling story of risk and sacrifice, profound ugliness and profound grace, defiance and almost unimaginable courage. This is a meticulously researched, insightful, beautifully written book, one that should be read, reread, and remembered."
—*Laura Hillenbrand, author of Seabiscuit*

The integration of baseball in 1947 had undeniable significance for the civil rights movement and American history. Thanks to Jackie Robinson, a barrier that had once been believed to be permanent was shattered—paving the way for scores of African Americans who wanted nothing more than to be granted the same rights as any other human being.

Only the Ball Was White

Director: Ken Solarz

Before Jackie Robinson broke the racial barrier in 1946, black American baseball players were restricted to playing in segregated leagues. *Only the Ball Was White* traces the birth and development of professional black teams, the incredible talent spawned there, and the throngs of faithful fans who flocked to the games. This documentary features an engaging look at legendary players Satchel

Paige, Roy Campanella, Buck Leonard, Jimmy Crutchfield, and other memorable black athletes. The documentary is based on a book by Robert Peterson.

Run Time: 30 minutes

—Sally Barber, All Movie Guide, *New York Times*

A League of Their Own, The Documentary
Director: Mary Wallace

The documentary that inspired Penny Marshall's film by the same title. Vintage film and stills along with interviews with the many of the original players. The actual charm school guide for players was located in the collections of the National Baseball Hall of Fame and can be accessed at the official site for the All-American Girls Professional Baseball League.

Run time: 35 minutes

www.aagpbl.org/league/charm.cfm

American Pastime
Director, Desmond Nakano

Powerful story about the dramatic impact WWII had in the home-front as Japanese American families were uprooted from their everyday lives and placed into internment camps in Western U.S. in the early 1940s. Faced with a country that now doubted their loyalty and struggling with their new situation, they turn to baseball as a way to handle their plight and find the strength to stand up for themselves, becoming a true symbol of honor and pride.

Run time: 107 minutes

www.youtube.com/watch?v=X-y_3c5Ma4I

Baseball, A Film by Ken Burns
The ultimate guide to baseball history on 10 DVD discs. A must for every school library.

Especially relevant: *Inning 5, Shadow Ball* and *Inning 6, The National Pastime.*

Baseball: Soundtrack
Thirty-one selections from the film.

National Baseball Hall of Fame and Museum
2006 Hall of Fame Induction Weekend

John "Buck" O'Neil welcomes the players and managers from the Negro Leagues into the Hall of Fame. Many were disappointed that Buck wasn't among those elected into the Hall, but upon learning he had not, his first impulse was to offer to speak. A moving tribute to the best of the best from the best of the best.

www.youtube.com/watch?v=LtE2I6jsung

There Was Always Sun Shining Someplace:
Life in the Negro Baseball Leagues

I'm a lifelong baseball fan, with a special interest in the Negro Leagues. I consider this the finest baseball documentary I've ever seen. The film exemplifies both technical expertise and great sensitivity to the subject matter. The interview sequence of the Pittsburgh Crawfords legendary outfield of Cool Papa Bell, Jimmie Crutchfield, and Ted Page stands as some of the best baseball footage ever. The director, Craig Davidson, has portrayed life in the shadows of black baseball with great brilliance and I give *There Was Always Sun Shining Someplace* my very highest recommendation.

VHS, Run time: 57 minutes

(amazon.com reviewer)

Diamond Cuts: 7th Inning Stretch

Seventh Inning Stretch is the seventh volume of the Diamond Cuts series of baseball song compilations. The collections are inspired by a passion for baseball, music, and helping others. Proceeds from sale of CDs benefit Hungry for Music's programs for disadvantaged youth.

The Post-Game Show

Celebrating in triumph, Steve Gromek and Larry Doby embrace and laugh after the fourth game of the 1948 World Series in Cleveland. Doby hit the home run which decided the outcome, 2-1, making Gromek the winning pitcher. The picture, one of the first to show affection between black and white athletes in the era of integration, became one of Doby's most cherished mementos. (Photo courtesy of Wide World)

They say that all good things must end someday. And true to that understanding, the Negro Leagues that had seen so many exceptional players, teams, and moments in baseball history, have receded into the distant past. What legacy did they leave behind? As might be expected, the answer is complicated. There is much to celebrate in the story of the people and events that made up the Negro Leagues. But, there is also much to lament about their passing.

No one would argue that the integration of baseball was less than the right thing to do. As early as the 1920s sports-writers for the black press had begun a campaign for integration that persisted up to the signing of Jackie Robinson and continued as they urged other teams to open their doors to African-American players. Indeed full integration into all avenues of American life was the goal of all civil rights activity for a century and more. But ushering in this new era in baseball history, for all the righteousness of its mission, would of necessity usher out the old. To call it anything less than a bittersweet transition would be less than honest. Although much was ultimately gained, much was lost.

Negro Leagues baseball was a multiplier industry for the entire black community. As the leagues grew, so did all of the adjacent enterprises necessary for servicing the teams, their travel needs, and their personnel. As a result, black-owned hotels and restaurants flourished. The black press had a steady audience because of its extensive coverage of the teams, the players, and the games; information that could not be found in the general circulation press. Stadiums were built, cars were bought, souvenirs were

Pitcher Steve Gromek hugging his rookie teammate Larry Doby after Doby's home run won game four of the 1948 World Series for the Cleveland Indians.

1. Robert Peterson, Lyle Wilson, Robert Buck, and Lawrence Hogan, "Forgotten Legacy," in Lawrence D. Hogan, *Shades of Glory: The Negro Leagues and the Story of African American Baseball,* (Washington, DC: National Geographic Press, 2006), p. 351.

2. *Ibid.,* p. 351

3. *Ibid.,* p. 352

4. *Ibid.,* p. 372.

5. *Ibid.,* p. 372.

6. *Ibid.,* p. 373.

sold, and the list goes on. These businesses, like the Negro Leagues and the black press were, "founded during segregation and served their people's cause well."[1] It is impossible to overestimate the impact of how much the Negro Leagues fueled the economies of the black community.

Wins & Loses

In short, "The Negro National League gave colored players a chance to develop skill and prowess and earn a lucrative salary when the majors had their doors barred."[2] Once considered to be unequal to the caliber of play in the major leagues, teams across the country competed for them. "Mel Goode, who had fought against segregation as a crusading journalist . . . witnessed the trade-offs that the struggle for equality sometimes entailed. He recognized that integration meant an end to the Negro Leagues. 'We gained something, but we lost something too. But what we gained was the greater. We got our self-respect, and you have to be black to understand what that meant.'"[3]

Over the course of the ten years following Robinson's historic signing, the Negro Leagues suffered an agonizing loss of players and revenues, until in 1958 the Negro American League had only four teams and "by 1963 black players were common—and dominant—in the major leagues."[4] Finally laid to rest was the notion that African-American baseball players would be unable to compete at the major league level. In every category of measurement these players showed themselves to be more than equal to the task. During the first decades of integration the Most Valuable Player Award went to black players eleven times. Jackie Robinson, the first Rookie of the Year, was followed nine out of the next ten years by former Negro League players. "Four of the top five players in the National League in 1963 were African Americans. All five league leaders for stolen bases were black."[5] Baseball gurus like Bob Feller and Larry McPhail, as well as the editors of the *Sporting News,* who had predicted that few black players would make it in the majors were forced to admit they were wrong. The African-American players not only excelled individually but they "changed the way in which baseball was played . . . reintroduc[ing] speed and base running into a game that had been dominated for three decades by power hitting."[6]

These achievements are offered only as a way of showing that major league baseball did itself a favor by integrating. And, in light of the documented and anecdotal evidence gleaned from the years of segregation, it is clear that the major leagues were fully aware of the talent these players had. They had competed against them and lost in too many exhibition games to harbor any conviction that the African-American players weren't superior athletes.

The Legacy

Their legacy, however, goes far beyond the impact they had on the national pasttime. As Buck O'Neil looked back on his years as both a player and manager in the Negro Leagues, he, like many others, saw the leagues as contributors to the progress of American society as a whole in becoming a land of equality for all.

> Yet when you look back, what people didn't realize, and still don't, was that we got the ball rolling on integration in our whole society. Remember, this was before Brown. . . . When Branch Rickey signed Jackie, Martin Luther King was a student at Morehouse College. We showed the way it had to be done, by just keeping on and being the best we could. . . . When I look at what happened to Jackie, I get a chill up my spine. But I also get a bittersweet feeling because I remember that a lot of people lost their whole way of life. That was another of those ironies, the hardest one. Not only did a black business die (the Negro Leagues) but other black businesses did too, the ones that were dependent on black baseball and black entertainment. The Streets Hotel (in Kansas City) had to close because it couldn't compete with the Muehlebach Hotel downtown.
>
> A way of life came to an end along with black baseball. But I guess it couldn't be any other way. The white-only hotels had to die, too, for integration to work, and that ended another way of life.[7]

7. John "Buck" O'Neil, quoted in Peterson, et al., p. 377.

For too long the history of the Negro Leagues has been, as Peterson, et. al., titled their chapter in *Shades of Glory*, a "Forgotten Legacy." Fortunately, that is changing. Ted Williams called for it in an unexpected exhortation to the National Baseball Hall of Fame in 1966 during his induction speech: "I hope that someday the names of Satchel Paige and Josh Gibson in some way could be added as a symbol of the great Negro players that are not here only because they were not given the chance." Five years later, the first of the former Negro Leagues players, Satchel Paige, was inducted into the National Baseball Hall of Fame with more to follow. These early inductees were players who were young enough when baseball became integrated to be able to play the necessary 10 years in the majors. Most Negro Leagues players never had that chance. However, since that time, in recognition of the fact that the qualifying rules of the Hall disqualified most of the Negro Leagues players, the rules have been revised so that players from the Negro Leagues who never played in the major leagues, can be considered. As a result, in 2006, sixteen players and one manager, Effa Manley, were inducted. Now over two dozen former Negro Leagues players have a home in the Hall. This is a start, but hardly redresses the years of discrimination or satisfies scholars who continue to advocate on behalf of players that are still not in the Hall like Frank Grant and Sol White who were discussed in Chapter One. At the time, many were disappointed that Buck O'Neil, baseball's acknowledged Ambassador of Goodwill, was not selected for induction into the Hall in 2006 when 17 worthy others were chosen. His biographer, Joe Posnanski, wrote what so many thought:

> His accomplishments as a player (a Negro leagues batting champion), a manager (his Kansas City Monarchs teams were the best in Negro Leagues baseball multiple times), a coach (he was the first African-American coach in baseball), a scout (signed Ernie Banks, Lou Brock, Joe Carter and Lee Smith, among others) and a celebrator of the game (impossible to sum up) were well-known. Everyone had seemed so sure that the committee would honor him—and I have little doubt that was the Hall of Fame's intention when it formed the committee—and the no vote on that day in February, when 17 others were elected, came as a jolt. I was there. I saw it.
>
> Buck handled it with dignity, of course. He was quiet for a little while. And then, just minutes after that, he started wondering if he might be asked to introduce the 16 dead men and one dead woman who were elected. And when I asked him why he would consider doing that—indeed, he DID introduce them in Cooperstown in one of his last public appearances—he said to me words that still echo in my head: "Son, what has my life been about?"
>
> What was Buck's life about? It was about baseball, of course. It was about love. It was about faith. It was about honoring those who, in their own small ways, had helped changed the world. And it was about doing his best to make sure people did not forget. Again and again, across the country, he would tell people small stories about Satchel Paige and Cool Papa Bell and Josh Gibson and Oscar Charleston and many others. He would talk about the pulse of neighborhoods in black communities in the 1930s and 1940s, with jazz playing on neon-lit Saturday nights and baseball on brilliantly bright Sunday afternoons.
>
> "And," he would always say, "we could play." [8]

8. http://joeposnanski. si.com/ 2011/02/23/ the-buck-oneil-award/

As the National Baseball Hall of Fame continues to redress years of exclusion, they've now placed a life-sized statue of Buck at the entrance to the gallery to acknowledge a lifetime of contributions to the game of baseball and created an award that bears his name. Buck would be pleased. But to all who might be saddened that he wasn't among the players that could transition from the Negro Leagues to the majors when integration began, he would say to them the words he often spoke and that are now engraved on his statue: "Waste no tears for me. I didn't come along too early. I was right on time."

Buck's legacy is, of course, about more than honors, and he had his share. When the nation got to know Buck in Ken Burns' epic nine-part documentary, *Baseball*, they were able to put a face on a past they knew little about. As Buck spoke in his comforting drawl, eyes crinkled at the corners with mischief, America opened their hearts to him, and by extension, to all the players they missed out on because of prejudice. In his way, and thanks to Ken Burns' work, a fresh layer of the civil rights story unfolded. This excerpt sums up Buck O'Neil's philosophy. He was asked, "What has baseball taught you?"

> It is a religion. For me. You understand? If you go by the rules, it is a right. The things that you can do. The things that you can't do, that you aren't supposed to do. And if these are carried out, it makes a beautiful picture overall. It's a very beautiful thing because it taught me and it teaches everyone else to live by the rules, to abide by the rules. I think sports in general teaches a guy humility. I can see a guy hit the ball out of the ballpark, or a grand slam home run to win a baseball game, and that same guy can come up tomorrow in that situation and miss the ball and lose the ball game. It can bring you up here but don't get too damn cocky because tomorrow it can bring you down there. See? But one thing about it though, you know there always will be a tomorrow. You got me today, but I'm coming back.[9]

In Service to the Cause

Examples of other former Negro Leagues players like Buck O'Neil and Jackie Robinson who used their talent and celebrity status to work on behalf of civil rights abound. He was not alone. Joe Black, a baseball pioneer, was the first African-American pitcher to win a game in the World Series and the only major leaguer to become a health and physical education teacher after his playing days were over. In retirement he became an executive with Greyhound Bus Lines and an ambassador for kids and baseball wherever he went. When John F. Kennedy won the presidency, Joe Black was among the first to contact him, volunteering his services to work with Kennedy and, "wanting to know how he could assist the new nations of Africa" on behalf of the United States.[10]

Another example of a player advocate is Curt Flood. Although not as well known as either Jackie Robinson or Joe Black, his efforts on behalf of baseball players forever changed the game as he took his message of equity into the board rooms of Major League Baseball. As George Will tells the story, "There was poetry and portent in the fact that Curt Flood's career blossomed in St. Louis, the city where Dred Scott had taken his case to court . . . to ask whether a man can be treated like someone's property. That is the question Curt Flood posed when the Cardinals tried to trade

9. *Ibid.*

10. Thurston Clarke, *Ask Not: The Inauguration of John F. Kennedy and the Speech that Changed America*, (New York: Penguin Books, 2011), p. 20.

11. George Will, "Dred Scott in Spikes," *Bunts*, (New York: Simon&Schuster, 1998) pp. 277-278.

him. They said he had to go wherever they decided to send him." Flood, like Scott, took his case against the "reserve clause" that denied players the right to negotiate the terms of their employment, to court and like Scott lost. But "he had lit a fuse. Six years later—too late to benefit him—his cause prevailed. The national pastime is clearly better because of that. But more important, the nation, because it has learned one more lesson about the foolishness of fearing freedom."[11] As he put it, "I am pleased that God made my skin black, but I wish he'd made it thicker."

America needed to learn how to adjust to a desegregated society and much of that learning began in baseball clubhouses and on the playing fields of America's ballparks. One way involved a candid snapshot of pitcher Steve Gromek hugging his rookie teammate Larry Doby after Doby's home run won game four of the 1948 World Series for the Cleveland Indians. At the time the picture was shocking to many Americans. In the same way that Pee Wee Reese's arm around Jackie Robinson quieted a raucous crowd, Gromek and Doby taught us that baseball, and by extension, life is bigger than racial barriers. The big difference between Pee Wee's gesture and the spontaneous hug in the clubhouse is that while Pee Wee's gesture was seen by the crowd at the stadium that night, the photo was broadcast on all the television stations around the country and printed in every newspaper. Although thought shocking at the time, it has become an iconic representation of the early years of an infant civil rights movement, doing its part to change hearts and minds.

There are countless other examples of the many ways African-American players advocated for and advanced the cause of liberty both on and off the playing field. How could they not? Their very presence was a challenge to the status quo and required all Americans to reassess their thoughts about race in American life; often while reading the morning paper's sports page.

The lessons that accompany this section are all about legacy and making connections to the past through the actions of today. To do this students will research the ball parks where so much of this history was made, participate in the Grave Marker Project, watch, listen, and respond to the documentary, *There was Always Sun Shining Someplace*, and take virtual road trips to the National Baseball Hall of Fame in Cooperstown, New York and the Negro Leagues Baseball Museum in Kansas City, Missouri.

Lesson 1: Legacy Projects
Stadiums and Cemeteries

Hinchliffe Stadium in Paterson, N.J., one of the last surviving stadiums that hosted Negro League baseball

There is perhaps nothing greener than the grass in a ballpark. You walk out from the dark interior of the stadium with its concession stands filled with the most enticing aromas a ballpark could offer—grilling hot dogs, popping corn, cotton candy—that waft through the air, you get dizzy from the utter sensuousness of it. But, all that falls away as you walk through the tunnel that will take you to your seat. There it is: the most brilliant blue sky you've ever seen and the greenest grass in the world. They stop you in your tracks and you gasp to see such a wonder. That world of hot dogs and baseball is also part of the grand legacy of Negro League baseball. For this project students can work in pairs or in groups to write the history of a baseball stadium, the teams that played there, or anything else about it that piques their interest.

Students can use a graphic organizer like the one below to take notes before creating a visual representation (collage, poster, drawing, etc.) of the park's "life."

NAME OF THE BALLPARK	WHERE IT IS (WAS) LOCATED	TEAMS OR GAMES PLAYED THERE	WHEN IT OPENED/ CLOSED	IMPORTANT MEMORIES ABOUT IT

The links below will take students to the websites for the ballparks.

Rickwood Field: www.rickwood.com/

Pop Lloyd Baseball Stadium:
www.pbs.org/opb/historydetectives/investigation/pop-lloyd-baseball-stadium/

Silver Stadium: http://en.wikipedia.org/wiki/Silver_Stadium

Comiskey Park: http://en.wikipedia.org/wiki/Comiskey_Park

Ruppert Stadium: www.oldnewark.com/sports/buildings/ruppert.htm *and*
http://en.wikipedia.org/wiki/Ruppert_Stadium_(Newark)

The Negro Leagues Baseball Grave Marker Project

Because so many of the players from the days of the Negro Leagues faded unsung into the past, a new project to honor their contributions to baseball and to civil rights history has begun.

• Students can, in this lesson, dig into history at the start of something big, The Negro Leagues Baseball Grave Marker Project. Students can follow this link: **www.nlbgmp.com/** to find out about the project, the players, and how to become involved.

After they've had the opportunity to read the information organized on the website, students should be ready to answer the questions:

Why was the project started?

Why do the people involved feel this project is important?

• More information on both the stadiums and the Grave Marker Project can be found at **www.nlbm.com/** the website for the Negro Leagues Baseball Museum.

• You will find another good source for commentary on the importance of the leagues and this project at **www.thegrio.com/black-history/sports/get-to-know-the-negro-leagues.php**.

The best way for students to become involved is to work toward a relevant and meaningful goal. As mentioned in Chapter 6, Connie Morgan's grave at the Mount Lawn Cemetery in Sharon Hill, Pennsylvania, remains unmarked. Knowing her story can inspire a personal commitment in students, helping them to see participating in the Graves Marker Project as a way to honor someone they care about. Done as a class project or school project, the effort to raise funds itself will raise awareness of this chapter in history. As a service-learning project, it will immerse students in an authentic, necessary, and relevant way to learn all the important lessons service learning can teach.

Lesson 2: Watch, Listen, and Reflect
Using Documentary Films

This highly acclaimed film released in 1989 has a run time of 58 minutes. Narrated by the inimitable James Earl Jones, this trip in the Wayback machine lets kids see and hear what it meant to be part of the Negro Leagues through rare archival footage of the games and through interviews with former players and managers. Its compact length also lends itself to being viewed in either a single class period or broken into smaller segments. Told through reminiscences and stories—bittersweet, humorous, and emotional—students will have the opportunity to develop authentic empathy with the folks they meet and get to know.

Because the film is so filled with stories, we would urge teachers to use this film as a way to allow students to think about the stories more than dig for discrete information. In other words, allow students to become immersed in the experiences they will be seeing and hearing about so that they can draw conclusions, formulate their own questions, and think about the America these players inhabited and its place in their own understanding about the American past.

Teachers can prepare students for viewing by reviewing a set of "things to look for" that the class can talk about later. A reflective analysis sheet with suggestions for this is included below.

After viewing the film, students can work with a

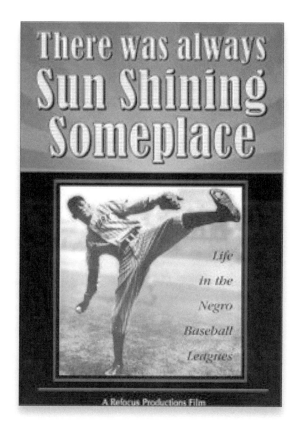

There Was Always Sun Shining
Someplace, Life in the Negro Leagues
Craig Davidson, Director
Narrated by James Earl Jones
Formats: DVD & VHS
Run time: 58 minutes
1984
America Library Assoc.:
www.ala.org/programming/
pridepassion/ppssn33

partner or in groups to talk about what they heard and listened to before participating in a full class discussion.

The real power of a film like this is to give faces and voices to historical events. As much as students can benefit from *reading* about the Jim Crow years, *seeing* a film such as the homecoming parade of the all-black 369th Infantry Division combat unit who fought in WWI under the French flag because they were not allowed to join American combat units, will make a deeper impression on them. Textbooks may say that African Americans were not allowed to join combat units during WWI, but they are unlikely to add that African Americans eager to fight were welcomed into French units. Where textbook versions leave the impression that no African-American men saw combat in WWI and were relegated to menial tasks only, documentary films clearly show this is only part of the story.

There Was Always Sun Shining Someplace, Life in the Negro Leagues is filled with those "rest of the story moments" that will surprise, outrage, and delight students. For example the story of a black team arriving at a café in Alabama and being turned away, no service for them, and being told the only thing they could have was a drink of water from the well out back. They got their drinks from a drinking gourd commonly used by southerners and began to leave, still hungry of course, only to look back and see the café's owner breaking the gourd to bits because they had used it. If this makes them angry, it should. Building care and concern for the past is critical to remembering and understanding it. When studying history elicits an emotional response, it's much more likely to be remembered. If we want students to remember what we teach, we need to teach, show, and talk with them about something memorable.

BUILD ANTICIPATION

1. Based on the picture on its cover, what do you think you'll see in this film?

2. What are some things you'd *like* to see in this film?

3. This film is in black and white. Why do you think that is?

4. Things to think about while you watch:

_____

_____

SURVEY REACTIONS

When it's over, we'll talk about what you think the filmmakers really want you to understand about this topic. What do you think the message is?

1. How do you think the filmmakers wanted you to respond to their film?

2. What are two or three things that you'll remember about life in America for African Americans during this time period?

3. Did *seeing* the film help you understand more about this time period than you would have by just *reading* about it? What?

4. What are some questions you'd ask the filmmakers or someone who was in the film, if you could talk with them?

5. How can you find out the answers to your questions?

6. Now that you've watched the film, why do you think the title is: *There Was Always Sun Shining Someplace*?

Lesson 3: Using Place as a Primary Source
Virtual Road Trips

Virtual Road Trips: Cooperstown, New York, and Kansas City, Missouri

Cooperstown, New York, and the **National Baseball Hall of Fame and Museum** are the yearly destination of baseball fans from all over the country. Although we know now that Abner Doubleday did not invent the game in Cooperstown, the legend was well in place by the 1930s and has remained ever since. You and your students may be interested in reading the story of how Cooperstown came to be the national shrine to baseball in this article by Eric Miklick and posted

on the website *19c Baseball:* **www.19cbaseball.com/game-2.html** or on the Wikipedia page: **http://en.wikipedia.org/wiki/Origins_of_baseball** to see how a fabrication became a legend and ultimately turned into reality.

http://baseballhall.org/

Most people are familiar with the National Baseball Hall of Fame and Museum at Cooperstown. Less well known is the **Negro Leagues Baseball Museum in Kansas City, Missouri.** According to the website it was "founded in 1990 as a privately funded, non-profit organization dedicated to preserving the rich history of African-American baseball."

www.nlbm.com/s/index.cfm

Each website offers a variety of exhibits and materials just waiting for students to explore. While it would be nice to be able to take students to each of the museums, it's not possible for most teachers. The next best thing is a virtual field trip. Like a walk through an actual museum, a virtual field trip should be perceived by students as a rich opportunity to see and enjoy new things. For that reason, it's really important to keep that in mind while designing a virtual field trip.

The keys to making virtual field trips valuable and pleasant learning experiences include clear goals for the work, careful preparation, and solid follow up. Without these in place, students are likely to be frustrated because they are unsure of what is expected or, worse, see computer lab time as free time. We have to raise their level of concern by making it clear that the virtual field trip is an essential element of their learning, and that they will be held accountable, through assessment of their work, for the learning experiences planned.

The first step requires that the teacher does an exhaustive advance search of the actual site. This gives you an opportunity to see what the site has to offer, how easy or not so easy the site is to nav-igate, what features may be especially engaging for students, and more. This first step is absolutely essential. And, because the National Baseball Hall of Fame and Museum is a huge site, this is even more important.

The next step is to work with the site so that you can give students precise directions for them to follow. For example, the film, "There Was Always Sun Shining Someplace," that students saw as part of lesson 2, has a segment about the influence that playing in Latin American countries had on baseball in the United States. If you would like to extend that learning with materials from the National Baseball Hall of Fame and Museum, you could just tell them to go to http://exhibits.baseballhalloffame.org/viva/ and answer the questions you've prepared. But, if you want them to practice finding materials on websites, you could have them begin on the home page first, then follow the directions below.

- Go to http://baseballhall.org/

- Highlight "Museum" on the locator bar

- Move the cursor to "Exhibits" in the drop-down menu

- Select "Viva Baseball" from the second drop-down menu

- Read the introductory material and then scroll to the bottom of the page to click on the link for "Viva Baseball online"

- Then tell them which of the links, History, Roster, or Timeline, you want them to follow so they can easily find answers to questions you've prepared.

Suppose you want students to find information about specific Negro Leagues players and the rules that govern future inductions of Negro Leagues players into the Hall. To locate the rules, you can save students an enormous amount of time by having them start on the home page.

- Highlight "Hall of Famers"

- Select "Rules for Election" from the drop-down menu

- Choose: "Eras: Pre-integration"

To find the complete list of current inductees who were members of the Negro Leagues is even easier. Once students are in the section of the web page dedicated to Hall of Famers, they can simply scroll

to the box in the lower right-hand corner of the page and click on "search." Since "Negro Leaguer" is the default setting, there's nothing further needed.

The website for the Negro Leagues Baseball Museum is smaller and easier to navigate. Solid preparation is still necessary but students are less apt to get "lost" here. Probably the most striking and daunting feature of this site is its wordiness. Features that students are apt to find interesting, however, would include the Legacy Awards and the Educational Resources found by clicking on "Education

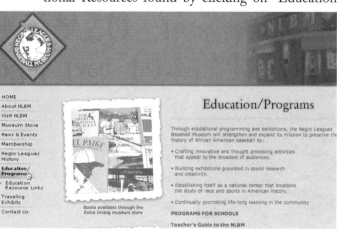

Programs." All of the education resource links open to beautifully illustrated materials with timelines, biographies, the history of baseball uniforms, and much more.

The Legacy Awards honor African-American players and are named in honor of the great Negro League players of the past like Cool Papa Bell, Oscar Charleston, Josh Gibson, and Buck O'Neil. For students who are now familiar with these names, seeing who has been honored by these awards will be especially meaningful.

The better the preparation and the clearer the directions, the less time will be wasted because students can't find what they are looking for. Without solid preparation a potentially powerful learning experience can become little more than an exercise in frustration for students and for you.

Setting clear goals is also important. How much

time you have available will determine how many goals you can meet, but when in doubt, have fewer rather than more. For students, trying to complete a worksheet bristling with specific questions to answer turns the experience into a stressful race against the clock. A better approach is to ask fewer questions and to keep them open ended. Of course, there will be specific features you'll want to draw the students' attention to, but beyond that, students should have some time to explore the site on their own so one of the questions you might ask could be, "What did you find that you especially liked or were surprised by? Tell a little about it."

A sample organizer is included below.

VIRTUAL TOUR GUIDE

- Where are you? _____

- What do you hope you'll see? _____

- If you are traveling with a friend, put his or her name here. _____

WHAT DO YOU ALREADY KNOW ABOUT THIS LOCATION?	WHAT DO YOU NEED TO KNOW?	WHAT DID YOU DISCOVER WHILE YOU WERE HERE?	WHAT QUESTIONS DO YOU STILL HAVE?

- What are some possible sources you can use to answer the questions you still have? _____

_____

_____

Sacrifice Bunts

The bunt is a ballet production all its own. As the batter squares to drop the ball in front of the plate, watch the first and third basemen come huffing toward home, kicking up dust; watch the second baseman stealing toward first to take the throw while the shortstop covers second and the outfielders charge in to back up the bases in the event of an overthrow. It takes a lot of years watching baseball to learn not to follow the ball every second. When everyone is in motion, it is like watching those delicate long-legged insects skim over calm water.[1]

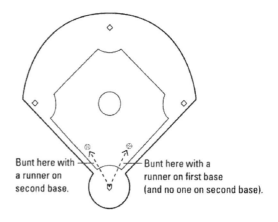

Bunt here with a runner on second base.

Bunt here with a runner on first base (and no one on second base).

In baseball a bunt is a "baby" hit. In this offensive strategy the batter holds the bat in front of him and taps the ball, grounding it toward the infield attempting to send it beyond the easy reach of the catcher and pitcher, forcing the infielders to run in for it and allowing the batter, if he's speedy enough, to reach first base. It requires dexterity, focus, knowledge of the fielders, and being able to read the pitches; not all pitches are good bunting pitches. It's one of the more demanding plays in the game. But a very important, potentially game-changing, kind of bunt is the sacrifice bunt. In this play the batter deliberately creates a productive out that will advance a base runner; exchanging the out for the chance to move the runner into scoring position, most often moving the runner from first base to second. Because a sacrifice bunt doesn't count as an official "at bat," it doesn't accrue any advantage for the batter, but can be critical to the success of the team.[2]

George Will offers an apt example of just how critical a successful sacrifice bunt can be in his Introduction to *Bunts*. The Baltimore Orioles and the Cleveland Indians were playing in the American League Championship Series for the right to represent their league in the World Series. Cleveland already had won three of the first five games of the seven-game series and needed only one more victory to advance. Both teams were scoreless in the seventh inning of Game Six and with the Oriole's pitcher,

1. W. P. Kinsella, *The Iowa Baseball Confederacy*, (Boston: Houghton Mifflin, 1986).

2. Joe Morgan and Richard Lally, *Baseball for Dummies*, www.dummies.com/how-to/content/bunting-in-baseball.html

Mike Mussina, in complete control of the Indian's bats, it was becoming increasingly clear that a single run could make the difference. The first two Oriole batters in the inning hit singles and the table was set for a sacrifice bunt that would move the base runners into scoring position and possibly plating the runner on second. Roberto Alomar, one of the Oriole's best bunters attempted to execute the play but his bunt was hit too hard, lobbing it directly to the charging third baseman who grabbed it, turned and threw it to the shortstop now covering third base in time to get the lead runner out. With one out and runners at first and second, the situation no longer called for a sacrifice bunt and the next batter was forced to swing away, promptly grounding into a double play that ended both the inning and the Oriole threat.

The game was still scoreless in the 11th inning when Joey Fernandez launched a walk-off home run into the night and the Cleveland Indians were on their way to the World Series as American League Champions. It was only their third hit of the game and serves to magnify the importance of the Oriole's failed opportunity to score in the 7th inning. Will and students of the game agree that the pivotal play of the game was the blown bunt attempt that shut down the Oriole threat and changed the momentum of the game. The rest is, of course, history.

3. George Will, *Bunts*, (New York: Touchstone Books) 1999.

As George Will remarks in wonderful understatement, "Bunts are modest and often useful things." And indeed they are. But in baseball, as in life, it is often the modest act that is the most useful.[3]

Inspired by Will's collection of short essays, we've gathered a collection of our own; a sampling of sacrifice bunts laid down by the men and women of the Negro Leagues and others of their era. In each, the "hero" essentially offers themselves up for the good of the cause: the broader goal of expanding civil rights in America. Each in his own way was moving the runners along. The useful concept of the sacrifice bunt can help students see the really important courage it took to be willing to make the small but critical sacrifices that ultimately overcame the institutional, customary, and statutory infrastructure of Jim Crow America.

Any researcher will readily admit that in the course of crafting a narrative, many stories are left behind for a variety of reasons, but mostly because they don't quite fit. Rather than discarding these stories, we decided to stitch together the best of them in order to let them speak about times and places we need to remember.

Lunch at the Jim Crow Diner

This first set of recollections recall the frustrations, humiliations, and satisfactions to be had in pursuing the simple act of having dinner.

Little Pieces

Monte Irvin was traveling through rural Mississippi with the Newark Eagles of the Negro National League when the team bus stopped at a small roadside café. He could already see a woman standing at the top of the stairs leading to the entrance—she was shaking her head. He walked over and politely asked: "Why are you shaking your head if we haven't asked for anything yet?" Her reply was simple and direct: "Whatever you want, we don't have any." Recognizing that they would receive no food service here, Irvin asked if any water was available. She directed the players to the back of the building where there was a well and a dipper made from a gourd. The players refreshed themselves and were returning to the bus when Irvin glanced behind. He saw that the woman had reached into the well to retrieve the gourd and was busy breaking it into little pieces.

John Virtue, *South of the Color Barrier: How Jorge Pasquel and the Mexican League Pushed Baseball Toward Racial Integration.* (Jefferson, NC: McFarland & Co., 2008), p. 43.

Jim Crow Silverware

The Indianapolis Clowns were accustomed to being kept waiting for service, particularly in the border states along the Mason-Dixon line, where restaurants would serve black clientele but in a decidedly hostile manner. The team devised their own strategy in response to this kind of discrimination—they referred to it as the "three strikes and you're out" rule. They would sit patiently at their table and after allowing five or more minutes to pass, would flag down a waiter. "In a minute" was the standard reply—strike one. Additional time would pass but the players remained patient, before again summoning a waiter. "Be right there" they were told—strike two. If additional time passed with continued neglect, one final attempt for service would be made from the table. A further dismissal signified "strike three." The players would proceed to take all the silverware from the table, put it in their pockets, and leave the restaurant. Upon returning home to Indianapolis, they would visit their favorite black hotel and make a gift to its owner of the pocketed "Jim Crow silverware."

Martha Ackmann, *Curveball: The Remarkable Story of Toni Stone.* (Chicago: Lawrence Hill Books, 2010), p. 153.

The Waste Riddance Fee

Alan J. Pollock with James A. Riley, eds. *Barnstorming to Heaven: Syd Pollock and His Great Black Teams.* (Tuscaloosa: University of Alabama Press, 2006), p. 144.

Felix "Chin" Evans was one of the top pitchers in the Negro Leagues during the 1930s and 40s. He was initially a part-time player, disdaining road trips in order to complete his teaching degree at Morehouse College. He assumed full-time status upon graduation, and went on to enjoy a stellar 16-year career. His many bus trips throughout the South and neighboring border states may have sensitized his eyes and ears to the Jim Crow segregation and discrimination he regularly encountered, but such treatment could not touch his heart, mind, or soul. And one day, he decided to make a statement.

Against his teammates' advice, Chin walked into a small restaurant in Washington, D.C., well known by the team for its disparaging treatment of black patrons—the sound of breaking china had been heard there by the team as it was leaving on more than one occasion. While the team bus waited outside, he seated himself at a table and was promptly approached by the restaurant's owner, who glanced out the window at the bus and muttered about the "damn nigger ball club" as he made his way back to the kitchen. Chin ignored the behavior and the derisive comments, ordered his lunch, and ate at a leisurely pace. Upon completion of the meal, he presented his host with a twenty-dollar bill, with instructions to "keep the change." Recognizing that the total cost of the meal came to less than one dollar, the surprised owner replied: "Pretty big tip for a nigger clown." Chin replied that it wasn't a tip at all: "It's a waste riddance fee." He proceeded to reach into his pocket and withdraw a hammer. With his other hand, he pulled the tablecloth up and over all the dinnerware and proceeded to smash every cup, plate, and saucer that had been on the table. Chin turned to the owner and smiled: "Just throw the nigger dishes out in the nigger tablecloth and keep the change." He walked out of the restaurant and onto the team bus, where he was greeted with the cheers of respect and admiration from his teammates.

Breakfast of Champions?

Aaron, Hank, with Lonnie Wheeler. *I Had a Hammer: The Hank Aaron Story.* (New York: Harper Torch, 1991), p. 47

Henry Aaron's exceptional baseball skills guaranteed him a relatively short tour through the Negro Leagues. His time was sufficient however, to acquaint him with the sounds of shattered dinnerware, and although quite young, shy, and inexperienced, he instantly understood the message being sent. Years later, he would recall such incidents with the hurt and anger that he was forced to suppress at the time. "If dogs had eaten off those plates, they'd have washed them." Jim Crow made certain that African Americans were treated as less than human.

Over There: African-American Troops in WWI

Approximately 380,000 African-American soldiers served in the United States' military in WWI. Of this number, some 200,000 served in Europe, with 48,000 participating in active combat. Perhaps most notable among the latter was the 15th Regiment from New York, reorganized as the 369th Infantry Regiment once they were stationed in France, and later to be christened "The Harlem Hellfighters." They earned the distinction of having served 191 days on the front lines, the longest such tenure of any Allied regiment in the war, and they were the first American regiment to reach the Rhine River. They distinguished themselves in several crucial campaigns and their courage and tenacity under fire came to be highly respected by their French comrades and highly feared by their German adversaries. However, distrust in their character and ability by American military officials helped to create yet another distinction—the inability to represent their own homeland. They were assigned to the French command for the duration of the war, marching into battle under the French flag, wearing French uniforms.

Anthony Gero,
*Black Soldiers of
New York State: A
Proud Legacy.*
(New York: SUNY
Albany Press, 2009)
p. 50.

Parléz-vous français?

The all-black 15th Regiment from New York was assigned to Spartanburg, South Carolina for their basic military training and racial tension was already in the air before they arrived. The city's mayor informed the issue: "I was sorry to learn that [they] were ordered here, for, with their northern ideas about race equality, they will probably be expecting to be treated like white men. I can say right here that they will not be treated as anything except Negroes. . . . This thing is like waving a red flag in the face of a bull, something that can't be done without trouble." The regiment's popular and accomplished marching band nonetheless provided a soothing and positive introduction, playing an outdoor concert on their first Saturday night in town. A large crowd of white citizens stood watch, muttering derisive comments to each other, but they otherwise listened without incident. The next day, the Spartanburg Chamber of Commerce contacted the unit to ask whether they'd be available to play the following Saturday at the local country club.

In the interest of keeping the peace, the black soldiers of the 15th Regiment agreed to follow local Jim Crow practice whenever they went into town and to do their best to look the other way when insulted. However, the soldiers of the white regiments also training in Spartanburg had made no such promise and many became unlikely allies of their fellow soldiers when they witnessed instances of discrimination and abuse. They routinely confronted and berated restaurant and store personnel when they refused to serve a black soldier. When a black private was physically assaulted for taking "too long" to leave a sidewalk that was occupied by several white residents, a group of white soldiers intervened and beat his attackers into submission. In another incident, the manager of a downtown hotel knocked a black soldier down for failing to doff his hat before buying a newspaper in the lobby. Military officers had to be called to keep a group of white troops from burning the place down. Such incidents prompted military officials to cut short their training and return the regiment to New York, with plans to resume the training once the unit was deployed in France. History thus records that a regiment of the United States Army was forced to complete its training in a foreign country—solely because it provided a safer and friendlier environment than did their own.[3]

Somewhere, Over the Rainbow

The 15th Regiment returned to New York City in the fall of 1917 to prepare for their deployment to Europe. They were considered part of New York State's contribution to the 42nd Division, a federally organized group of 26 National Guard units, each representing a different state. Douglas MacArthur was instrumental in its creation and is said to have remarked of the Division that it "stretches like a Rainbow, from one end of America to the other"—it was thereafter commonly referred to as "The Rainbow Division." On December 17th, the Division marched proudly through the streets of New York to the cheers and applause of the many thousands who turned out to bid them farewell. One unit was missing however—the all-black 15th Regiment was not allowed to participate. When their commanding officer protested the snub he was reportedly told: "Black is not a color of the rainbow."

A Different Drummer

Jazz–A Film by Ken Burns
www.pbs.org/jazz/time/time_wwi.htm

New Year's Day, 1918—The 15th Regiment landed in Brest, France, and their regimental band struck up its distinctive version of *Marsellaise* to a welcoming crowd of soldiers, sailors, and citizens, all of whom seemed surprised to see an all-black regiment under the American flag. Perhaps even more surprising was the spirit and rhythm with which the band performed, so much so that it took the French eight to ten bars to recognize that they were listening to their own national anthem! A band member recalls that "there came over their faces an astonished look," quickly followed "by alert snap-to-it attention and a salute by every French soldier present."

The French who were present that day learned what a number of American military personnel and civilian music enthusiasts already knew—this was no ordinary military marching band. A significant number of the regiment's soldiers were accomplished musicians who brought their cultural style and experience to the band. They were led by Lieutenant James Reese Europe, who, prior to the war, was the most sought-after society band leader in New York City and the man who had introduced the fox-trot to America. The band's musical style was one of orchestrated ragtime, adapted for marching, and although improvisation was not allowed, the arrangements included many elements of a developing American style of music known as "jazz." The band played for numerous military and civilian audiences in France and created an intense curiosity and excitement with their style and their energy. They are, in fact, credited as among the first to introduce and popularize jazz in Europe.

A Word to the Wise

The attitudes that helped to keep the "Harlem Hellfighters," as well as several other all-black units, from representing their homeland abroad came from the top. General John G. Pershing, the commander of American forces in Europe, issued a secret communiqué to the French military stationed with the American Army on August 7, 1918. Entitled "Secret Information Concerning Black American Troops," it warned of the dangers of relying on black soldiers and offered a detailed rationale. Pershing was specific in defining the black man as being "inferior" to the white, that he lacked a "civic and professional conscience," and that he was a "constant menace to the American," [as if to strongly imply that a black American was not a "real" American.] His instructions to the French spoke to a complete segregation of the races: "We must not eat with them, must not shake hands with them, seek to talk with them or to meet with them outside the requirements of military service. We must not commend too highly these troops, especially in front of White Americans."

Pershing's continual use of the word "we" strongly implied a perceived

Black Americans In The US Military From The American Revolution To The Korean War: World War I & The "Harlem Hellfighters" http://dmna.ny.gov/ historic/articles/ blacksMilitary/ BlacksMilitaryWW1. htm

camaraderie with the French along the lines of racial attitudes and opinion. He seemed to anticipate an agreement based on the assumption that the French and Americans were on the same side of things, as both being "white." Pershing didn't realize however, that the French already had black troops (mostly Senegalese and Algerian natives from her African colonies) serving under her command. These soldiers had fought commendably in several major engagements and had earned the respect of their commanders as well as from their German adversaries. The French treated Pershing's memorandum with indifference.

Thanks for the Memories

Anthony Gero,
*Black Soldiers of
New York State: A
Proud Legacy.*
(New York: State
University of New
York Press, 2009)
p. 50.

The National
Archives
www.archives.gov/
education/

Cameron
McWhirter, *Red
Summer: The
Summer of 1919 and
the Awakening of
Black America.*
(New York: Henry
Holt, 2011).

Although the 369th Regiment was highly respected by both the French and German armies, formal acknowledgment from their own country was significantly absent. Of the 183 decorations awarded to the regiment, only 12 were issued by the United States military; the other 171 medals came from the French in the form of the Croix de Guerre, the "French Cross." U.S. military officials forbid the regiment from marching in France's huge Victory Parade through the streets of Paris in July 1919 and further American pressure resulted in their exclusion from the newly-erected French War Memorial. Their return to New York City in February 1919 was received by an expressionless unit of military police who had been instructed not to salute any members of the 369th.

Their white commanding officer however, Colonel William Hayward, the man who two years earlier had been told that "black is not a color of the rainbow" and forced to watch in anger a farewell parade that excluded his soldiers, made sure that this time, his men would be appropriately honored. "Damn their going away parade! We'll have a parade of our own when we come home, those of us who come home—and it will be a parade that will make history." He followed through on his promise in grand style. A crowd estimated to be 250,000 strong cheered wildly as the unit marched up 5th Avenue to the New York Armory, where a celebratory lunch had been prepared. Following the meal, the unit reformed and marched into Harlem, where the *New York Times* reported that their arrival "threw the population into hysterics." For the final mile of their march, friends, relatives, spouses and girlfriends, joined the ranks and marched arm-in-arm with the soldiers.

The Service record of the 369th, as well as the parade itself, was a source of tremendous pride to the black community and was often cited by those championing the cause for civil rights. The 369th Regiment maintained an active presence in Harlem over the next two decades, reappearing annually for an organized march through Harlem on their way to their summer training camp and marching back through the neighborhoods two weeks later. The celebration, since renamed the Martin Luther King Jr./369th Regiment Parade, was revived in 1959, and remains an annual event each May.

¿Hablas Espanol?

One of the most confusing and contradictory aspects of the exclusion of African Americans from the game of white baseball was the fact that players of Hispanic origin or heritage were allowed to play. A wide variety of skin tone within the Hispanic culture meant that some of these players were actually darker in color than the African Americans who were denied. The irony becomes complete when one considers that a foreign-born citizen of a Latin American country, who might come to America under a temporary visa, perhaps with little or no comprehension of the English language, could play in major league baseball while an English-speaking American citizen, was denied the same opportunity. It is safe to conclude that it wasn't a "whites only" policy that was being followed, rather a specific rule applied to one specific group of people. Within this context, it appears that one's spoken language could frequently hold the key to the clubhouse.

John Virtue and Monte Irvin, *South of the Color Barrier: How Jorge Pasquel and the Mexican League Pushed Baseball Toward Racial Integration.* (Jefferson, NC: McFarland & Co., 2007) p. 43.

The Cuban Giants are generally considered to have been the first African-American professional baseball team. Formed in 1885 at a summer resort on Long Island, the Argyle Hotel, the club was made up of the black wait staff employed at the hotel—none of the players were actually Cuban. The hotel's owner may have thought that the "Cuban" label lent an exotic flavor to his establishment but it was more likely an attempt to avoid referring to the players as "black" or "Negro," a common practice at the time. In an interview in Esquire magazine in 1938, baseball historian and former Negro League player Sol White stated that "when the team first began playing away from home, they passed as foreigners." In the effort to sell this deception, they talked to each other in the field in a nonsensical gibberish, hoping that it sounded like Spanish.

Casey's Strategy

John Virtue and
Monte Irvin.
p. 41.

Casey Stengel's strong belief that insults could unnerve an opposing player were well known, and he was not shy about using them. He was once alleged to have yelled "Cuban nigger" at an opposing player and although he denied the accusation, his apparent guilt was enough to prompt a punch from the comment's target. As manager of the New York Yankees, he once asked infielder Willy Miranda to shout insults in Spanish to an opponent, Minnie Minoso. What Stengel didn't realize was that the two Cuban players were best friends. What Miranda shouted while the White Sox first baseman was in the batter's box was in reality an invitation to dinner. Recognizing the ploy and playing along with it, Minoso paused and called for a time-out. "I stepped out of the box and shook my fist at Miranda and shouted that I understood and I'd see him at dinner." Stengel was quite pleased with the exchange until Minoso later hit a game-winning triple. He then regretted having "upset" the Cuban player.

Certified Castilians

John Virtue and
Monte Irvin.
p. 41.

Clark Griffith owned the National League Cincinnati Reds in the early 20th century and in 1911 signed his first Cuban players, Armando Marsans and Rafael Almieda. Their physical characteristics caused African-American newspapers to consider them both to be black and their presence in the lineup led some African-American players to believe that integration of the major leagues was a possibility. According to baseball historian Peter Bzarkian, Griffith was so worried about the rumors and their implications that he "sent off to Cuban officials for documents to certify that the two imports were of Castilian and not Negro heritage." Both players were subsequently "certified" as Castilian and the perceived crisis was averted.

Toni and the Klansman

Martha Ackmann,
*Curveball: The
Remarkable Story
of Toni Stone.*
(Chicago: Lawrence
Hill Books) 2012;
Fred Lieb, *Baseball
As I Have Known It.*
(New York: Grosset
& Dunlap, 1977).

Charles "Gabby" Street was born for the game of baseball. His major league debut as catcher for the Cincinnati Reds in 1904 marked the beginning of a 34-year career in baseball as both player and manager. Even his retirement from on-the-field activity couldn't keep him from the game he loved and he continued as a color commentator on radio broadcasts for several more years. Though spirited and colorful, his playing career was rather undistinguished. As catcher and mentor to Hall of Fame pitcher, Walter Johnson, and as the winning manager of the 1931 World Series Champion St. Louis Cardinals, he was more often noted for who he was associated with rather than for his own accomplishments. But Gabby loved the game and he loved to tell stories, and he loved working with young boys, teaching them both the fundamentals and intricacies of the sport. So it was that he and Toni Stone crossed paths in the spring of 1936.

Street's personal background would not have prepared him well for the relationship that was to develop. He was born in 1882, just 17 years removed from General Lee's surrender at Appomattox, and raised in rural Alabama. A product of his time, his community, and his family, it was not surprising that he grew up with a racist attitude toward African Americans. His nickname, "Gabby," in fact, owed its origin to his childhood experiences in the Jim Crow South. "We used to call the colored boys 'Gabby' down in Alabama. . . . If you see a black boy, and want him, and you don't know his name, you yell: "Hey Gabby!" . . . To me, all black boys have been 'Gabby' and I got my nickname from the use of that word . . . not because I'm a chatterbox." His racial attitudes followed him into adulthood and as a major league player he once confided to sportswriter Fred Lieb that he was in fact a member of the Ku Klux Klan. By the 1930s however, Street's life experiences had softened his stance just a bit. He was able to be friendly and respectful of individual African Americans, while at the same time denigrating the group to which they belonged.

In 1936, Toni Stone was the 14-year-old "Tomboy Stone," just beginning to achieve some notoriety for her athletic skills in her hometown of St. Paul, Minnesota. Gender and race were daily challenges for her. As chance would have it, Gabby Street was in his first year as manager of St. Paul's minor league baseball team. On the side, he operated a baseball school for teens, an all-white all-boys enterprise, the former requirement a function of the time and the latter reflecting another of his prejudices. "Baseball is a good thing for boys," he would say, it helped to bring out their best qualities and to become "professional," in relation to both character and in playing the sport. African Americans and women had no place in the all-white "man's game" of base-ball as far as he was concerned. Typical of her own spirited nature, "Tomboy Stone" ignored the obstacles—"professional" was the only word she needed to hear—and she began hanging around Gabby's school.

Toni initially stayed apart from whatever group Street was working with but she always remained within earshot, eager to hear his stories and gain some of his baseball wisdom, always carrying her baseball glove, always hoping to get noticed. Persistent in her attendance, her boldness grew to approaching him with repeated requests to become part of the school and to have a chance to show her ability. Such requests were repeatedly denied, with the admonition that she should go home, that she didn't belong there. But Toni was nothing if not head-strong and determined, and she continued to show up at the school. Impressed by her persistence and putting his prejudices on hold, Gabby finally relented and gave her an opportunity to play. "I just couldn't get rid of her until I gave her a chance," he recalled, "Every time I chased her away, she would go around the corner and come back to plague me again." Given the opportunity, Toni immediately impressed and won the old Southerner's respect, if not some of his heart as well. He took a certain pride in her ability to "show those boys up" and they soon developed a close relationship. As Toni recalled, Street went so far as to intimate to her that if it was up to him, racial and gender lines would not exist in the game of baseball, a truly remarkable admission coming from a card-carrying member of the Klan.

Only Gabby could have said with any certainty what effect his relationship with Toni Stone that summer had on him. Perhaps it helped him to see things differently, perhaps his own attitudes had already softened to the extent that he was able to see beyond gender and race and to regard her as a person rather than as an object. For Toni however, the impact of that relationship was life-long and deeply felt. For her 15th birthday that summer, Gabby gave her a pair of baseball shoes, the first she had ever owned. "It was like a miracle," she recalled. For those shoes were not simply a piece of equipment, but a validation—a belief that she could go forward in baseball. Charles "Gabby" Street passed away in 1951—he was not present to witness the realization of Toni Stone's dream to play professional baseball two years later. But Toni would not hesitate to tell you—he was there.

Pictures Tell the Story:
The Legacy of Ernest C. Withers

Anthony Decaneas, ed., "Diamonds Within Diamonds," Daniel Wolff, *Negro League Baseball: Photographs by Ernest C. Withers.* (New York: Abrams, 2004) p. 39.

Ernest C. Withers was a black commercial photographer in Memphis, Tennessee, striving to support his family in post-World War II America. His photographic style was simple—black-and-white images, always taken with a standard lens, usually developed at home with the assistance of his wife. The motto that defined his work—"Pictures Tell the Story"—was written across the front window of his small studio for all to see.

Withers had been drawn to baseball as a child when, employed as a "seat duster" and "bird boy" at his hometown Russwood Field, he would be allowed to stay and watch the Negro League Memphis Red Sox play their games and exhibitions. With the exception of himself and the other young "dusters," the park was strictly segregated and he recalled hearing white fans encourage batters to "hit it in the coal field," referring to the stands behind the right field fence where blacks were allowed to sit. His interest in photography began in his teens and was cultivated during the war when he received training in the Army School of Photography. Upon returning home, he parlayed his earlier association with the Red Sox into per-diem publicity assignments for the team and soon gained regular access to all their games and related activities.

Memphis in the 1940s and 50s was at the crossroads of the civil rights movement and Withers soon began an association with the movement that would span his career. He developed close relationships with its leaders and was present at many of its seminal and historic moments. He was the only photographer allowed access to Emmett Till's funeral and his numerous photographs of events and their leaders, both public and candid, have played an important role in documenting the history of the movement.[4]

Back home in Memphis, Withers' attention turned to Beale Street and baseball. His simple photography proved to be profound in its depiction of black culture and society, as reflected in the blues and on the diamond in his hometown. His images documented the astonishing culture that African Americans had managed to create within the white man's world and helped to dissolve the simplistic Saturday night/Sunday morning stereotypes that informed much of America's prejudice. In so doing, Withers was able to cast a bright light upon that which had previously been hidden, capturing the joy and the pride of an entire community.

In the spring of 1947, Ernest journeyed to Sportsman's Park in St. Louis, the home of the National League St. Louis Browns; Brooklyn was in town and he had come to see Jackie Robinson. From his seat in the press box, he snapped a panoramic view of the ballpark, a scene that upon first glance appears rather unremarkable, an oft-repeated view quite familiar to baseball fans and casual observers alike, one that rarely prompts more than a cursory glance or comment. This particular photograph was far more significant however, as it represented a completely new perspective, taken as it was from the vantage point of the press box—until then off limits to black sportswriters and photographers. This was, quite simply, a view that a black photographer or journalist had never been allowed to have. It was a simple, matter-of-fact, black-and-white photograph—but one that documented a changing America.

When Withers returned to Russwood Park in the spring of 1960 to take photographs of an exhibition game, it would turn out to be his final visit to the place where he had spent so many hours of his youth and adulthood. Despite his reputation and long association with the ballpark, "They wouldn't let me in the front. Because I was colored. Send me around to the colored gate. It was the condition of yesterday. We didn't go home mad." But he remembered walking home that evening and wishing aloud that Russwood "would just burn down." Later that night, the stadium did indeed catch fire and was reduced to ashes. He smiled when recalling the event. "I never did tell anyone what I'd been thinkin'."

It Didn't Make a Difference: WWII

Steve Jacobson,
*Carrying Jackie's
Torch: The Players
Who Integrated
Baseball and
America.* (Chicago:
Chicago Review
Press, 2009), p. 5.

Buck O'Neil served in the United States Navy during World War II. His unit, as were all branches of the U.S. military at that time, was segregated according to race. He recalled being assigned to a train carrying German prisoners of war from Virginia to Fort Leavenworth, Kansas. The prisoners rode in the front of the train while the American Negro sailors rode in the back. Even though the German soldiers were prisoners, they sat ahead of the men guarding them. "Pitiful," O'Neil remarked, "the American uniform didn't make a difference."

Dear Mom . . .

James Horton,
"Patriot Acts: Public
History in Public
Service," *Journal of
American History,*
Dec. 2005.

Henry McPeak recalled his own experiences with segregation in the military during his service in the Army Air Corps in World War II. Stationed at Keesler Field near Biloxi, Mississippi, he found that the Post Exchange (PX) was off limits to black troops, as were all the restaurants and theaters on the base. African-American newspapers were banned, as they were frequently critical of the country's practices of racial discrimination and segregation and their targets included the U.S. military. As a consequence of this ban, McPeak was instructed to inform his mother that should she send him any cookies or other treats from home, she should take care not to wrap them in any African-American newspaper or magazine. Such packages would be confiscated.

Veterans' Day, 1944—

German prisoners of war during World War II were often transported by train to the various military camps used for their detention. Despite their status as "captured enemy," these passengers were generally provided with more respect, consideration, and service than an African American in military uniform. Army Air Corpsman Henry McPeak, although dressed in full formal military attire, was forced to watch from the entrance to the railway's dining car as German prisoners ate graciously and in comfort within, its venue and service denied to him because of the color of his skin. One conductor told him that he might have been allowed to eat there if a curtain had been available to separate him from the other diners, as if his very presence might disturb the enjoyment of others. James Horton recalls hearing stories from his father, a military police-man frequently assigned to escort German prisoners, told from the same vantage point as McPeak's. Guard duty began and ended at the dining car's door.

Originally published in *Yank* magazine as a letter from Timmingham, cited in "Citizen Soldiers: Jim Crow and Black Segregation,"

www.
worldwar2history.
info/Army/Jim-
Crow.html

Converted for the web from *Citizen Soldiers: The U.S. Army From the Normandy Beaches, To the Bulge, To the Surrender of Germany,* by Stephen E. Ambrose

The Best American . . .

The elevated position of the German prisoner over the African-American soldier was not limited to a military environment. Army Corporal Rupert Timmingham recalls his experience with eight fellow GIs as they traveled through the South in full military uniform in 1944. "We could not purchase a cup of coffee." They finally encountered a lunchroom manager at a small Texas railroad depot who told them they could go around to the kitchen in the back for a sandwich and coffee. As they did so, he recalls what happened next: "About two dozen German prisoners of war—with two American guards—came to the station. They entered the lunchroom, sat at tables, had their meals served, talked, smoked, and in fact had a swell time. I stood on the outside looking on, and I could not help but ask myself, why are they treated better than we are? . . . If we are fighting for the same thing, if we are to die for our country, then why does the Government allow such things to go on?"

Despite the bitter disappointment and resentment that resulted from continuing instances of racial discrimination and segregation, the African-American soldier does not appear to have vented his frustration on his German counterparts. Stephen E. Ambrose interviewed a number of German ex-prisoners of war for his book, *Citizen Soldiers,* and encountered universal testimony that they received better treatment from their black guards than from their white captors. The POWs even had a saying among themselves: "The best American is a black American."

Buck O'Neil: Baseball's Ambassador of Good Will

John Jordan "Buck" O'Neil enjoyed a 17-year career in the Negro Leagues as both player and manager, all but one with the Kansas City Monarchs. Five times he hit over .300 for a season and he played in three East-West All-Star games. His career statistics were otherwise unremarkable and his enduring legacy is more clearly defined by his subsequent service to the game. Following his retirement from the Negro Leagues in 1955, he was hired as a scout for the major league Chicago Cubs and went on to become the first African-American coach in major league history in 1962. He was given a prominent role in Ken Burns' 1994 documentary, *Baseball*, where his quiet dignity and humility captured a national audience and catapulted him to legendary status as both spokesman and ambassador for black baseball. He traveled America preaching its gospel until his death in 2006 at age 94.

Welcome!

John Virtue and Monte Irvin, *South of the Color Barrier: How Jorge Pasquel and the Mexican League Pushed Baseball Toward Racial Integration,* (Jefferson, NC: McFarland & Co., 2007), p. 44.

Negro League teams came to expect various segregation-related difficulties during their road trips through the South, but even then, there were occasional surprises. Buck and the Kansas City Monarchs arrived at the stadium in Macon, Georgia early one evening for an exhibition game with the local team. "I got off the bus and went into the dugout and here's the Wizard of the Ku Klux Klan! . . . So he says, 'You boys aren't going to play here tonight. We're going to march here tonight.' I say, 'Yessir.' So we got back on the bus and go on. . . . That's just the way it was."

This Ain't No Ballgame

Joe Posnanski, *The Soul of Baseball: A Road Trip through Buck O'Neil's America,* (New York: William Morrow, 2008), p. 172.

During one scouting trip, Buck and fellow scout, Piper Davis, found themselves in rural Louisiana; it was nighttime and they were unfamiliar with the area. They drove the dark country roads for some time before finally sighting a brightly lit baseball field. Buck drove over to two men who were standing by the entrance. "This must be where the game is," Buck said to them. One of the men smiled and replied: "Oh yeah, this is where it is, all right." O'Neil parked the car and the two scouts entered the stadium but as they neared the field, they soon realized that something was not right. They saw a number of men standing on the field but none were in baseball uniforms. Instead, all those present in the stadium were wearing white robes and their heads were covered by white hoods. Buck's attention was drawn to the pitcher's mound, where a truck was parked and a man in more elaborate costume stood on the flatbed and appeared to be preaching to the crowd. A pig was being barbequed in a nearby fire pit. Buck turned to his companion and with sudden urgency and recognition announced: "No, Piper, this ain't no ballgame." With a shared panic fueling their flight, they ran back to their car and sped from the lot, leaving gravel and dust in their wake. As they were leaving the stadium, Buck glanced behind and saw that the two men who had invited them in were rolling on the ground in laughter. Once safely down the road, the two scouts burst into laughter of their own.

Look, But Don't Touch

Buck's spoken words often had the cadence of poetry according to his biographer, Scott Posnanski, and the poetry was wistful as he recalled his wife Ora's encounter with Jim Crow when she wanted to buy a new hat. Never one to harbor bitterness, "That's just the way it was," he would say. He told the story this way:

Joe Posnanski,
*The Soul of Baseball:
A Road Trip through
Buck O'Neil's
America,*
(New York: William
Morrow, 2008),
p. 173

My wife, Ora, wanted a hat.

So she went downtown

To a store called Woolf Brothers

Where black women could shop

But could not eat.

At the counter.

Ora was allowed to look at the hats,

Imagine how they might sit

On her head.

But if she touched one,

Touched a hat,

She had to buy it.

A black woman could ruin a hat

By touching it.

So degrading,

So degrading.

That's what racism was.

Not surprisingly, Ora, and many other African-American women, frequently made their own hats, and exchanged or sold them amongst themselves.

A Game-Saving "Catch"

Jonathan Eig,
*Opening Day:
The Story of Jackie
Robinson's First
Season,*
(New York: Simon &
Schuster, 2007),
pp. 229–230.

http://online.wsj.
com/article/
SB11752903
0001654993.html

and recounted in
poetry in
Maryann Lorbiecki,
Jackie's Bat, (New
York: Simon &
Schuster, 2006).

The St. Louis Cardinals were the chief rivals of the Brooklyn Dodgers for National League supremacy during the late 1940s. Jackie Robinson's personal rivalry with the team proved to be particularly intense and it extended well beyond wins and losses; it actually began before he played a single inning for the Dodgers. St. Louis was the southernmost city in the National League. The majority of its roster was made up of players who hailed from the South and the stands at Sportsman's Park in St. Louis were segregated until 1944. Jim Crow was neither stranger nor unwelcome guest in their locker room and rumors circulated throughout the spring of 1947 that players had circulated a petition against Robinson's expected debut and that the team was threatening to strike if he were to be allowed to play.

The air was thick with tension as the two teams met in May. During his first at-bat, Robinson and the St. Louis catcher, Joe Garagiola, began talking and talk escalated into a back-and-forth argument. Tempers quickly cooled and the game resumed, but the incident was noted by both teams. There was no such thing as a "minor" skirmish in the racially-charged atmosphere of Robinson's appearance in the opening game of the three-game series.

In mid-July, the teams met again. In his first at-bat of the series, future Hall of Famer Enos Slaughter, rumored to have been one of the ringleaders of the locker-room strike talk that spring, hit a routine groundball to the shortstop. He was out by many feet but in crossing the first-base bag, Slaughter spiked Robinson in the thigh. No minor injury, play was halted while the Dodger trainer worked to repair a 7-inch gash to Robinson's leg. Later commenting on the injury, the trainer remarked, "It's lucky [Jackie] wasn't maimed." Slaughter contended the incident was unintentional; Robinson strongly disagreed. "All I know is that I had my foot on the inside of the bag. I gave Slaughter plenty of room."

By mid-September, Brooklyn held a five-game lead over the second-place Cardinals and the tension was high as they arrived in St. Louis to begin a 3-game weekend series. Once again, the tension hung thick over the field from the start. In the bottom of the second inning of the first game, it was again the catcher, Garagiola, at the center of controversy. In running out what was again a routine groundball in the second inning, Garagiola spiked Robinson at first base. There was no injury—only Robinson's shoe was torn—but the stage was set for another confrontation and it didn't take long for it to arrive. The two began talking at the start of Robinson's next at-bat and this time, there was nothing minor about the exchange. Tempers quickly escalated and the home-plate umpire had to intervene, physically holding back Garagiola to prevent the loud, animated exchange from progressing any further.

The teams split the first two games of the spirited and hard-fought series. In the bottom of the eighth inning of the pivotal third game, Brooklyn held to a 6-4 lead, but the Cardinals had already scored twice in the inning and had runners on first and second with two outs. It was a pivotal moment in the game but in a much broader sense, a crucial moment in the season for both teams. Pinch-hitter Nippy Jones came to the plate and lifted a twisting foul ball toward the Dodger dugout; Robinson took off in hot pursuit.

Jonathan Eig picks up the story:

"He reached the top of the dugout steps and with no more room to run, abandoned any concern for his personal safety and hurled his body down the concrete steps. He stabbed at the ball with his glove and in that instant, Dodger pitcher Ralph Branca left his seat on the bench and hurled himself at the diving player. The ball, the pitcher, and Robinson arrived simultaneously. The ball dropped into Robinson's glove for the third out to end the inning and the Cardinal threat. Meanwhile, Branca's arms had encircled Robinson's waist and the pitcher's momentum carried both players out of the dugout and onto the surrounding grass. As the jubilant Dodger players left their positions and trotted into the dugout, hugs and hearty slaps on the back were visited upon both men. No one was more surprised than Robinson by Branca's grab: 'I tried to break my fall but I don't know what would have happened if Ralph Branca hadn't tackled me.'"

The Dodgers went on to win the game and never looked back, winning the National League pennant by five games over the second-place Cardinals. Students of the game will tell you, however, that on another sunny Sunday afternoon in St. Louis, a footnote in the history of a memorable and historic year, the "Branca catch" was the moment that baseball, once more, opened our eyes to the possibilities and the potential of a changing America. When the season began six months earlier, Jackie Robinson "could not have been sure that anyone would have cared enough to break his fall."

In the Year of the Boar and Jackie Robinson

Jonathan Eig, "The Real Jackie Robinson Story," available at: http://online. wsj.com/article/ SB117529030001 654993.html

The long-term consequences of the Garagiola-Robinson spat were less predictable, and beyond the imagination of anyone involved. In 1984, a Chinese-born American named Bette Bao Lord published a slender book of fiction intended for young readers. She called it *In the Year of the Boar and Jackie Robinson.* The autobiographical story describes a young girl's passage from China to America, and her adjustment to life in Brooklyn in 1947. The story's hero doesn't know English and makes few friends—until she discovers Jackie Robinson and baseball, and learns that America really is the land of opportunity.

A staple of elementary school classrooms, *In the Year of the Boar and Jackie Robinson* has been read by countless thousands of children, establishing Garagiola as a bigot in the minds of a generation that never saw him play. When Garagiola's grandchildren read the book, they were stunned, asking him "Was that you, Papa?" Why had he hated Jackie Robinson, they wanted to know."

In recent interviews, Garagiola begged for his encounter with Robinson to be forgotten. He seemed pained and confused, shocked at how a seemingly forgettable bit of ballpark bickering from ages ago continued to haunt him. "Look," he said, his voice breaking, "Jackie was a firebrand. Even in '47, he was a competitor. You're fighting for the pennant, and who cares what color he is. . . . He said something to me. I said, 'Why don't you just hit!' And then here comes Clyde Sukeforth. I've lived with this thing unfairly. It was a little bit of jockeying to break his concentration, that's all. . . . It wasn't even an argument. . . . You just don't know the grief and aggravation this has caused."

Casual Racism

Happy Birthday, Pee Wee!

Carl Erskine and Vin Scully. *Tales From the Dodger Dugout: Extra Innings.* (New York: Sports Illustrated Publishing, 2004) p. 124.

The Brooklyn Dodgers of the 1940s and 50s represented the heart and soul of the Brooklyn community. The players were not simply members of a team, they were members of a family, and their feelings toward the borough were mutual. So it was that on the evening of July 22, 1955, the Ebbets Field faithful paused during a game to wish their beloved shortstop, Pee Wee Reese, a happy birthday. The stadium lights were turned off, the fans lit matches, and 30,000 people rose as one to sing to him. The Brooklyn Dodgers, the acknowledged leader in baseball's integration, with three of their African-American players on the field that evening, had planned an additional tribute. When the lights were restored, it was revealed that all the flags atop the roof of Ebbets Field had been replaced with Confederate flags, in "tribute" to Reese's southern heritage.

The irony of the situation went unnoticed by many, but not by Jackie Robinson. Carl Erskine recalls that, "Back in the clubhouse, [he] was livid. He was so upset by the display of Confederate flags that he was loudly protesting in front of his locker. He denounced the act and continued to berate those responsible. Any attempt to console Jackie at this point was impossible; a few of us spoke with him and assured him we were on his side but thought that in this particular case he would lose more supporters than he would gain."

Robinson was a close friend of Pee Wee Reese, which could have only made the unfortunate display that much harder to endure.

Just for Luck

The Brooklyn Dodgers were on their way north by train to open the 1947 baseball season and several of the players were playing cards together in the train's club car; Jackie Robinson sat alone nearby, quietly reading a newspaper. Pitcher Hugh Casey, a southern native, was not doing well in the game that evening, losing each and every hand without offering much competition. Without saying a word, he stood up, walked over to where Robinson was sitting, and before Robinson could stop him, rubbed the top of his head several times before returning to his seat at the table. No one said a word.

Cal Fussman, *After Jackie* (New York: ESPN Books, 2007), p. 78

Jackie Robinson and the Power of Aggregation

Aggregation *n.* 1. The act of bringing together, as into a mass, sum, or body. 2. A collection into a whole.

Many who consider Jackie Robinson to be a preeminent figure in the civil rights movement base their assessment upon but one event—his breaking of the Major League color line when he took the field for the Brooklyn Dodgers in the spring of 1947. As significant and courageous as this action was however, it simply marked one more step forward for a man already committed to the practice of social activism.

Robinson was honorably discharged from the United States Army in 1944

Steve Jacobson, *Carrying Jackie's Torch.* (Chicago: Lawrence Hill Books, 2007), pp. 11-12.

as a Second Lieutenant. He had only been able to achieve officer status because he and a fellow recruit, African-American heavyweight champion Joe Louis, successfully petitioned for entrance into the previously all-white officer candidates' school at Fort Riley, Kansas, where they were stationed. In his role as platoon leader, his unit's morale officer, Robinson made it a point to actively confront many of the segregationist practices he encountered at his post. He argued for more complete access to post exchange (PX) services for African-American soldiers and at one point refused a request to play football for the post because he had not been allowed to play on its all-white baseball team. When his commanding officer reminded him that he could be ordered to play, Robinson agreed that might be so, but remarked that he could not be ordered to play well. His honorable discharge was in jeopardy until he was acquitted in court martial proceedings that stemmed from his refusal to move to the back of an Army bus he was riding.

Armed with a college education, a four-year career in the military, and experience on the national stage as a collegiate sports star, Robinson was no ordinary rookie when he joined the Kansas City Monarchs in 1945. Teammate Buck O'Neil immediately noticed the difference. "We just accepted segregation as the way it was," he recalled, but we could see that Robinson had a different mind-set, that he was unwilling to accept the Jim Crow practices that the rest of the team had learned to tolerate. So it was that the Monarchs left Kansas City one morning on the way to their next game in Oklahoma. Their bus pulled into the same gas station they had been using for two decades, the same station that had a "Whites Only" sign hanging above their restroom. Buck O'Neil recalls the scene:

> The man comes out, puts the hose in the tank. He says, … "You boys played baseball last night, filled up the ballpark, put on a great show." Jackie gets off the bus and starts for the restroom. "Where you goin' boy," the man says.
> "I'm goin' to the restroom."
> "Boy, you know you can't go to that restroom."
> Jackie says, "Take the hose out of that tank."
> Man thought awhile now because we got a 50-gallon tank on this side and we got a 50-gallon tank on that side. He's not going to sell that much gas at one time on any day soon. You know what he said: "You boys can go to the restroom, but don't stay long."

A small victory for the moment, but a much larger one was in store.

As the bus was pulling away, Robinson's surprised and jubilant teammates asked him why he had acted as he did. "We live in a capitalist society," he replied, "the man's gotta sell his gas." And with that remark, Robinson's teammates were activated. Their ensuing discussion focused on their collective economic power, an asset that had previously gone unrealized. Through the aggregation of their resources—presenting themselves as a team rather than as a group of individual patrons—they were able to achieve the kind of economic power that improved their condition.

Buck O'Neil recalled that after that incident, the Kansas City Monarchs traveled just a little better than other Negro League teams. They always found a hotel that would take the kind of money that comes from booking rooms for an entire baseball team. They always found a restaurant that would take the kind of money that comes from feeding an entire baseball team. And with two 50-gallon gas tanks to fill, they always found a gas station that would let them use the bathroom. It was 1945, and Jackie Robinson had only just begun.

Appendix 1: Learning Standards

Overarching Themes

Jim Crow America was a national phenomenon that offered a full constellation of restrictions to African Americans between the end of Reconstruction and the Civil Rights era.

The restrictions and limitations imposed on African Americans acted as a catalyst for creative resistance that resulted in a parallel world of exceptional achievement within the black community.

As one of the most financially successful institutions of the black community, the Negro Leagues experience brought to the black community economic stability, pride, and an alternative narrative of American history.

Essential Questions

In what ways and to what extent were the restrictions and limitations known as "Jim Crow" a national phenomenon?

Who, what, where, when, and how was the black community, in particular the Negro Leagues, bound by these limitations and restrictions?

Who, what, where, when, and how did the black community, in particular the

Negro Leagues, resist these limitations and restrictions?

In what ways and to what extent did the Negro League's owners, managers, and players actively challenge the limitations of Jim Crow America?

In what ways and to what extent did the black press actively challenge the limitations of Jim Crow America?

In what ways and to what extent did these everyday challenges to the system of Jim Crow presage the activism of the Civil Rights era?

National Social Studies Standards

*NCSS Standard Two: Time, Continuity and Change
from the published learning standards of the National
Council for the Social Studies*

Students will be able to use their knowledge and understanding of the past in order to enable them to analyze the causes and consequences of events and developments, and to place these in the context of the institutions, values and beliefs of the time period between the end of Reconstruction and the Civil Rights era. This study of the past will enable them to evaluate and draw conclusions about the ways in which African Americans were viewed and how they viewed themselves and their society.

NCSS Standard Five: Individuals, Groups, and Institutions

Students will be able to evaluate the role of the Negro Leagues as an institution within the African-American community and how it was an important organizational embodiment of the core social values of the community, and played a variety of important roles in socializing individuals and meeting their needs, as well as in the promotion of societal continuity, the mediation of conflict, and the advancement of civil rights issues.

NCSS Standard Ten: Civic Ideals and Practices

Students will be able to demonstrate through written, artistic, musical, and oral responses and presentations, an understanding of civic ideals and practices as critical to full participation in society. All people have a stake in examining civic ideals and practices across time and in different societies. Through an understanding of both ideals and practices, it becomes possible to identify gaps between them, and to study efforts to close the gaps in our democratic republic and worldwide.

Students will be able to demonstrate a historical and contemporary understanding of the basic freedoms and rights of citizens in a democracy, and learn about the institutions and practices that supported those rights and freedoms and those that undermined them in the case of African Americans, as well as the important historical documents that articulate them.

Students will be able to begin answering questions such as:

What are the democratic ideals and practices of a constitutional democracy?

What is the balance between rights and responsibilities?

What is civic participation? How do citizens become involved?

What is the role of the citizen in the community and the nation?

How have Americans over time developed the concept of civil disobedience and practiced civil disobedience?

National History Standards
Era 9 –Postwar United States (1945 to early 1970s)
National Standards for Civics and Government

Standard II.A.2 Students will be able to explain the extent to which Americans have internalized the values and principles of the Constitution and attempted to make its ideals realities.

Standard III.B.1 Students will be able to evaluate, take, and defend positions on issues regarding the purposes, organization, and functions of the institutions of the national government.

National Geography Standard One

Students will use maps and other geographic representations, tools and technologies to acquire, process and report information from a spatial perspective.

NCTE Literacy Skills

Adapted from the National Standards of the National Council of Teachers of English

Students will expand their understanding of the political, social, and cultural environment of the United States during the years between the end of Reconstruction and the Civil Rights era.

Students will read a variety of materials from the time period drawn from a variety of sources and genres in order to build an understanding of the African-American experience during this time period.

Students will apply a wide range of strategies to comprehend, interpret, and evaluate print and non-print text materials.

NCTE Critical Thinking Skills

Students will be expected to evaluate data, synthesize information, and draw conclusions throughout the activities.

Students will be expected to generate hypotheses and support their hypotheses with evidence in order to formulate a compelling and persuasive response to the activities.

Appendix 2: Works Cited and Resources for Teaching

Primary Sources

The Chicago Defender

The California Eagle

The New York Afro-American

The Pittsburgh Courier

The Amsterdam (New York) News

The Atlanta Daily World

Freedom's Journal (New York City)

The Norfolk (Virginia) Journal and Guide

The Crisis

Jet

Ebony

Secondary Sources

Carroll, Brian. "From Fraternity to Fracture: Black Press Coverage of and Involvement in Negro League Baseball in the 1920s," *American Journalism,* Vol. 23, No. 2, 2006.

Clarke, Thurston. *Ask Not: The Inauguration of John F. Kennedy and the Speech that Changed America,* (New York: Penguin Books, 2011).

Cottrell, Robert Charles. *The Best Pitcher in Baseball, The Life of Rube Foster, Negro League Giant,* (New York: NYU Press, 2001).

Dixon, Phil S. *Andrew "Rube" Foster: A Harvest on Freedom's Fields,* (New York: Xlibris Corp., 2010) 114.

Frommer, Harvey. *Rickey and Robinson,* (New York: MacMillan, 1982).

Gibson, Robert A. *The Negro Holocaust: Lynching and Race Riots in the United States, 1880-1950,* (New Haven: Yale, 1979) and at www.yale.edu/ynhti/curriculum/units/1979/2/79.02.04.s.html

Goodwin, Doris Kearns. *Wait Till Next Year: A Memoir,* (New York: Simon & Schuster, 1998) p. 202.

Graham, Hugh Davis and Gurr, Ted Robert. *Violence in America,* (New York: Praeger, 1969).

Harnischfeger, Mark and Corey, Mary E. "Cap, Jackie, and Ted: The Rise and Fall of Jim Crow Baseball," *OAH Magazine of History,* April, 2010.

Hiss, George L. and Bostic, Joe. *The First Black American Radio Announcer,* (Bloomington, IN: Authorhouse, 2006).

Hogan, Lawrence. *Shades of Glory, The Negro Leagues and the Story of African American Baseball,* (Washington, D.C.: National Geographic, 2006).

Holway, John. *Voices from the Great Black Baseball Leagues,* (New York: Dodd, Mead, 1975).

Kahn, Roger. *Baseball as America,* "We Never Called Them Bums," (Washington, D.C.: National Geographic Society, 2002).

——————. *Beyond the Boys of Summer* (New York: McGraw-Hill, 2005).

Kinsella, W. P. *The Iowa Baseball Confederacy* (Boston: Houghton Mifflin, 1986).

Klein, Herbert S. *African Slavery in Latin America and the Caribbean,* (New York: Oxford University Press, 2007).

Ladson-Billings, Gloria. *The Dreamkeepers, Successful Teachers of African American Children,* (San Francisco: Jossey-Bass, 1994 & 2009).

Lamb, Chris. "What's Wrong With Baseball": The Pittsburgh *Courier* and the Beginning of its Campaign to Integrate the National Pastime," *Western Journal of Black Studies,* Vol. 26, No. 4, 2002

Lanctot, Neil. *Negro League Baseball: The Rise and Ruin of a Black Institution,* (Philadelphia: University of Philadelphia Press, 2004).

Lester, Larry. *Black Baseball's National Showcase, The East-West All-Star Game, 1933-1953,* (Lincoln, NE: University of Nebraska Press, 2001).

——————. *Rube Foster in His Time: On the Field and in the Papers with Black Baseball's Greatest Visionary,* (Jefferson, NC: McFarland, 2012).

Loewen, James. *Lies My Teacher Told Me,* "Handicapped by History: The Process of Hero-making," (New York: Touchstone Books, 1995).

——————. *Teaching What Really Happened,* (New York: Teachers College, 2010).

Long, Michael G., ed., *First Class Citizenship, The Civil Rights Letters of Jackie Robinson,* "Editor's Introduction," (New York: Henry Holt, & Co., 2007)

McWhirter, Cameron. *Red Summer: The Summer of 1919 and the Awakening of Black America,* (New York: Henry Holt & Co., 2011).

Myrdal, Gunnar. *An American Dilemma: The Negro Problem and Modern Democracy,* (New York: Harper Brothers, 1944).

National Baseball Hall of Fame, *Baseball as America: Seeing Ourselves Through Our National Game,* (Washington, D.C.: National Geographic Society, 2002).

Peterson, Robert, *Only the Ball Was White: A history of legendary black players and all-black professional teams,* (New York: Oxford University Press, 1970).

Pollock, Allen J., *Barnstorming to Heaven: Syd Pollock and His Great Black Teams,* (Tuscaloosa: University of Alabama Press, 2006).

Posnanski, Joe. *The Soul of Baseball: A Road Trip Through Buck O'Neil's America,* (New York: Harper, 2007).

Prince, Carl E., *Brooklyn's Dodgers: The Bums, the Borough, and the Best of Baseball, 1947–1957.* (New York: Oxford University Press, 1997).

Reisler, Jim. *Black Writers/Black Baseball: An Anthology of Articles from Black Sports-writers Who Covered the Negro Leagues,* (Jefferson, NC: McFarland & Company, 1994).

Ribowsky, Mark. *A Complete History of the Negro Leagues, 1884-1955,* (New York: Citadel Press, 2002).

Ruck, Robert. *Sandlot Seasons: Sport in Black Pittsburgh* (Champaign, IL: Univ. of Illinois Press, 1993).

Simon, Scott. *Jackie Robinson and the Integration of Baseball,* (Hoboken, NJ: John Wiley & Sons, 2002).

Tannenbaum, Frank. *Slave and Citizen,* (Boston: Beacon Press, 1946).

Thelwell, Michael, in Morrison, Toni, Ed., *Race-ing Justice, En-gendering Power,* "False, Fleeting, Perjured Clarence: Yale's Brightest and Blackest Go to Washington," (New York: Pantheon Books, 1992).

Tuttle, William M. *Race Riot: Chicago in the Red Summer of 1919,* (New York: Atheneum, 1970).

Tye, Larry, *Satchel: The Life and Times of an American Legend,* (New York: Random House, 2009).

Wiggins, David K. "Wendell Smith, the *Pittsburgh Courier-Journal* and the Campaign to Include Blacks in Organized Baseball, 1933-1945," *Journal of Sport History,* Vol. 10, No. 2 (Summer, 1983).

Will, George. *Bunts,* "Dred Scott in Spikes," (New York: Simon & Schuster, 1998).

————. "Taking a Bat to Prejudice," *Washington Post,* April 15, 2007.

Films

Burns, Ken. *Baseball, A Film by Ken Burns,* Inning 5, "Shadowball."

The Sun Was Always Shining Somewhere (vintage footage and reminiscences of former Negro League players)

¡Viva Baseball!, documentary

Sugar (A young player from the Dominican Republic comes to the United States to play baseball)

Beisbol, The Latin Game, documentary

American Pastime (Baseball in a Japanese Internment Camp)

Websites

The Black Press, Soldiers Without Swords: www.pbs.org/blackpress/

Viva Baseball!: http://exhibits.baseballhalloffame.org/viva/index.asp

The History of Keokuk, Iowa website (honoring Bud Fowler): www.keokuk.net/baseball/index.html#1885

The Life and Times of Cap Anson, Chapter 4, "Cap's" Great Shame" www.capanson.com/chapter4.html

WWI, 369th Infantry: www.archives.gov/education/lessons/369th-infantry/

Caribbean slavery: www.digitalhistory.uh.edu/database/article_display.cfm?HHID=78

Latin American Baseball: www.andrewclem.com/Baseball/LatinAmerican_Leagues.html

National Baseball Hall of Fame and Museum: http://baseballhall.org/

Negro Leagues Baseball Museum: www.nlbm.com/

Historic American Newspapers, Library of Congress: http://chroniclingamerica.loc.gov/

ProQuest Historical Newspapers: www.proquest.com/en-US/catalogs/databases/detail/pq-hist-news.shtml

Acknowledgments

This book is not just the result of three years of research, but rather the product of a lifetime of passion and experience. As such, it would be impossible for us to thank every person who made this work possible. It would have to include ticket takers, popcorn venders, hot dog hawkers, aging veterans of the game and fresh-faced rookies; Freedom Riders and foot soldiers, children facing water cannons; teachers who inspired and a grandfather who rarely encountered a competent umpire—a list as varied as it would be endless, a blending of the worlds of baseball and human rights that have combined to forge a unique historical perspective. For all those who have ever played the game, watched it, or dreamed about it, for all those who have ever helped another or saw a wrong and tried to right it, for all those who never took "no" for an answer and persevered in the face of adversity, our heartfelt thanks—you're all in here somewhere.

Regarding our actual work, we can be much more specific and so wish to personally thank the following:

First, all kinds of gratitude go to Anne Kilgore of Paperwork, our book designer, cheerleader, friend, guide, and sister who believed in us from the start and stayed with us to the end to help shape and deliver the final product. We didn't know what we didn't know and probably still wouldn't without her infinite patience and expert guidance. We couldn't have done it without you. Many thanks also to Doris Walsh founder and head of Paramount Market Publishing who read with her veteran editor's eye no fewer than three versions of the work in progress. It is significantly improved because of her comments and suggestions.

Special thanks must go to another of those who saw value in the project from the start, LeRoy Ashby, Regents Professor Emeritus at Washington State University, for his enthusiastic acceptance for publication of a portion of our early manuscript,

"Cap, Jackie, and Ted: The Rise and Fall of Jim Crow Baseball," in the prestigious *Magazine of History* published by the Organization of American Historians. His was just the best kind of encouragement. And, we want to thank him too for his willingness to read an advance copy of the complete manuscript and for offering spot-on comments and suggestions we were happy to use. The work is much stronger for his efforts on its behalf.

Many thanks to Ora Jerald of Dreammakers, Inc., of Birmingham, Alabama, whose encouragement and excitement about our work was simply infectious and helped to inspire the final stages of the project. And, we will always be grateful to you for introducing us to Reverend William Greason. Perhaps at the time you didn't know how inspiring those long talks on the phone were—we hope you do now.

To Reverend William Greason, a remarkable man of profound accomplishment, dignity, and grace, who honored our work with his own words of inspiration, many thanks. Your belief in our project strengthened our own.

Rick Mosely of Tuskegee University, creator of the Negro Leagues board game, "Legends of the Game," brought enthusiastic support and valuable recommendations, including his willingness to introduce us to Ora Jerald. Your help establishing a network of "friends of the work" was truly a blessing.

Obtaining copyright permissions can be an arduous and exhausting task. Lerner Books and The National Baseball Hall of Fame were particularly gracious in their accommodations of our requests. Particular thanks go to the Giamatti Research Center and Pat Kelly, the Photo Archivist who was so helpful. Special thanks also to Sarah Marquardt at Lerner. In spite of a very busy schedule, whenever we spoke she made it clear that assisting us with our project was her most important job and her most important concern was taking care of our requests.

Our spiritual guide throughout has been John "Buck" O'Neil who helped us to remember our best day in baseball, "Hang on to your day. If you hang on to that day, you'll stay young. Keep it in your heart." Thanks Buck. We feel younger already.

Thank you also for the on-going support of the Education and Human Development Department at The College at Brockport. Their support made it possible for Mary to travel to archives, attend conferences to present the work, and take a sabbatical leave in order to complete the first full draft of the manuscript.

We can't forget to thank our most important support—family and friends who endured endless work sessions instead of golf; pizza instead of real dinners; trips to archives and conferences instead of vacations; and much more. We hope our work is worthy of your sacrifices.

Excitement is not a solitary emotion—it is born to be shared. It is only through sharing the experience that it becomes truly alive and able to reach its full potential. So it is that we come to share our excitement about this project with you. Publication marks the end of a long and winding road for us, but we hope it marks the beginning of new roads and interesting journeys for you.

Index

About the Authors

On October 16, 2003, in the 11th inning of game 7 of the American League Championship Series, at Yankee Stadium, Aaron Boone of the New York Yankees stepped to the plate to face veteran Red Sox pitcher, Tim Wakefield who had already pitched a scoreless 10th inning. Boone entered the game as a pinch runner and it was his first at bat. Wakefield's perfect knuckleball should have stopped him cold, but instead Boone launched it into the stadium's left field seats and the lights went out all over Boston—again—and I became a Red Sox fan.

—M.E. Corey

When you've been a Pirates fan all your life, you learn infinite hope . . . and patience.

—M. Harnischfeger

This book is the result of a collaboration by two history nerds and baseball nuts. Several years ago we began a conversation on a subject entirely unrelated to either history or baseball. The topic was inclusive classrooms. As we talked about the elements necessary to constructing learning spaces and strategies that "fit" rather than enlarge already-bloated state curriculum requirements, we began thinking out loud about what parts of the American history curriculum offered promising sites for culturally relevant enrichment. We had already identified the places where African-American history was included in curriculum standards: 1.) the era of slavery, 2.) during Reconstruction, 3.)during the Harlem Renaissance, and 4.) during the Civil Rights era. We began calling them The Big Four. It quickly became clear that by far the most promising time frame was between Reconstruction and the Civil Rights Movement. This was the time when the incremental changes occurred that ultimately became the civil rights movement, and the time when African Americans increasingly, acting on their own behalf, accumulated the power to challenge the political, social, economic, and cultural structure of the nation. Of all the settings where these challenges occurred, the one that was both local and national, the one with the power to have the greatest economic impact, and the one that was the most visible throughout the time period, was Negro League baseball. For these reasons, we have created a curriculum that spans this time period and incorporates all of the important historical themes, events, and people of the times, but does it through the lens of Negro Leagues baseball.

Mary E. Corey is an associate professor of history and social studies education at The College at Brockport, State University of New York where she directs the program in social studies education. Her work combines scholarly interests in women's and civil rights history and over 15 years of teaching American History at the secondary and Advanced Placement levels, with a personal love of baseball.

Dr. Corey is also a faculty consultant for the Advanced Placement Exam in United States History through the College Board and serves on the Board of Trustees of the Brockport Community Museum where she has developed a series of teaching modules for the education section of the museum's web page. These include "Early Industry, Agriculture, and Transportation in Brockport, New York;" "Hometown Heroes, Teaching with Historic Markers: Frances Barrier Williams;" "Finding Local Heroes, Brockport and the Vietnam War," and "Walking into Local History: Reading Communities as Primary Sources."

Her work also includes workshops for secondary teachers, and she also has conducted AP Workshops; "Using Artifacts in the Social Studies Classroom" at The Summer AP Institute at St. John Fisher; and a walking tour of Seneca Falls, New York, and workshop, "Weaving Women into the Curriculum" as part of a Teaching American History Grant.

Mary lives in Hilton, New York, with the dowager queen, Althea Kitty Cat.

Mark Harnischfeger has taught in the Rochester City School District and several surrounding districts following a three-decade career in community mental health. The two constants in his life have been his passion for both history and baseball, a loving legacy from his father, that culminated in his Master's thesis, *The Way We Were: Brooklyn, Ebbets Field, and the Dodgers.* He holds a Master's Degree in education from the SUNY College at Brockport, with certifications in Social Studies (5-12) and Inclusive Education (7-12).

Mark is the proud father of three, each as passionate within their own field of interest as he is about baseball. He resides in Rochester, New York, with his faithful cat Max, who graciously allows him to share his home.

Together they have also published "Cap, Jackie, and Ted: The Rise and Fall of Jim Crow Baseball" that appeared in the April 2010 issue of the Organization of American Historians' *Magazine of History*. They have presented widely at local, state and national conferences including the July 2011, Jerry Malloy Negro Leagues Annual Conference in Birmingham, Alabama, sponsored by the National Society for Baseball Research.